Working for Equality

Working for Equality
THE NARRATIVE OF HARRY HUDSON

Harry L. Hudson

EDITED BY
Randall L. Patton

The University of Georgia Press
ATHENS

Paperback edition, 2019
© 2015 by the University of Georgia Press
Athens, Georgia 30602
www.ugapress.org
All rights reserved
Designed by Kaelin Chappell Broaddus
Set in 10.25/13 Ehrhardt MT Regular by Graphic Composition, Inc.

Most University of Georgia Press titles are
available from popular e-book vendors.

Printed digitally

The Library of Congress has cataloged the
hardcover edition of this book as follows:

Hudson, Harry L., 1925–2003.
  Working for equality : the narrative of Harry Hudson / Harry L. Hudson ;
edited by Randall L. Patton ; foreword by Gavin Wright.
    pages   cm
  Includes bibliographical references.
  ISBN 978-0-8203-4800-1 (hardback) — ISBN 978-0-8203-4838-4 (e-book)
  1. Hudson, Harry L., 1925–2003. 2. Lockheed-Georgia Company—
Employees—Biography. 3. African American supervisors—Georgia—
Biography. 4. African Americans—Georgia—Biography. 5. Discrimination
in employment—Georgia—History—20th century. 6. African
Americans—Georgia—Social conditions—20th century. 7. Civil
rights—United States—History—20th century. 8. United States—Race
relations—History—20th century. I. Patton, Randall L., 1958- II. Title.
  HD9711.U63L6485 2015
  331.7′62913334092—dc23
  [B]

                                                              2014040841

Paperback ISBN 978-0-8203-5688-4

Dedicated to all the people who were co-workers and business associates over the years who have passed over the end of the last runway.

Don't stand behind the fan (jet that is).
—H. L. "HAP" HUDSON

Contents

FOREWORD xi   PREFACE xiii

EDITOR'S ACKNOWLEDGMENTS xvii

INTRODUCTION 1

Chapter One 34   Chapter Two 42   Chapter Three 59

Chapter Four 74   Chapter Five 84   Chapter Six 94

Chapter Seven 100   Chapter Eight 105   Chapter Nine 114

Chapter Ten 129   Chapter Eleven 138 Chapter Twelve 145

Chapter Thirteen 153   Chapter Fourteen 157   Chapter Fifteen 162

Chapter Sixteen 167   Chapter Seventeen 170 Chapter Eighteen 176

Chapter Nineteen 181   Chapter Twenty 187   Chapter Twenty One 193

Chapter Twenty Two 199   Chapter Twenty Three 202   Chapter Twenty Four 205

EPILOGUE 209   NOTES 211

INDEX 215

Foreword

Randy Patton's discovery of Harry Hudson's memoir is the historian's dream. In the course of conducting interviews for a study of racial integration at the Lockheed plant in Marietta, Georgia, Patton's inquiries prompted Hudson's family to rummage through long-forgotten boxes in the attic. One of them contained a real prize: an eyewitness account by a frontline participant in the revolution in workplace race relations that transpired from the 1950s to the 1970s.

Having studied the civil rights era from the standpoint of economic history, I can testify to the rarity of Hudson's manuscript. The civil rights movement is rich in historical narratives and memoirs, supplemented by superb oral history collections at universities all over the South. By comparison, the business and employment chronicles are relatively thin. Once the political tide had turned, employers were understandably reluctant to acknowledge their pre-integration racial practices, and most new black workers were not practicing writers documenting their experiences. In this setting, a first-person account by a racial pioneer whose narrative is both observant and articulate is worth its weight in gold. Adding to its value, Hudson's employment history stretches back to the early 1950s, when "everything was black or white and not gray in between," and few could have anticipated the epochal changes of subsequent decades.

Hudson's story bristles with gripping moments: the early altercation with the egotistical but ignorant new boss Mr. Hal, who was determined to "prove to some of those halfass characters from California that he could handle 'Negras'"; the confrontation with "the great Sam" over Hudson's advice to two white office workers to stay away from an Atlanta jazz club for their own protection; the black man with graduate training in psychology assigned to "drilling holes and shooting rivets"; Hudson's skeptical response to an invitation to take part in an "experiment" to determine whether "a Negro could supervise a mixed crew in the South without friction." In each of these episodes and others, the reader may suspect that we are hearing only one part of a more complex story. But what we do hear comes from an on-the-ground source and has the ring of heart-felt authenticity. Hudson was making history and wanted to leave a record of his experience for posterity.

One might wish for a better storybook ending to Hudson's tale, for more of the "feeling of ultimate triumph" that Michael Honey found in his Memphis interviews with retired black workers in *Black Workers Remember* (2002). But perhaps it is fitting that the concluding pages express a complex mixture of feelings: on the one hand, Hudson's pride in his accomplishments and, on the other, resentment that he did not get the promotions he felt he had earned. Both of these perspectives are part of the larger and still ongoing national narrative. At least Harry Hudson received well-deserved recognition from corporate and civic leaders at his retirement and could say that in the end "the good overruled the bad."

We can now be grateful to Harry Hudson for keeping this journal, to his family for preserving and unearthing it, and to Randy Patton for bringing it to a wider reading public.

Gavin Wright
Stanford University

Preface

When I went to work for the Lockheed-Georgia division in September 1952 I had no idea that this would end up being my life's work. I thought that I would be there for about three years at the most. The war in Korea was going full bloom and when it came to a close then that would be the end of that job. I was wrong.

For some reason I decided to keep a record of my employment. These documents grew with the years. After about five years I started to make tapes and type up memos. I did not save anything that could not be considered my personal records. I saved just about everything in writing that reflected on me. As the years rolled by my records grew, most of the tapes dry-rotted, but my notes and the other documents remained intact. I finally had two boxes full of material. I collated the information and decided that I would try and write a book. As I went over my material I found myself able to project back into that timeframe and my memories became very clear. I feel that 90 percent of the actual statements made by others as indicated are verbatim.

I sat down and began to talk out the story and came to the conclusion that this book would be a narrative. The documents I had accumulated—work reviews, training certificates, cost-saving awards, and miscellaneous correspondence—helped me reconstruct my experiences. I have included some examples of these in the narrative. The experiences related here represent only a few of the thousands I lived through during those years. I tell them as I lived them. I don't bite my tongue in relating incidences as they occurred. This narrative is about me, myself, and I. My opinions were developed from these experiences and I will not hold back on expressing those opinions. Some words seemingly profane are simply aircrafters' language expressing emphasis. This method of emphatic expression is found at all levels in all industry around the United States and the world. I can say that from experience. Ninety percent of the time there is nothing personal in the use of such words.

If there is any social significance to this narrative it will have to be the gradual reduction of discrimination over the years (appearance, skin color, and so-called races) and the economic uplift that an organization such as Lockheed provided for the community. Technologically, things have advanced so far that at present younger workers of today would wonder how we did most of the things that we accomplished. I do not feel satisfied with the changes that younger "gung-ho" managers have initiated. From what I hear the attitudes and morale levels have dropped sharply because of a feeling of insecurity. The workers seem to have a feeling of constant intimidation. In my opinion this goof called "downsizing" is going to explode all over the economy by the turn of the century. So be it, this is another generation.

This is a true narrative of working in the aircraft industry for almost thirty-six years. There have been books written on the automotive industry and most other areas of endeavor but I have never seen one about an aircrafter who rose from an hourly position on the factory floor up to management and then to a position as a buyer dealing with a network of suppliers. There are over two hundred thousand working and retired aircrafters out there and I hope this will be of interest to them and any others (like a million) who may find this book interesting. I hope all of the manufacturers and suppliers who support the aircraft companies will have the opportunity to also read this story. There are millions of people who work as members of a team, permitting the United States to maintain its air and space superiority. They can never be forgotten.

If you read between the lines you will understand the subtle evolution of the American original philosophy of the melting pot of different cultures and so-called races becoming one as the true American, as spelled out in the Declaration of Independence and the Constitution. This won't happen in my lifetime but will occur eventually in the next fifty or one hundred years. If you were born in this country then you are one of those people. Basically, all of us evolved from immigrants or slaves. If we continue the effort to classify ourselves as races (or castes) instead of Americans this will only delay the fulfillment of the Founding Fathers' dreams. The American Indians must be recognized as the true Americans and treated accordingly. Without this recognition we will be the shortest-lived dynasty in world history. Try and explain that to some politicians.

I would like to express appreciation to the following:

To Edith, my ex-wife, who handled the home front and got me to work during those years.

To Jackie, my present wife, who encouraged me to keep working on this book in many ways.

To Harry Jr. and Mike (my sons), Charles Frye (my stepson), and Sharon (granddaughter-in-law), all of whom were of tremendous help in acquiring, setting up, programming, correcting, and maintaining my computer.

To all of the people at Lockheed-Georgia and our affiliates within the

Lockheed Corporation for their help and influence (good or bad) on me. This includes all departments and divisions, especially the folks who worked directly with me over the years.

To all of the suppliers and vendors with whom I was associated for so many years. My records indicate about 95 percent of you but if I attempted to list you it would take at least ten pages. Your efforts in supporting Lockheed as to quality, delivery, and competitive cost were always at a high level. Your salesmen and manufacturing representatives were some of the best. Read this paragraph as personal, for I am talking about each of you. Those efforts supported me in maintaining my level of merit, thus securing my job.

To all of my instructors in all the classes that you taught. Every bit of that information was used at one time or another.

To the American Red Cross Blood Banks for the opportunity to recruit, donate, and receive blood for me and my family when needed.

My thanks to you all.

Harry L. Hudson, 2003

Editor's Acknowledgments

I would like to thank a number of people for their help in fulfilling Harry Hudson's goal of publishing his memoir of a working life at Lockheed. First and foremost, I appreciate the willingness of Harry L. Hudson Jr. and his family to donate the manuscript to the Kennesaw State University Archives. Harry shared some of his recollections of his father and also generously allowed the use of family photographs and his father's records, including work evaluations. I believe that Harry Jr. and the family are pleased that Harry Sr.'s story will be preserved and made accessible to students, scholars, and the general public in this edited volume.

Tamara Livingston, KSU's Director of Archives, offered encouragement for this project from the beginning and granted permission to publish the manuscript. Archivist Anne Graham and History and Philosophy Department secretary Megan MacDonald facilitated the project with their work in creating a digital version of the original manuscript.

Mick Gusinde-Duffy saw the potential for this volume early on and enthusiastically welcomed the proposal. The readers who evaluated both the editor's introduction and Hudson's narrative offered valuable suggestions that improved the manuscript (though any errors or misjudgments are the property of the editor).

My wife, Karen, and sons, Randall and Matthew, offered encouragement and relief as usual.

Most of all, I should thank Harry L. Hudson for having written this memoir. Sources such as this as are all too rare, and we are indebted to him for recording this piece of the history of civil rights and American business in the Cold War era.

Working for Equality

Introduction   On March 31, 1952, President Harry Truman announced that he would not seek re-election. The *Atlanta Daily World*, the nation's first successful African American daily newspaper, solicited reactions from members of Atlanta's black community. The paper published responses from a variety of African American citizens of Atlanta, including political activists, a club woman, a political science professor, a pharmacy employee, and a service station proprietor. Harry L. Hudson, the co-owner of Hudson's Service Station, observed that despite "all the corruption and graft in the present administration, President Truman was the only man to stand for complete democracy. Regardless of what the Southern or any other Democrats said, President Truman stood pat for his civil rights program," Hudson insisted. Truman's civil rights program represented "one of the pillars of democracy—equal rights for everybody." If Truman changed his mind and decided to seek re-election, Hudson declared, "I would vote for him."[1]

Just a few weeks after Truman's announcement, the *Daily World* reported on its front page that the National Association for the Advancement of Colored People (NAACP) was searching for candidates to apply for employment with the Lockheed Aircraft Corporation, which had recently reopened a vacant facility in nearby Marietta, Georgia. Atlanta NAACP President C. L. Harper told the *Daily World* that the restricted employment opportunities for Atlanta area African American citizens would soon "loosen up" at the massive airplane manufacturing plant. As the Korean War fueled government demand for military aircraft, the NAACP and its local chapters looked to use the leverage of potential manpower shortages to crack the Jim Crow system of segregation in employment, opening more jobs and job categories to black workers.[2]

Harry Hudson probably had no inkling in May 1952 that within a few months, he would become a foot soldier in the African American freedom struggle that had won the Truman administration's attention in the late 1940s. Yet by September 1952, Hudson was enrolled in a training program at the Lockheed facility. He would go on to spend the remainder of his working life with the company, retiring in 1988 after thirty-six years of service. Along the way, Hudson recorded a number of firsts with Lockheed. He would be "the first member of his race"[3] to serve as a supervisor at Lockheed-Georgia in 1953. Five years later, Hudson would become the first black supervisor to manage an integrated crew. In 1961, Hudson became the first African American to serve as a buyer, or purchasing agent, thus moving from working inside the factory to a position in which he represented Lockheed to suppliers of the endless stream of materiels and supplies consumed by the largest employer in the southeastern United States in the 1960s.

Harry Hudson was aware that his story might hold some interest for those who came after. He began saving documents, writing notes, and even tape recording his recollections shortly after he accepted the job at Lockheed. After his retirement, Hudson began composing a memoir of his working life at Lockheed. Though some of the documents and all the tape recordings were lost, Hudson's remarkable memoir survived. Harry Hudson Jr., Harry's eldest son, discovered the manuscript in a box in his attic in the summer of 2012. Hudson's memoir offers a rare, ground-level glimpse at the process of desegregation within the American workplace in the era of the modern civil rights movement.

Yet it is very much a personal story of Hudson's working life. He makes very few detours, particularly in the first half, outside his own experience at Lockheed. Hudson offers very few details about his private life, family, naval experience, public school years, or time at Morehouse. The civil rights movement forms a key component of the context for Hudson's story, but he maintains his focus solidly on his own experiences within the confines of Lockheed-Georgia. Likewise, Hudson observed that he maintained a "Gemini personality," split between a warm and loving father at home and a tough, unsentimental business persona at the office. Hudson's insistence that he developed dual personalities for work and home was in some ways reminiscent of Paul Laurence Dunbar's famous formulation presented in the poem "We Wear the Mask," and might superficially resemble W. E. B. Dubois's "double consciousness." Hudson's "Gemini personality" seems to be something rather less racially tinged; that is, it appears to be a work-home distinction that is perhaps familiar to a great many who have labored in corporate America.[4] As important as his family was in his life, however, Hudson only rarely mentioned his domestic life.

At the close of World War II, racial discrimination and white supremacist attitudes remained entrenched in southern law and American culture. Harry Hudson grew up in a segregated city embedded within a network of racially segregated labor markets. Segregated labor markets constricted economic opportunities for African Americans and, in turn, contributed to prevailing ideas about the limited potential of black workers. This feedback loop helped create and maintain a vicious cycle. Black workers, so the conventional wisdom assured, were not suited for highly skilled labor or professional work, especially skilled or professional work that required interaction as equals with whites. Educational facilities for African American youths were limited and underfunded in the late nineteenth and early twentieth centuries, yet even when the funding gap began to close in the 1930s (in response to challenges to segregation), the new funds largely were devoted to expanding traditional offerings. The essence of the dilemma was captured by the New York railroad entrepreneur and philanthropist William H. Baldwin Jr. in 1899: "It is a crime for any teacher, white or black, to educate the Negro for positions which are not open to him." Even in the 1920s and 1930s, when the Rosenwald Fund conducted surveys to try and demonstrate a need for black high schools, "in place after place the response indicated that there were no black jobs for which a high school education would be useful."[5]

Harry Hudson was born in Atlanta in 1925. His father, Perry, came of age in a segregated economy that defined black labor as less capable and therefore less valuable. By the 1920s, though racial discrimination was endemic in the American economy, racial segmentation defined the economy of the American South. The federal Bureau of Labor found in a 1937 survey that "nearly 60% of southern firms reported hiring only whites or blacks." Entire industries in the southern states were nearly closed to African Americans by the early 1930s; blacks constituted less than 10 percent of the workforce in southern textile mills, furniture and shoe factories, printing establishments, and railroad shops. The limited black employment in these industries was further restricted by a racial skill hierarchy. The 1930 Census reported that only 4 out of more than 5,000 loom fixers (the apex of skilled employment in textiles) and fewer than 50 out of almost 15,000 railroad engineers in the southern states were black.[6]

Perry Hudson occupied a relatively high-status position within the African American community as an employee of the U.S. Postal Service. Federal employment and professional work within the confines of a segregated society offered most of the scant opportunities for advancement into a black middle class in the early twentieth-century South. Hudson listed his occupation as "letter carrier" in the 1930 Census. By 1940, Hudson had moved up to "clerk." The Post Office remained one of the few arenas in which black men might find professional work in much of the South. Though discrimination permeated the Postal Service as other areas of American life, "the post office in the post-Reconstruction South became a scene not of black surrender but rather a contested site." Republican control of the patronage machinery of the federal government for most of the half-century following the end of Reconstruction, though not a panacea, served to protect at least some opportunities within the federal agency. By the 1920s, African American letter carriers and clerks were commonplace in larger post offices around Georgia, especially in Atlanta and Athens.[7] The Hudson family income, which consisted wholly of Perry Hudson's postal salary, amounted to $2,100 in 1939, well above the national average for all families of $1,368. This placed the Hudson family solidly within the black urban middle class. After World War II, Perry Hudson would open a service station in partnership with his son, Harry, financed in large part by the elder Hudson's savings and credit rating. Such entrepreneurial endeavors represented another possible, though difficult, path to social mobility in a segregated economy.[8]

World War II marked a turning point in government policy toward employment opportunity. African American demands for a fairer share of industrial jobs quickened with the rapid economic recovery from the Great Depression sparked by military production in 1940 and 1941. Pressured by A. Philip Randolph and other African American leaders, President Franklin Roosevelt issued Executive Order 8802. FDR's order required that all defense-related government contracts must contain a provision prohibiting racial discrimination in employment and created a Fair Employment Practices Committee (FEPC) within the War Production Board to oversee and enforce these contract provisions. Though the committee had little enforcement power, it managed to achieve tangible results, opening up more jobs than might have been accounted for simply by wartime labor shortages. The economist William J. Collins sharply differentiated FEPC's work in the South from its experiences in the northern states. The committee's work was difficult everywhere, but met with intransigence in the South. The region's history of de jure segregation and disfranchisement of black voters coupled with its deeply segregated labor market made FEPC's work nearly impossible.[9]

The aircraft industry was among the most resistant to penetration by black workers in the late 1930s and early 1940s. It was also the industry that perhaps benefited more than any other from massive wartime demand and, after the war, the permanent mobilization that characterized the Cold War era. No firm benefited more than Lockheed Aircraft, the company that provided the corporate setting for most of Harry Hudson's working life. Lockheed Martin is the current corporate identity of a pair of pioneer firms in American aviation. Allan and Malcolm Loughead, innovative mechanics with a passion for the newfound technology of flight, founded the Alco Hydro-Aeroplane Company in 1912, at about the same time that Glenn L. Martin founded his eponymously named company. The Loughead brothers' firm went through several incarnations, with the brothers eventually settling on a phonetic spelling of the family name—Lockheed—for the firm in 1926. The two companies merged in 1995 to form Lockheed Martin. For Harry Hudson's career, however, his corporate home was simply Lockheed Aircraft Corporation.

The Loughead brothers had some success during the World War I years, but struggled financially until their firm developed the Vega in 1927. The company introduced the Vega just six months after Charles Lindbergh's historic transatlantic flight demonstrated the viability of long-distance air travel. The Lockheed Vega, a six-passenger plane designed without the familiar struts that helped support wings on early aircraft, hit the market just as the Lindbergh-induced aircraft boom took off. Lindbergh himself flew the Vega in a series of flights crafted to test potential commercial airline routes, and sales boomed. The Vega quickly became a cultural icon. Amelia Earhart would become the first woman to fly across the Atlantic in a bright red Vega 5B, and Wiley Post would fly his modified Vega 5C around the world. Both planes are familiar sights today at the Smithsonian Air and Space Museum in Washington, D.C. Harry Hudson recalled building models of these iconic aircraft as a child. The models and the adventurous images they conjured formed his earliest memoires of the company that would define his working life.[10]

Lockheed and the entire aircraft industry grew exponentially during World War II, making the firm and the industry prime targets of interest by civil rights activists and FEPC. Aircraft manufacturers' output "increased by an astounding 13,500 percent during the war," the Lockheed historian William Hartung noted, as Lockheed, Douglas, Convair, Bell, and other firms rolled more than three hundred thousand planes off their assembly lines. The government not only bought every plane manufacturers could produce during the war, Washington also supplied investment capital to build new state-of-the-art plants, including the largest aircraft manufacturing plant in the world in Marietta, Georgia. Robert Gross informed an investor that while the enormous demand of wartime could not be sustained indefinitely, Lockheed's stockholders would "be pleased to learn that we ended [1944]. . . with our company in the best financial position it has ever enjoyed." With profits of 4 to 9 percent on such volume production, this was a model of understatement.[11]

Robert C. Weaver, the Harvard-educated economist, activist, and member of FDR's "black cabinet," coordinated a number of studies of African American employment opportunities before, during, and in the aftermath of World War II. "Perhaps the most significant, and certainly the earliest, example of a sound approach to the integration of Negroes in aircraft production,"

Weaver observed in a 1945 article, "occurred at the Lockheed-Vega Plant in Southern California." Like virtually all other firms in the aircraft industry, Lockheed employed no black workers in the spring of 1941. The company responded quickly to FDR's executive order, Weaver noted, developing a comprehensive plan.[12]

Lockheed introduced the first black workers into its California plants in August 1941. About 1,000 African Americans had found employment at Lockheed by the end of 1941. As of March 1942, the firm employed 2,500 black workers, many in skilled and semiskilled production jobs. The numbers were small relative to the company's size: Lockheed's total employment peaked at more than 90,000 in 1943 before falling to 63,000 in 1944 due to improved efficiency.[13]

Weaver concluded that his study of the aircraft industry during World War II "illustrated clearly that when economic necessity and governmental pressures require the introduction of minorities into new types of work, it can be achieved." Activist government policy combined with a tight labor market (itself perhaps manipulated by the state) could open job training and employment opportunities for minorities, overcoming systemic racial discrimination. Beyond government policy and high levels of employment, the most important factor "in effecting relaxations in the color caste system in employment" was "the strategic position of management." Lockheed served as perhaps the best example of Weaver's insistence that management commitment and planning could crack the walls of employment segregation. The aircraft industry "also illustrated that, given economic necessity, relaxations in traditional bars to Negro employment are most easily and extensively achieved in industrial centers outside the South, where the color caste system is least firmly entrenched." While employment segregation was a national and not merely a regional problem, Weaver found that plants in the South proved tougher to penetrate. "The picture in Southern aircraft plants is uniformly bad," he wrote, though he found that the Bell Aircraft–operated plant in Marietta, Georgia, was among "the least bad."[14]

The manufacturing facility that would serve as the home of Lockheed-Georgia during Harry Hudson's career originated during World War II. "The decision to build a bomber plant in rural Cobb County," the historian Tom Scott wrote, "was the result of fortuitous circumstances and the hard work of visionary local statesmen determined to lead the area out of the Great Depression." The local attorney and businessman James Carmichael, General Lucius Clay, and Mayor Rip Blair were "champions of industrial growth," opposed the race-baiting associated with the Eugene Talmadge faction in Georgia politics, and "saw a positive role for government [at all levels, local, state, and national] in improving education, building a modern infrastructure, and actively recruiting" outside industry. During the preparedness campaign of 1941, Marietta's development coalition successfully sought federal support first for the construction of Rickenbacker Field, a modern airstrip. With the outbreak of war in December, the army stepped up its production demand for the massive Boeing-designed B-29 bomber. The production runs required for the new planes—indeed, for all aircraft during World War II—necessitated that Boeing license its plans to other manufacturers to meet the military's demand. Marietta's development team won over Bell management. The plant would be constructed with federal funds, managed by Bell Aircraft, and tasked with producing B-29s for the army.[15]

Bell operated the plant for less than three years, from the plant's completion in the spring of 1943 until it closed its doors, seemingly for good, in January 1946. At its peak, Government Aircraft Plant No. 6 (later Air Force Plant No. 6) employed more than 28,000 workers in late 1944, including about 2,000 African-Americans. Black workers were strictly segregated from whites, working in separate areas. Many of the black workers were employed in janitorial, loading, materiel handling, and other "traditional" black jobs, but some eventually received training and performed semiskilled and skilled manufacturing work, albeit still within a segregated framework. Bell at first refused to hire black workers for any jobs beyond unskilled labor. Eventually, pressure from FEPC and the Atlanta Urban League (AUL) produced some cracks in the segregated labor market. By late 1944, Bell had trained and employed eight hundred African Americans in skilled manufacturing positions. The skilled black workers continued to labor, however, in segregated areas, some at feeder locations miles away from the main plant. Indeed, the most knowledgeable historian of the Bell factory and Cobb County in this period has observed that "the company was so effective in its segregationist policy that few white workers were aware that blacks performed skilled jobs." Blacks made up about 8 percent of the workforce at the plant, though African Americans accounted for 16 percent of Cobb County's population. Strict segregation along departmental lines also drastically curtailed black workers' chances for advancement and promotion. James Carmichael, who served as plant manager for Bell, finally negotiated an agreement with FEPC to open more training opportunities for black workers, but, faced with declining demand for aircraft, began to reduce total employment at the plant as early as the end of 1944.[16] With the end of the war in August 1945, the fate of the plant was sealed. The short-lived demobilization of the immediate postwar years forced the closure of the Marietta factory in January 1946.

Jennifer Delton has offered the most complete analysis of the complex interrelationships among civil rights activism, government policy, and corporate America. Prior to World War II, organizations such as the National Urban League had focused on negotiating agreements with employers that tried to open new opportunities for black workers in "non-traditional" (i.e., higher skilled or higher profile) jobs. In the early days, such negotiations often led to informal quotas or numerical targets, and such targets nearly always became de facto maximums, and little beyond symbolic headway had been made by World War II. In fact, it was such an arrangement that had opened the limited opportunities at Marietta's Bell plant. In the wake of World War II, the NAACP and other civil rights organizations shifted toward an emphasis on "fair employment," reflecting the aims of the wartime Fair Employment Practices Committee. After the war, "FEPC activists" turned their attention toward "ending barriers to black employment" and away from the earlier goal of simply "securing jobs for blacks." When Congress failed to create a permanent FEPC after the war, activists pressed for the creation of state-level agencies to promote fair employment. Many northern state legislatures responded with state FEPCs. Civil rights activists argued that if the government promoted full employment via vigorous macroeconomic policies and focused on encouraging employers to eliminate overt barriers to equal employment, further intrusive action by the state to require racially based hiring targets would be unnecessary.[17]

The World War II experience led to modest economic gains by black workers and limited political momentum toward continued progress in much of the country. Gavin Wright found that "black occupational attainment as of 1950 in northern states—limited as it was—markedly exceeded that of black southerners." FEPC, as noted above, had a positive effect on black employment outside the South. The migration of large numbers of southern blacks to northern cities and the subsequent political mobilization of African American communities in the North helped sustain the limited momentum of FEPC by securing passage of fair employment laws (creating state-level versions of FEPC) in a number of northern states. Outside the South, a number of corporate leaders, generally quietly and without fanfare, began implementing anti-discriminatory personnel policies. In Dixie after the war, however, Wright observed that "the white South dug in its heels in defense of its racial order." Widespread disfranchisement of black voters in the South removed much of the internal political pressure that might have disciplined southern politicians. Though a relatively vigorous moderate faction contended for influence, the winners in Georgia's public square reflected the regional mood. Embodying the regional spirit, Georgia's Senator Richard Russell secured passage in June 1944 of an amendment to require congressional approval of any funding for any agency created by executive order that lasted more than one year. This was a death warrant for the wartime FEPC, as it subjected even an agency created by executive order to the senatorial filibuster. "On matters of policy," Wright concluded about the immediate postwar South, "there was little sign or promise of change."[18]

Perry Hudson and his family had no connection with the Bell Aircraft experience during World War II. Harry Hudson, one of Perry's six sons, was born in 1925. Harry enlisted in the navy in 1943 after graduating from high school. He mustered out in January 1946 just as Bell closed. Harry Hudson attended Morehouse College, a historically black institution, on the GI Bill. The GI Bill (the Servicemen's Readjustment Act) is generally hailed as a watershed social revolution in American life, but the bill's legacy has been more complex for African Americans. In short, the GI Bill enhanced opportunities for education, training, housing, and employment for whites and for blacks outside the South. Within the South, African Americans found it difficult to take advantage of GI Bill benefits. Lack of adequate facilities and the local control and administration of the bill's programs limited its effectiveness. The South's black colleges were small, underfunded, and unable to accommodate the rapid influx of potential students. Very few offered any post-baccalaureate programs; none offered advanced degrees in engineering. For black veterans unwilling to leave the South, the GI Bill offered limited benefits. Gavin Wright has observed that, ironically, the economic lot of many black southerners actually worsened in the first decade and a half after World War II. The disparate impact of the GI Bill helped account for this "widening [of] the gap" between blacks and whites, boosting proportionately many more whites through education while leaving many blacks behind.[19]

Harry Hudson was one of the fortunate black southerners able to take at least partial advantage of the GI Bill. Hudson spent the late 1940s attending Morehouse as tensions between the United States and the Soviet Union grew. By the time Hudson graduated with a degree in biology in June 1951, the Korean War was a year old. The Cold War erupted in a limited but vicious hot war on the Korean peninsula in June 1950. After initial communist success in the war's early days, followed by a near-total victory by UN/U.S. forces in the fall of 1951, Chinese intervention pushed the front lines back to the starting point around the 38th parallel, where the war ground down to a bloody stalemate. The Korean War created the conditions that brought together black demands for greater employment opportunity, the Cold War, a corporation with massive government contracts, a federal government moving (tentatively) toward more inclusive civil rights policies, and Harry L. Hudson.

On January 4, 1951, the day Seoul fell to communist forces for the second time in the Korean War, Lockheed President Robert Gross announced that the company had reached an agreement with the U.S. government to reopen a large aircraft manufacturing facility in Marietta, Georgia—mothballed since the end of World War II—to aid in the refitting of B-29s and to build the Boeing-designed B-47. (Lockheed, Boeing, and Douglas had engaged in such collaboration during World War II, and the Korean War seemed to call for such cooperative ventures again.) It would take "some time" to get the plant up and running, Gross observed. Reopening the old facility would clearly generate thousands of high-paying manufacturing jobs in the heart of Dixie, a region in the midst of an economic transformation "from cotton belt to sun belt," as one historian characterized it.[20] Lockheed's reopening of Air Force Plant No. 6 also started a chain of events that helped lead to stronger action by the federal government on equal opportunity employment which, in turn, helped lead to Harry Hudson's employment at Lockheed-Georgia.

Responding to increasing pressure from civil rights organizations to take action to guarantee fair employment in the defense industries rapidly expanding with the hot eruption in Korea of the Cold War after 1950, the Truman administration issued an executive order in December 1951 creating the Committee on Government Contracts (CGC) to "improve the means for obtaining compliance" with existing anti-discrimination policies. In essence, the CGC became the successor to the FEPC at the federal level. Truman's CGC was to confer with employers to help determine the best ways to eliminate discrimination, but was given no enforcement powers beyond a vague ability to make recommendations to the Defense Department and the president.[21]

The *Atlanta Daily World*, the city's preeminent African American newspaper, reported in September 1951 that Lockheed's Marietta, Georgia, facility would "follow southern tradition" and operate on a segregated basis. Lockheed-Georgia Vice President and General Manager James V. Carmichael elaborated on the company's policy. Carmichael was widely "recognized as a liberal-minded (within the southern context) former Georgia gubernatorial candidate." The Marietta attorney-businessman's background and reputation as a racial moderate perhaps made him the perfect messenger for the corporate policy he announced, at least within the Marietta area. Carmichael's statement clearly crystallized the consensus of white opinion in the South and revealed the narrowness of the spectrum on issues of race. "We intend to live in the Southern tradition here," Carmichael declared. Lockheed's Georgia division would "employ colored people according to their ability, but they will not be mixed with white people on assembly line operations. They will be hired for work for which they are qualified or can be trained."[22]

Carmichael insisted that Lockheed would not be discriminating, simply hiring according to ability. The underlying message that Carmichael intended to deliver seemed clear, however. By emphasizing that African Americans would be hired "for work for which they are qualified or can be trained," Carmichael offered a nod and a wink to the prevailing prejudice that black workers were inherently inferior to whites. Lockheed signaled that the traditional southern system of segregating the labor market would continue, as would racial separation on the factory floor. In his narrative, Harry Hudson bitterly recalled hearing rumors that Carmichael had stated the company's policy in more explicit terms.

The *Atlanta Daily World* followed a more cautious line in interpreting Carmichael's remarks, perhaps justified by later events. After his initial comments had touched off protests from the NAACP, Carmichael argued that his comments had been misinterpreted. Carmichael met with representatives of the NAACP in early November 1951 and assured them that Lockheed aimed for "the use of available labor at all levels of employment without regard to race." The *Daily World* expressed confidence (perhaps as much to encourage or pressure as to express simple concurrence) that Carmichael's true intent reflected a commitment to equality of opportunity, albeit within the complex segregated world of the workplace in early 1950s Georgia.[23]

The Atlanta branch of the NAACP protested Carmichael's apparent flouting of federal government pledges of nondiscrimination among defense contractors. In November 1951, C. L. Harper, president of the Atlanta NAACP, and C. W. Greenlea, chairman of the Atlanta branch's War Mobilization Committee, met with Carmichael to discuss these concerns. Carmichael told Harper and Greenlea that Lockheed would work to offer black employees expanded opportunities within a segregated framework. Atlanta NAACP leaders expressed their dissatisfaction with Carmichael's response by going over his head to Lockheed President Robert Gross. Harper and Greenlea informed Gross that they had raised concerns about Carmichael's statements on segregation in the plant. Carmichael had assured NAACP leaders that "discrimination was not the intent of the Marietta plant's policy." After the meeting, Greenlea and Harper drafted a letter rejecting Carmichael's offer of more opportunity within a segregated system. The NAACP "cannot commit itself to a policy of segregation in any field of activity," they insisted, and added a Cold War–related argument. "Moreover, if Lockheed is to produce planes to defend America, now threatened by Russian Communism, certainly we cannot afford, through discrimination in employment, to give our enemies a cold war weapon more powerful than guns, planes, or battleships."²⁴

As the Cold War intensified in Africa and Asia, sensitive observers noted that it would be difficult for the United States to win the hearts and minds of people of color while carrying the social and political baggage of racial discrimination. Paul Robeson remarked in the 1950s that when he visited the Soviet Union, "it was the first time I felt like a human being." Few wanted to emulate the Soviet system, yet a great many wondered how a nation that openly touted itself as a bastion of freedom and democracy could systematically deny legal, social, and political equality to racial and ethnic minorities within its own boundaries.²⁵

The Atlanta Urban League and the NAACP received numerous complaints from black job applicants. Essentially, Lockheed did not allow black applicants to fill out applications at the employment office. African American applicants were routinely told to take the applications home and fill them out and return on Fridays for interviews. When the black applicants returned on Fridays, they were "told that no interviews are being held and that no jobs are available." As of December 1951, NAACP officials declared to Gross, "only one Negro person is employed in other than a maintenance capacity" at the plant.²⁶

Grace Towns Hamilton, president of the Atlanta chapter of the Urban League, and the AUL's Employment Opportunities Committee met with Carmichael and Lockheed Director of Industrial Relations James Lydon in January 1952 to discuss employment opportunities at Lockheed. Hamilton asked Carmichael about "the present status of Negro employment at Lockheed." According to minutes of the meeting, Carmichael "replied there had been some cutbacks in scheduled plane production by Washington. He indicated that these cutbacks may be attributed to the fear of over-production." Carmichael went on to describe in some detail the status of black workers at Lockheed. He also described plans currently being implemented to employ more black workers, albeit on a segregated basis. Beneath the superficial façade of 25 percent African American employment at the plant, virtually all black workers were confined to job categories that would have fit the definition of traditional jobs for blacks within a segregated labor market. Acknowledging this fact, Carmichael frankly "*stated that the employment of Negroes in skilled and technical jobs would be resented by other plant personnel. Therefore, it would seem advisable to utilize skilled and technical Negro personnel as supervisors of future Negro employees*" (emphasis added).²⁷

Skilled black workers would work on a segregated line assembling a section of the B-47 bomber, built by Lockheed under a license agreement with its designer, Boeing. This could allow black workers to develop skills and work experience in higher-paying job classifications while minimizing racial friction in the workplace. It would, however, also establish separate lines of advancement and make it difficult for African Americans to progress into management positions. "Messrs. Carmichael and Lydon also revealed that between 130–159 occupational skill[s] will be used in the fabrication of the 43 section of the B-47 plane. Again Negroes will be employed under similar circumstances as mentioned above."[28]

Harry L. Hudson was among those African Americans hired as part of the arrangement between Lockheed and the Atlanta Urban League. Hudson described a visit paid by Robert Kennon to the Hudsons' service station. Hudson noted that as of that Sunday in August 1952, he did not know that Lockheed had opened the World War II-era Bell Bomber Plant to produce airplanes for the U.S. war effort in Korea. It is doubtful that Hudson had never heard anything of the plant opening—it was widely reported in the region's newspapers—but it is plausible that it made little impression on him. Hudson would not have thought of Lockheed as a potential employer. Aircraft manufacturing was skilled, highly paid, highly respected work that occurred outside the confines of the segregated African American economy. Such opportunities were clearly limited for men like Harry Hudson, and he knew this all too well.

Hudson certainly knew of James Carmichael, Lockheed's initial plant manager. Carmichael was a local Marietta attorney who had played a role in helping convince the U.S. government to locate a mammoth aircraft manufacturing facility in Marietta early in World War II. Carmichael also served as the plant's general manager during the war. Hudson characterized Carmichael as a typical southern segregationist politician. Hudson's brief characterization belied the complexity of the South's racial politics in the post–World War II era, yet it conveyed an elemental truth. The die-hard commitment to segregation in the South was symbolized by the short-lived Dixiecrat political movement in 1948. Though the Dixiecrats faded, opposition to threats to white privilege did not. The emergence of white massive resistance to the postwar civil rights movement around the region coincided with an economic boom that helped create the Sunbelt South by the 1970s. Carmichael was seen as a moderate on the race issue in the 1940s and 1950s within the context of Georgia politics. Georgia politics was dominated by the specter of the Talmadges, Eugene and Herman. Eugene Talmadge had served several terms as governor of the state in the 1930s and faced James Carmichael in a bitterly contested Democratic primary (the only election that mattered) in 1946.

The U.S. Supreme Court struck down the Texas white primary in 1944 in its *Smith v. Allwright* decision. Yet Georgia and other southern states attempted to continue to use the racially exclusive primary, leading to a series of related federal court decisions and attempts to recast the white primary through legislative subterfuge, as when South Carolina repealed all state laws regarding the primary election in 1945. Among the chief issues in the campaign was the fate of Georgia's whites-only primary, struck down by federal courts in 1945. Talmadge favored trying to revive the white primary by legal subterfuge and further pledged to defend legalized segregation in Georgia from the increasing attacks of the NAACP and the intrusive federal government. Carmichael downplayed the race issue and emphasized economic growth and stability, though he remained publicly committed to segregation. Talmadge lost the popular vote but won the all-important county unit vote (a bizarre Georgia tradition that resembled a state version of the electoral college). He died before taking office, thus touching off the "three governors controversy," which eventually resulted in a special election for governor, won by his son, Herman Talmadge, in 1948.[29]

Herman Talmadge made large new commitments to public education but coupled this with threats to close public schools rather than integrate during the 1950s and other measures of massive resistance. He publicly and vigorously opposed federal civil rights legislation, voicing a white supremacist agenda. Talmadge pledged to revive the white primary in some form and do "all within my power to help defeat" President Truman's proposed permanent FEPC. The leader of Georgia's dominant political faction assured Georgia's white working-class voters that "I don't want your wives or your daughters to work under a Negro foreman or beside a Negro." The statewide political environment in Georgia in the early 1950s was not hospitable to overt threats to the established segregationist order.[30]

Harry Hudson commented on Lockheed's economic impact on Georgia and the South, observing that the thousands of high-paying manufacturing jobs created a revolution in the region. Though Hudson did not appreciate the subtle differences between Carmichael and Talmadge, the eventual victory of the boosters—politically and economically—clearly made a critical difference in the region's history. Gavin Wright has observed that while the politics of the post–World War II South did not produce an interracial coalition advocating social democracy, the economy promoted by the boosters "did offer access to the rewards of that regime to substantial numbers of black as well as white southerners, and this is no small matter."[31]

Carmichael and his colleagues in Marietta's development coalition were New South boosters, searching for ways to bring the region out of its economic stagnation. Boosters pursued an approach that James C. Cobb famously labeled "the selling of the South." Numan Bartley, Patricia Sullivan, Jacquelyn Dowd-Hall, and Glenda Gilmore have, in somewhat different terms, emphasized the narrowing of political debate that accompanied the emergence of race as a national issue in the postwar years and the richness of the radical traditions that existed in Dixie before the emergence of the Cold War and the second Red Scare. The potential for a class-based interracial coalition, something like a southern version of the northern elements of the New Deal coalition, according to these historians, went unrealized. Politicians such as Carmichael's erstwhile mentor in the 1946 governor's race, Ellis Arnall, seemed to represent the just left-of-center tip of a potential iceberg. After the race-baiting campaigns of the late 1940s and the emergence of massive resistance to civil rights reform, the only remaining potential opponents (within the political mainstream) of the Talmadges of the South were the New South boosters, businessmen and business cheerleaders committed to little beyond economic growth.[32]

Hudson and others of his generation pioneered and suffered, benefited but bumped into limits yet to be overcome. Hudson saw Carmichael simply as a typical southern segregationist politician. White liberals (a quite small but somewhat hardy lot led by writers such as Lillian Smith) would have had their own quibbles with Carmichael (he was no friend of organized labor, for example, and Smith certainly thought he was too conservative on the race issue), but would certainly have seen him as clearly preferable to Talmadge.[33] Yet it should not be surprising that such hair-splitting meant little to a great many Georgians of African American descent: in the end, Carmichael was a segregationist, too; he just promoted a "kinder, gentler" version of southern apartheid. But the boosters Carmichael represented perhaps did, at least, represent the possibility of a kind of progress.

The National Urban League conducted a survey of employers with major defense contracts in July 1952. The results demonstrated the extent of the race problem that existed within the U.S. labor market both inside and outside the South. Texas and California had developed concentrations in aircraft and related manufacturing. Texas facilities owned by Consolidated Vultee Aircraft (popularly known as Convair) and Bell Aircraft "employ[ed] Negroes in unskilled but not skilled production jobs." Those firms also "refuse[d] to employ Negroes for technical and clerical jobs, nor [did] they accept Negroes in training programs conducted by them." The situation was slightly better in California, but Douglas Aircraft, North American Aviation, and Northrop Aircraft "refuse[d] to employ Negroes in technical and clerical jobs." General Electric's aviation division shared that problem but also "refuse[d] to accept Negroes in training programs" and did not hire blacks for skilled production work.[34]

The Urban League survey criticized Lockheed-Georgia for limiting black workers to unskilled jobs in the production area. "Promises have been made that Negroes will be upgraded into semi-skilled jobs" but noted that "they will be maintained in segregated areas."[35] The program that James Carmichael and Jim Lydon had outlined to the League's Atlanta chapter seemed to be the basis of the survey's findings. The following month, August 1952, Harry Hudson would join a small group to begin crossing the color line in skilled aircraft work at Lockheed, albeit within a segregated framework.

Hudson described the recruitment and training of black workers for skilled positions at Lockheed in the opening pages of his memoir. Hudson's account emphasizes the perhaps excessive training and too-simple elementary instruction offered to a group of probably overqualified African American men. The *Atlanta Daily World* reported on the progress of Lockheed's black trainees in December 1952. In a front-page story, the staff writer Lerone Bennett Jr. and the city editor Robert Johnson politely confirmed Hudson's assessment. "Untrained workers are given a personal interview and a battery of tests," they observed, and, like Hudson, "most of the trainees have attended college." In a follow-up story, Bennett and Johnson reported that "all officials at the plant pointed out that the educational achievements of Negro workers are much higher than those of white workers." According to the labor relations representative Robert Kennon, all of the black workers were high school graduates and three-fourths had at least two years of college.[36]

Hudson's opening pages effectively tell the ground-level story of the beginnings of workplace desegregation in the South. Robert Kennon, a young African American personnel representative from Lockheed, was a regular customer of the Hudsons' station. He recruited Harry as part of his job. Kennon, a Morehouse graduate, was "the only Negro employed in the administrative section" at Lockheed. Hugh Gordon, employed at Lockheed in the personnel department from the early 1950s through the late 1980s, confirmed Hudson's contention that Kennon was recruiting black workers. Gordon recalled that sometime in 1952, "word came down from above" that personnel "needed to hire a Negro recruiter." Though he did not recall the finer details sixty years later, Gordon clearly remembered that some sort of directive had come down from upper management. Kennon's main job was to recruit qualified black applicants for skilled work at Lockheed and to assist in coordinating their training and retention. The *Daily World* reported in December

1952 that "approximately 40 Negroes [including Harry Hudson] are now enrolled in the corporation's earn while you learn program." In addition, Lockheed intended to hire an additional twenty black workers per week until an unspecified "employment schedule" was reached. The training program paid workers $1.55 per hour while they learned (average hourly earnings in all U.S. manufacturing in 1952 amounted to $1.59, while the minimum wage was 75 cents). This program represented the fulfillment of the pledges made by Carmichael and Lydon to the Atlanta Urban League earlier in the year.[37]

Lockheed hired Hudson's "super Negroes" (highly educated black men) with the specific intent of training them in skilled aircraft work. Some or all of these original ten were viewed by management as potential candidates to become the first black supervisor for the company. Harry Hudson distinguished himself in training, demonstrated leadership once on the factory floor, and quickly became a "lead man"—still an hourly manufacturing employee, but this classification placed a great deal of responsibility on its holder and was often a stepping stone to promotion to supervisor. A production supervisor became a member of management.

In September 1953, Harry Hudson became the first African American supervisor at Lockheed-Georgia and, he believed, within the entire firm. This may appear surprising given the longer history of black workers with the firm in California, coupled with the fragmentary evidence that Lockheed had a better reputation than other aircraft companies. Yet employment discrimination was a fact of life nationwide in the postwar era. Attitudes and management traditions that restricted blacks to certain job categories were slow to change. In 1961, the chairman of the NAACP's West Coast Labor and Industry Committee, William Pollard, charged that racial exclusion was the norm in supervisory positions. At that point, there were no supervisors among the 1,500 black workers employed by Lockheed in California. It is difficult to make a definitive conclusion, but Hudson's view, apparently held by many within the company, is eminently plausible.[38]

Hudson's "breakthrough job" made him something of a celebrity. In 1957, the Pet Milk Company featured the Hudson family in an advertisement targeted at black newspapers. "Pretty Edith Hudson," the ad copy began, "is the center of an active, happy family—her successful husband [Harry], a graduate of Morehouse College, and four husky boys." The ad featured pictures of Edith Hudson, the Hudson family seated at the dinner table, and Harry Hudson rough-housing with his boys on the living room floor. The Hudsons appeared in every respect a typical middle-class American family. Edith Hudson "loves cooking for them [Harry and her sons] and she always uses PET

Evaporated Milk to make her meals extra rich, extra nourishing, and extra delicious." The Hudsons enjoyed entertaining in their "large backyard," with Harry playing a steel guitar to accompany group singing at parties.[39]

The Pet Milk ad reflected the growing significance of the African American market. As early as the late 1920s, market researchers had identified the small but growing black urban middle class as a prime target for increased advertising campaigns. Pet Milk developed a remarkably successful campaign focused on the Fultz quadruplets, the first recorded set of African American quadruplets, in the late 1940s. The idea for the ad, according to Harry Hudson Jr., came from one of his father's Morehouse classmates, at the time in the advertising business.[40]

Hudson's example notwithstanding, progress was painstakingly slow for African American workers at Lockheed. NAACP Labor Secretary Herbert Hill reported on conditions at the Lockheed-Georgia plant in March 1957. The plant employed 17,350 total workers, of whom 1,350 were black. Almost 1,000 of them were concentrated in two departments. "The overwhelming majority of Negroes employed in these two departments are classified as 'structural assembly helpers.'" Lockheed specified 450 job classifications in the plant; African Americans could be found in "no more than 20." A majority of supervisors in the all-black departments were white. "The Company's policy is to have a limited number of Negroes in 'lead man' positions only in the Negro departments; therefore, because Negroes can only be promoted to supervisory jobs within the Negro work force, the opportunities for Negro promotion are extremely limited."[41]

Despite public criticism such as that from Hill and the NAACP and private pressure via representatives from Eisenhower's government contracts committee, Lockheed continued to move slowly. Hudson crossed another color line at Lockheed in 1959. Lockheed made Hudson the first African American to supervise an integrated crew. Hudson was allowed to pick his crew. He focused on older workers, men with families who had a larger stake in keeping their jobs. Hudson's responsibilities expanded until he was supervising eighty-seven black and white workers. By 1961, Hudson believed he was in line to become a department manager. Yet Hudson's story was still very much the exception.

What accounted for the slow pace of progress? At least three factors played a role. Hudson amply documented the most obvious possible explanation— the accumulated traditions, assumptions, attitudes, and practices of a segregated society and economy. Even accounting for the distortions that always accompany eyewitness accounts, there seems little doubt that Hudson and other black workers faced a tough uphill climb at Lockheed. Managers and fellow workers alike generally discounted the potential of black workers, and Hudson provided a number of examples. Hudson seemed to have been convinced that top management at Lockheed favored integration and racial equality while many within what might be called middle management favored maintaining the status quo. Hudson singled out Dan Haughton, who served in a variety of high-level management capacities, including general manager of the Marietta plant, before assuming leadership of the corporation.[42]

There were notable exceptions as well. Hudson's account of the inspector who had been instructed to grade down the workmanship of Hudson and his fellows is genuinely moving. Hudson, his fellow workers, and the white inspector were all individual players caught up in a much larger drama. The experience of exaggerating or falsifying the flaws in the black crew's rivet holes moved the inspector eventually to refuse to participate in an activity that degraded everyone involved, and the very idea of quality workmanship as well. As difficult as the experience was for all concerned, the accumulation of thousands of small experiences such as this played a part in breaking down the mental barriers that had been erected to defend segregation.

In addition to the barriers created by the assumptions and practices of a segregated society, the economic fortunes of Lockheed in the 1950s made consistent progress in black employment difficult. Black workers entered the workforce at Lockheed more slowly than whites at the beginning; thus when layoffs struck, black workers were, as usual, among the last hired and first fired. Lockheed's Georgia workforce fluctuated in the 1950s, topping 17,000 in May 1955, but slipping to less than 14,000 in late 1961. Employment rose and fell with the company's ability to procure new contracts from the Defense Department—the C-130 Hercules in the 1950s; the C-141 Starlifter in the early 1960s; and the ill-fated C-5A in the late 1960s. The most rapid progress in black employment and advancement dated from the period after the C-141 contract in 1961, when the workforce ballooned to almost 33,000 in 1969. As Robert Weaver had observed in 1945, rapid employment growth could help smooth the way for desegregation.[43] Stagnant or declining employment intensified the problem.

Lockheed's Jim Lydon acknowledged the impact of both these factors in October 1954. Harry Alston, director of the National Urban League's Southern Field Division, met with Lydon, Lockheed's personnel director, that month to review the company's progress on "the utilization of Negro personnel." Alston reported that Lydon "expressed a rather doubtful point of view relative to expanding employment opportunities" for black workers at the Marietta plant. Lydon told Alston that there were two main reasons for the gloomy prospects: "the repercussions to the Supreme Court's decision relative to segregation in public schools; and the limited budget with which Lockheed has to work." Though Lockheed was at that time near its 1950s employment peak, Lydon well knew that the projected workforce would be contracting rather than growing over the foreseeable future, so that the prospect of financing (in the moral as well as financial sense) integration from growth, as the firm had done in the early 1950s, would not be an option. Lydon perhaps implied that pressing ahead with plans to hire more blacks for skilled jobs and advance black workers into supervisory positions would meet with greater hostility within the community and from the white workers. He also strongly implied that the backlash against the *Brown* decision would make black advancement at the plant a sensitive local issue.[44]

Lydon cited the backlash against the *Brown* case as a limiting factor, but school desegregation took second place among racial issues in Cobb County in the mid-1950s. The Amos Reece case dominated local headlines. Reece was arrested and convicted of raping a white woman in October 1953. Reece went through multiple trials, the last one coming when the Supreme Court overturned Reece's conviction on the basis that African Americans were excluded from the grand jury pool in Cobb County. The county revised its procedures, and a new grand jury with two black members indicted Reece again in 1955. Reece was executed in January 1957.[45] The Reece case played out concurrently with the *Brown* case, and both contributed to an atmosphere of retrenchment in Georgia and the South.

Georgia was home to prominent politicians who posed as titans of massive resistance to civil rights reform, including Herman Talmadge and Marvin Griffin. While Talmadge had publicly criticized fair employment legislation and openly opposed integration on the factory floor, in reality he and his segregationist successor, Marvin Griffin, said nothing (as far as can be determined) about the advancement of black workers at Lockheed. Georgia political leaders voiced frequent criticism of federal legislation aimed at equal employment opportunity, but generally avoided any overt criticism of Lockheed or other private employers. Local newspapers also seemed to ignore developments at Lockheed. While the *Atlanta Constitution* covered Lockheed's first few years in Georgia voluminously, it carried no announcement of Hudson's promotion to supervisor in 1953. The *Marietta Daily Journal* followed suit, offering no mention of the event. Hudson had made the front page of the *Daily World* and rated a notice in *Jet* magazine.

Organized labor also played a complicated role in the progress of African American workers. Many of the unions with the longest history of racial discrimination—the International Association of Machinists (IAM) and the building trades, for example—were associated with the American Federation of Labor (AFL), yet the old federation also was home to A. Philip Randolph's Brotherhood of Sleeping Car Porters. The Congress of Industrial Organizations (CIO) adopted an exceptionally progressive national stance on race, yet some affiliated CIO unions and locals engaged in racially discriminatory practices. By the early 1950s, both major federations had voiced support for equal employment opportunity and the growing civil rights movement. On balance, organized labor appeared to be a net positive force in the struggle for racial equality by the 1950s. Lockheed's workers were represented by IAM, a union with a particularly troubled past in terms of racial exclusion. Though the machinists union made progress on race in the postwar years, it was often slow. In fact, IAM established separate local unions for black and white members at Lockheed-Georgia.[46]

Throughout the 1950s, NAACP officials charged that white workers dominated skilled positions, while black workers were concentrated in semiskilled "assembly helper" jobs. The color line in employment moved up a bit, but remained, according to critics. The white local's control over the highest-rated skilled positions also gave it control over apprenticeships in those job categories. Without access to union apprenticeships, black progress was limited. Lockheed would operate with separate black and white IAM locals until the early 1960s, when the units merged under pressure from the federal government.[47]

Hudson spent a little more than a year as a union member at Lockheed before his promotion to supervisor made him a member of management. The bulk of his experiences with the union came as a member of management. Hudson vividly recalled two bitter strikes at Lockheed in 1958 and 1977. He offers colorful descriptions of his experiences as a member of management during both strikes. In each case, Hudson and his management colleagues had to hit the assembly lines to try and keep production moving. The second strike lasted seventy-seven days and created tremendous hardships for Lockheed production workers. Hudson believed both strikes had accomplished nothing except to create difficulties for a great many workers.

Hudson's career stalled, it seemed, as Lockheed struggled. Hudson recalled President Eisenhower's famous warning about the emerging "military-industrial complex" in his discussion of his experiences in the 1970s. There was no better example of Eisenhower's complex than Lockheed, for good and ill. Lockheed had developed a series of aircraft that fulfilled key functions for the Department of Defense in the 1950s and 1960s, from open conflicts in Korea and Vietnam to top-secret long-range reconnaissance (the SR-71 Blackbird). The C-5A contract led Lockheed into a quagmire of cost overruns, massive losses, government loan guarantees, and a bribery scandal involving foreign governments. All of these activities were well above Harry Hudson's pay grade, but he imbibed the company line. Lockheed officials consistently blamed unrealistic contract requirements imposed by a new system adopted in the mid-1960s.[48]

Lockheed's prime position at the apex of the military-industrial complex made the company an obvious target for equal employment activists as well. Lockheed won a contract for the C-141 Starlifter in March 1961. The contract was announced just after the new Kennedy administration issued Executive Order 10925. Kennedy had promised tougher action on employment discrimination among government contractors. Executive Order 10925 required that contractors go beyond simply removing barriers to discrimination and take "affirmative action" to guarantee equality of opportunity in employment.[49] Almost immediately, the NAACP and a group of black workers at Lockheed filed grievances with the president's committee on contract compliance, claiming that Lockheed had systematically denied equal opportunity since its inception in Georgia and should be denied the contract. Out of this controversy, Lockheed and the president's committee developed a "plan for progress," in essence, a desegregation plan that called for an end to "white and colored" facilities and segregated production lines. It also committed Lockheed to a broader program of recruitment, training, and effort to retain minority workers. This initial plan became the basis for the voluntary Plans for Progress initiative introduced later in 1961.

The Plans for Progress voluntary program has received generally harsh treatment from scholars. "Enforcing JFK's affirmative action order [10925], obviously, was a problem that was not going to be resolved by voluntary plans," observed the author of a recent comprehensive history of affirmative action in the United States. Terry Anderson noted that the president's committee under JFK "put pressure on companies" but it "never canceled a contract." Numerous examples could be found of companies continuing past policies of discriminatory hiring, training, and promotion, in spite of having signed a Plan for Progress. With a few high-profile exceptions such as Lockheed, Chrysler, and Westinghouse, the private sector's "record was mediocre."[50]

The Harvard sociologist Frank Dobbin has offered a somewhat more positive assessment of Plans for Progress. By 1963, Dobbin noted, Plans for Progress participating firms "were hiring 10 times the number of blacks they had hired just three years earlier." Whitney Young of the Urban League had been a vocal critic of the voluntary program in its early days. But by late 1963 Young "announced that 115 companies in Plans for Progress had hired nearly 15,000 new blacks in the third quarter of that year—25 percent of new workers in these companies were black. Before Plans for Progress, blacks had never made up more than 3 percent of new workers in any quarter."[51] Dobbin argued that federal laws staked out grand goals but left implementation to the imagination of individual firms. Personnel managers at Lockheed and other large companies defined what equal opportunity was at the firm level. Courts accepted widespread "best practices" at major corporations as meeting the definition of equal employment opportunity.

Lockheed has generally been cited as one of the few examples of firms that made real efforts at desegregation during the early 1960s. Lockheed also continued to play a leading role in promoting private-sector initiatives to increase minority employment, retention, and promotion. Lockheed executives such as Howard Lockwood, E. G. Mattison, and the personnel director Hugh Gordon offered their time to Plans for Progress and other voluntary initiatives during the 1960s. Lockheed played a leading role in these initiatives.[52] Acting on behalf of Lockheed's top management, Gordon organized the Atlanta area Merit Employment Association (MEA) in 1965. Evangelizing for a method he had used at Lockheed for years, Gordon used the MEA to persuade businesses to recruit actively in the African American community. MEA also urged businesses to set up training programs to help black workers who might be poorly prepared (because, Gordon said, of the "historic discrimination in education" that had plagued the region since slavery days). *The New York Times* took note of the Atlanta MEA's early success in 1968, reporting on a recent MEA survey showing that "some 1500 Negroes are employed now by 53 Atlanta area companies in 451 job classifications that were not open to Negroes in 1966." Gordon cautioned the *Times* that while this represented progress, "the job ahead is so big we should not stop to congratulate ourselves."[53]

Hudson mentioned none of these events or initiatives in his memoir. He was not alone among Lockheed's black employees in missing or failing to recall specific initiatives such as Plans for Progress. Charles Ferguson had been hired at Lockheed in 1951, before Hudson's "Super Negroes" had arrived. Ferguson followed a familiar, if depressing trajectory in his first few years at Lockheed. Despite having a year of college, Ferguson was hired as a groundskeeper. Under the same agreement that brought Hudson and his colleagues into training programs, Lockheed began opening its training programs to some of the early black employees from janitorial and groundskeeping. Ferguson, like Hudson, took advantage of every available training opportunity and by the mid-1950s had worked his way into semiskilled and then skilled job categories. Ferguson was among the handful of black supervisors who followed Hudson in the late 1950s (though Hudson remained the only one to manage an integrated crew until after the Plan for Progress). Ferguson eventually received training in complex electronics, moved into highly skilled work, and spent a long career at Lockheed. Like Hudson, Ferguson did not recall much about the precise timing of desegregation at Lockheed, nor did he remember the efforts made by Hugh Gordon to spread the idea of equal employment opportunity within the broader community.[54]

Ferguson and Hudson grew up in a segregated society and faced discrimination at nearly every turn. It is not surprising that, just as Hudson admitted little difference between the moderate James Carmichael and the arch-segregationist forces of the Talmadge faction in Georgia politics, black workers at Lockheed saw little to praise in the painstakingly slow progress made by Lockheed's management. Moreover, while Lockheed's upper management may have been committed to opening the workplace for minorities, the day-to-day experiences of Hudson and Ferguson involved little interaction on that level. Black workers faced daily difficulties with co-workers and immediate supervisors. Whatever the view from the clouds may have been of the progress at Lockheed, it would almost inevitably have looked quite different at ground level.

Hudson reported occasional visits to Lockheed by committees from Washington or the NAACP. He noted periodically throughout the first half of the narrative that observers were frequently present. Men in suits or uniforms who were not part of management floated around Lockheed's facilities, apparently checking on the status of black workers. He vaguely referred to increasing government demands for action on equal employment and related that to increasing opportunities, but he seems to have been disconnected from these processes. Hudson observed that at some point shortly after becoming a buyer, he was interviewed by representatives of a government committee. This was almost certainly JFK's President's Committee on Equal Employment Opportunity. Hudson left the interview less than impressed with the efficacy of the committee. Hudson believed that such committees made routine visits to Lockheed and other employers but required little more than token desegregation. Yet Hudson's own experience owed something to these observers and the government supervision they implied. Lockheed signed its Plan for Progress in May 1961. By September, Hudson had been moved to purchasing as a buyer. Hudson took pains to make clear that this was not a promotion but a lateral move. He retained the higher salary he carried from his position as a supervisor in manufacturing. Hudson believed that he was moved to clear a path for a white beneficiary of favoritism to move up to department manager. One of Lockheed's goals, established by the Plan for Progress, was to open a wider array of job categories to minorities. As the only black supervisor to work with an integrated crew, Hudson was perhaps uniquely qualified at Lockheed to move into an all-white department and work with other white buyers as an equal. While the position of buyer may not have been a promotion, it did involve representing the company to a variety of outside interests. The buyer served as the face of the company to suppliers. In addition, Lockheed had also pledged to increase its purchases from minority-owned firms, and Hudson described such efforts in his early days as a buyer. By moving Hudson to purchasing, Lockheed increased the visibility of African Americans within the company. Positions such as this had traditionally been among the toughest to penetrate for minority workers. Hudson again served as a pioneer.

Hudson recalled that a group of NAACP representatives visited Lockheed (later in the 1960s). These investigators were apparently counting black employees in various job categories. One of them told Hudson he could not be counted because he was too light-skinned. Hudson briefly allowed himself to reflect on what must have been numerous experiences with being "in between." Hudson's father and paternal grandmother were both described in the Census of 1920 as "mulatto," a designation indicating a light-skinned person of African American descent (the use of the insulting term was discontinued by the Census Bureau in 1930). Hudson's consciousness of the complexities of race is evident in his narrative.[55]

Hudson suffered discriminatory treatment, yet his career also may have reflected the internal hierarchy of skin color within the black community. It is tempting to speculate that Hudson's invitation to become the first African American to supervise an integrated crew was in part conditioned by his skin color as well as his race. It would have been an unspoken assumption of white superiors that a lighter-skinned African American man would have an easier time managing white workers in the Deep South than a darker-skinned supervisor. If skin color played a role in his selection, it is also clear that Hudson had proven his ability to manage people and achieve high productivity. A recent study of racial categories and earnings from early twentieth-century U.S. Census materials indicated that social perceptions of race mostly trumped perceived skin color distinctions within the black community. Roy Mill tracked individuals coded as "Black" and "Mulatto" and found that the "within-family earnings difference [was] substantially lower than the Black-Mulatto earnings difference in the general population, suggesting that skin color in itself played only a small role in the racial earnings gap." Specific family background factors such as wealth and education played far greater roles, it seemed, in determining future incomes than intra-race skin color distinctions.[56] A full exploration of the complexities of the issue is beyond the scope of this introduction, but Hudson's awareness of this issue certainly did not lessen his conviction that he was a race pioneer.

Lockheed pioneered early affirmative action policies and played a leading role in defining those policies for corporate America in the generation after the classic victories of the civil rights movement in the mid-1960s. The company's policies emerged from a mix of motivations, but a number of Lockheed executives and managers matched deeds with words by working to open American—and southern—workplaces to racial and ethnic diversity. As Jennifer Delton has argued, many Americans "had hoped that the civil rights movement and racial progress would deliver us from the sterile materialism and structured inequality embodied in the phrase "corporate America."[57]

Some historians, notably Glenn Eskew and Manning Marable, have argued that many civil rights leaders opted for a conservative strategy that left behind the African American masses. Eskew has argued that middle-class African Americans took control of the civil rights movement in the early 1960s and steered toward the goal of inclusion within the existing U.S. political economy. This opened some opportunities for middle-class African Americans, but left behind the impoverished black masses. Marable described this bourgeois vision, contending that middle-class African Americans came to define freedom as "social acceptance and upward mobility within the very centers of corporate power." One perspective on light refracting through the prism of Harry Hudson's story could serve as an illustration of these arguments. Yet different angles of view reveal other aspects of the complex narrative of race and employment in America.[58]

As it happened, the trajectories of economic growth, class inequality, and racial discrimination in the workplace developed in complex and interrelated ways. Deep social transformation may have eluded reformers during the civil rights era, but the corporate world of the Cold War era offered an arena within which even narrow conceptions of equality and opportunity could lead to significant material gains for African Americans. Such gains should not be minimized. Delton insisted that corporations and management should receive greater recognition for the role they played in "actually devis[ing] and implement[ing] the policies that integrated the workplace" and achieved at least a limited social transformation of American corporate culture.[59]

Those who persevered through the first generation of racial integration in corporate America—those who climbed the ladder—should be remembered as well. Harry Hudson's perhaps too-slow climb up the ladder at Lockheed typified the experiences of many middle-class African Americans in the postwar years. The materialism that many decried in the 1960s perhaps contributed, through boosterism of various kinds, to breaking down barriers of racial discrimination within the confines of corporate America. Executives and government bureaucrats, pressured by protest but also responding to ethical imperatives and the perceived demands of efficiency, developed policies that transformed the workplace. African Americans like Harry Hudson struggled to rise within the system. They both took advantage of the small cracks in the edifice of segregation and, by their small successes, helped widen those cracks. The process of social change may not have matched the ideals of civil rights reformers, but the change was real.

His career prospects were limited by his race, yet Hudson and his generation passed through a historic phase of civil rights protest and economic transformation, and the two were not unrelated. Gavin Wright's careful analysis of the economics of the civil rights revolution in the South indicates that African Americans achieved significant—indeed, revolutionary—progress in terms of employment, education, and income in the post–World War II years. Just as significantly, rapid and widespread economic growth generated dramatic gains in living standards.[60] Hudson noted the change himself, observing that Lockheed's presence in the Atlanta area helped transform the South. "Most southerners were beginning to realize that one cannot advance when one has to stand in the ditch holding down another," Hudson observed of the early days of Lockheed-Georgia. "They slowly understood if both left the ditch the path to a better future was on the level land of opportunity." The rising tide lifted a great many boats because protest movements demanded change and the federal government implemented policies that led to a broad distribution of economic gains, including equal employment policies.

Hudson's narrative offers eloquent testimony to both the efficacy and the limitations of individual initiative. Like an individual soldier in the American Civil War or World War II, Hudson and millions like him were caught up in events they could not clearly comprehend, let alone control. In the end, the actions of men and women like Harry Hudson, considered together, helped move the American workplace toward a greater degree of democracy and opportunity. Hudson's early career began a process of opening doors. He felt a deep sense of pride and accomplishment in at least two senses. Hudson expressed pride in his contributions to Lockheed, the nation's defense effort, and his own accomplishments. He also understood his role as a racial pioneer and expressed pride in playing some part in helping the country begin to move beyond racial discrimination. Yet he also expressed frustration at not climbing as high on Lockheed's corporate ladder as he thought he should have. Hudson's story is, in that respect, a quintessentially post–World War II career narrative. Hudson was an organization man. He believed that some combination of his race and his unwillingness to bear insults silently had held him back, but maintained a respect for the corporation that had formed the context for his working life.

Harry Hudson retired from Lockheed in 1988. After a divorce from his first wife, Edith, Hudson married Jacqueline Frye. Hudson worked on his memoir during his fifteen years of retirement. He died in August 2003, leaving behind the draft memoir presented here. It is a shame that Hudson himself did not survive to see his memoir in print. He was survived by his first wife, Edith (who was still living in 2014), and their six sons—Harry Jr., Michael, Ronald, Wayne, Albert, and Mark. Hudson's second wife, Jacqueline, passed away in 2010, but her children—Harry's stepchildren—survived: Charles Frye, Beverly Malone, and Jacqueline Roberson. Though Hudson himself did not live to see the publication of his memoir, many members of his family will see his project come to fruition. Hudson's spouse during his time at Lockheed, his children, his stepchildren, and his grandchildren can view his accomplishment with pride.

In 2001, two years before Harry Hudson's death, Lee Rhyant became the first African American to serve as executive vice president and general manager of Lockheed-Martin's Georgia division. He ran the operation for ten years (a company record for the division) before handing the reins to Shan Cooper, who became the second African American and the first woman to serve in the position.[61] Rhyant and Cooper surely followed their own paths, but as Hudson observed in his memoir, "no one succeeds on their own." Harry Hudson was only one of millions of foot soldiers in the struggle for civil rights in American business. Most of those stories have survived only as tales told within families and among friends. We are fortunate that Hudson chose to share his story.

Notes

1. "Truman's Decision Wise, Negroes Say," *Atlanta Daily World*, April 1, 1952, 1, 5.
2. "War Job Seekers Get NAACP Help," *Atlanta Daily World*, May 10, 1952, 1.
3. "Hudson Gets Supervisor's Post," *Atlanta Daily World*, October 25, 1953, 1.
4. For an exploration of Dunbar's poetry focused on masking and identity, see Willie J. Harrell Jr., ed., *We Wear the Mask: Paul Laurence Dunbar and the Politics of Representative Reality* (Kent, Ohio: Kent State University Press, 2010), esp. Harrell's introduction and Lena Ampadu, "The Poetry of Paul Laurence Dunbar and the Influence of African Aesthetics: Dunbar's Poems and the Tradition of Masking."
5. Gavin Wright, *Sharing the Prize: The Economics of the Civil Rights Revolution in the American South* (Cambridge, Mass.: The Belknap Press of Harvard University Press, 2013), Kindle location 811–15.
6. Ibid., Kindle location 616.
7. Philip Rubio, "There's Always Work at the Post Office: African-Americans Fight

for Jobs, Justice, and Equality at the U.S. Post Office, 1940–1971" (Ph.D. diss., Duke University, 2006), 38.

8. Fifteenth Census of the United States, 1930, and Sixteenth Census of the United States, 1940, accessed via Ancestry.com, February 15, 2013.

9. William J. Collins, "Race, Roosevelt and Wartime Production: Fair Employment in World War II Labor Markets," *American Economic Review* 91 (March 2001): 283–84. See also Wright, *Sharing the Prize*, Kindle location 1186.

10. William Hartung, *Prophets of War: Lockheed Martin and the Military-Industrial Complex* (New York: Nation Books, 2011), 37–39; Walter Boyne, *Beyond the Horizon: The Story of Lockheed* (New York: Thomas Dunne Publishers, 1998), 55. On government financial assistance to Lockheed, see John B. Rae, "Financial Problems of the American Aircraft Industry, 1906–1940," *Business History Review* 39 (Spring 1965): 110.

11. Hartung, *Prophets of War*, 49.

12. Robert C. Weaver, "Negro Employment in the Aircraft Industry," *Quarterly Journal of Economics* 59 (August 1945): 608–9. On Weaver's background as an activist, scholar, and public servant, see Francine Rusille Wilson, *The Segregated Scholars: Black Social Scientists and the Creation of Black Labor Studies, 1890–1950* (Charlottesville: University of Virginia Press, 2006), 230–45; Cecilia Conrad and George Scherer, "From the New Deal to the Great Society: The Economic Activism of Robert C. Weaver," in *A Different Vision: African-American Economic Thought*, ed. Thomas Boston (New York: Routledge, 1996), 290–301.

13. Weaver, "Negro Employment in the Aircraft Industry," 610; Boyne, *Beyond the Horizons*, 131.

14. Weaver, "Negro Employment in the Aircraft Industry," 620–24.

15. Thomas A. Scott, *Cobb County, Georgia, and the Origins of the Suburban South* (Marietta, Ga.: Cobb Landmarks and Historical Society, 2003), 110–11. Scott's chapters 5 and 6 detail the recruitment and development of the facility under Bell management. See also Jeffrey Holland, *Under One Roof: The Story of Air Force Plant 6* (Wright-Patterson Air Force Base, Ohio: Aeronautical Systems Center, 2006), 3–9.

16. Scott, *Cobb County*, 168–71. For a discussion of FEPC's efforts at Bell, see Merl Reed, "Bell Aircraft Comes South: The Struggle by Atlanta Blacks for Jobs During World War II," in *Labor in the Modern South*, ed. Glenn Eskew (Athens: University of Georgia Press, 2001), 102–34. Reed's analysis of FEPC records on Bell is congruent with Weaver's assessment, cited earlier.

17. Jennifer Delton, *Racial Integration in Corporate America, 1940–1990* (New York: Cambridge University Press, 2009), 28–36. Delton observes that this policy preference remained intact in spite of contrary evidence throughout the 1950s and into the late 1960s, when civil rights groups slowly came to the realization that simply announcing an end to discrimination and promoting full employment did not lead to significant improvement in "fair employment."

18. Wright, *Sharing the Prize*, Kindle location 165; Delton, *Racial Integration in Corporate America*, chapter 2. On the Russell amendment, see William G. Howell, *Power Without Persuasion: The Politics of Direct Presidential Action* (Princeton, N.J.: Princeton

University Press, 2003), 132. For a useful account of the stubborn persistence of the politics of white supremacy in postwar Georgia, see Michelle Brattain, *The Politics of Whiteness: Race, Workers, and Culture in the Modern South* (Athens: University of Georgia Press, 2004; reprint of 2001 Princeton University Press edition).

19. Wright, *Sharing the Prize*, Kindle location 1128–37; David Onkst, "'First a Negro. . . . Incidentally a Veteran': Black World War Two Veterans and the G. I. Bill of Rights in the Deep South, 1944–1948," *Journal of Social History* 31, no. 3 (Spring 1998): 517–43; Sarah Turner and John Bound, "Closing the Gap or Widening the Divide: The Effects of the G.I. Bill and World War II on the Educational Outcomes of Black Americans," *Journal of Economic History* 63, no. 1 (March 2003): 145–77.

20. The phrase is drawn from the title of Bruce Schulman, *From Cotton Belt to Sun Belt: Federal Policy, Economic Development, and the Transformation of the South* (New York: Oxford University Press, 1991). See also Gavin Wright, *Old South, New South: Revolutions in the Southern Economy Since the Civil War* (Baton Rouge: Louisiana State University Press, 1996; reprint of 1986 edition), esp. chapter 8.

21. *The New York Times*, December 4, 1951, 26; Delton, *Racial Integration*, 32.

22. *Atlanta Daily World*, September 14, 1951, 1; *Atlanta Constitution*, September 14, 1951, 1. Carmichael's remarks gained new currency after President Truman issued an executive order creating a new agency to police discrimination among government contractors. See, for example, *Rome News-Tribune*, "Lockheed Sees no Need for Truman FEPC Order," December 9, 1951, 5.

23. *Atlanta Daily World*, November 7, 1951, 6.

24. C. L. Harper and C. W. Greenlea to James V. Carmichael, November 24, 1951, 1951, Folder 7, Box 275, Atlanta Urban League (AUL) Papers, Robert W. Woodruff Library, Atlanta University, Atlanta, Georgia. On the relationship between U.S. foreign policy and the civil rights movement, see Mary L. Dudziak, *Cold War Civil Rights: Race and the Image of American Democracy* (Princeton, N.J.: Princeton University Press, 2000).

25. Robeson quoted in testimony before the Committee on Un-American Activities, "Investigation of the Unauthorized Use of U.S. Passports," 84th Congress, Part 3, June 12, 1956.

26. Harper and Greenlea to Gross, December 4, 1951, Folder 7, Box 275, AUL Papers.

27. "Memorandum: Lockheed Conference," January 30, 1952, Folder 7, Box 275, AUL Papers.

28. Ibid. The B-47 was a Boeing design, but Lockheed would build the plane under a license agreement to help meet wartime demand. Merl Reed argued that Bell had made important steps toward beginning to open more training opportunities for black workers by late 1944, but demobilization and plant closure cut short the possibility. Reed, "Bell Aircraft Comes South," 132–35.

29. This is a very brief summary of Georgia's political narrative in the late 1940s. For greater depth and analysis, see Numan V. Bartley, *The Creation of Modern Georgia* (Ath-

ens: University of Georgia Press, 1990), 200–207; Jennifer Brooks, *Defining the Peace: World War II Veterans, Race and the Remaking of the Southern Political Tradition* (Chapel Hill: University of North Carolina Press, 2004), 113–38. For the story of Georgia's white primary, see Laughlin MacDonald, *A Voting Rights Odyssey: Black Enfranchisement in Georgia* (New York: Cambridge University Press, 2003), 49–54.

30. Talmadge quoted in Harold P. Henderson, "M.E. Thompson and the Politics of Succession," in *Georgia Governors in an Age of Change*, ed. Harold P. Henderson and Gary Roberts (Athens: University of Georgia Press, 1988), 64.

31. Gavin Wright, "The Economics of the Civil Rights Revolution," in *Toward the Meeting of the Waters: The Civil Rights Movement in South Carolina*, ed. Winfred O. Moore Jr. and Orville Vernon Burton (Columbia: University of South Carolina Press, 2007), 401.

32. This discussion draws on Numan Bartley, *The New South, 1945–1980* (Baton Rouge: Louisiana State University Press, 1995); Patricia Sullivan, *Days of Hope: Race and Democracy in the New Deal Era* (Chapel Hill: University of North Carolina Press, 1996); Jacquelyn Dowd-Hall, "The Long Civil Rights Movement and the Political Uses of the Past," *Journal of American History* 91, no. 4 (March 2005): 1233–63; Glenda Gilmore, *Defying Dixie: The Radical Roots of Civil Rights, 1919–1950* (New York: Norton, 2009).

33. On Smith and southern liberals, see Randall Patton, "Lillian Smith and the Transformation of American Liberalism," *Georgia Historical Quarterly* 76 (1992): 373–92.

34. "Allegations of Discrimination Made by National Urban League at Hearings before the President's Committee on Government Contract Compliance," July 9, 1952, Committee on Government Contract Compliance Case Files Re: Charges, Box 9, Record Group 325, National Archives and Records Administration, Washington, D.C. For a detailed discussion of the complexities of fair employment in the Texas aircraft industry during World War II, see Joseph Abel, "African-Americans, Labor Unions, and the Struggle for Fair Employment in the Texas Aircraft Manufacturing Industry, 1941–45," *Journal of Southern History* 77, no. 3 (August 2011): 595–638.

35. "Allegations of Discrimination."

36. Lerone Bennett and Robert Johnson, "Fair Job Plan at Lockheed," *Atlanta Daily World*, December 18, 1952; "Lockheed Plan Seen as a Big Economic Gain for Negroes," *Atlanta Daily World*, December 19, 1952, 1.

37. *Atlanta Daily World*, December 18, 1952, 1; author interview with Hugh Gordon, February 15, 2013.

38. Pollard's statement reported in *Jet*, November 16, 1961, 61.

39. Advertisement in *Washington Afro-American*, October 19, 1957, 18. Available via Google Newspapers, http://news.google.com/newspapers?id=F7k9AAAAIBAJ&sjid=5ysMAAAAIBAJ&pg=6668%2C16943418.

40. Author interview with Harry Hudson Jr. On marketing to the African American community, see Jason Chambers, *Madison Avenue and the Color Line: African-Americans*

in the Advertising Industry (Philadelphia: University of Pennsylvania Press, 2011); and the Moss Kendrix pages at the website of the Museum of Public Relations, http://www.prmuseum.com/kendrix/moss1.html, accessed June 16, 2013.

41. Herbert Hill, "Status of Negro Workers at Lockheed Aircraft Corporation," *The Crisis*, March 1957, 146–48.

42. Scott, *Cobb County*, 216–17, 220–26.

43. Holland, *Under One Roof*, 54.

44. Harry L. Alston to James C. Evans, October 20, 1954, "Committee on Government Contract Compliance Case Files Re: Charges," Box 9, Record Group 325, National Archives and Records Administration, Washington, D.C.

45. Scott, *Cobb County*, 250–62.

46. On race and the labor movement, see Robert Zieger, *For Jobs and Freedom: Race and Labor in America since 1865* (Lexington: University of Kentucky Press, 2010), esp. chapters 4 and 5; and Paul D. Moreno, *Black Americans and Organized Labor: A New History* (Baton Rouge: Louisiana State University Press, 2007).

47. Frank Dobbin, *Inventing Equal Opportunity* (Princeton, N.J.: Princeton University Press, 2009), 53. Hudson mentioned a union election at Lockheed in 1952, and there was an election. IAM, an AFL member union, already represented Lockheed's workers, but the CIO-affiliated International Brotherhood of Electrical Workers challenged the existing union's jurisdiction. IAM won the election, and the merger of the two federations in 1955 ended such internecine warfare. *Atlanta Daily World*, September 24, 1952, 1.

48. See Hartung, *Prophets of War*, chapters 4–6, for a critical assessment of Lockheed and the scandals of the late 1960s and 1970s; for the company's perspective, see Boyne, *Beyond the Horizons*, 331–69.

49. On the new executive order, see Judson McClaury, "President Kennedy's E.O. 10925: Seedbed of Affirmative Action," *Federal History*, no. 2 (January 2010), online journal accessed January 15, 2012, http://shfg.org/shfg/publications/federal-history-journal/past-issues/issue-2-january-2010/.

50. Terry Anderson, *The Pursuit of Fairness: A History of Affirmative Action* (New York: Oxford University Press, 2004), 64–65. An even bleaker assessment is offered in Nancy Maclean, *Freedom is Not Enough: The Opening of the American Workplace* (New York: Russell Sage, 2008), 44.

51. Dobbin, *Inventing Equal Opportunity*, 48–49.

52. See Gordon, Kruse, Wentzel Collection Scope and Content, Kennesaw State University Archives, Kennesaw, Georgia, available at http://archon.kennesaw.edu/?p=collections/findingaid&id=197&q=&rootcontentid=2099.

53. "Atlanta Showing Gains in Negro Employment," *The New York Times*, May 5, 1968, F17.

54. Charles Ferguson, Oral History, conducted by Brent Ragsdale, History 4425 Bell/Lockheed Oral History Series, No. 17, Kennesaw State University, November 17, 2007. See also Susan Reed, *The Diversity Index: The Alarming Truth About Diversity in*

Corporate America and What Can Be Done About It (New York: American Management Association, 2011).

55. An excellent introduction to the complex subject of varying skin color within the African American community is Kathy Russell, Midge Wilson, and Ronald Hall, *The Color Complex: The Politics of Skin Color Among African-Americans* (New York: Anchor, 1993). On discrimination based on skin tone as opposed to race, see Jennifer Hochschild and Vesla Weaver, "The Skin Color Paradox and the American Racial Order," *Social Forces* 86, no. 2 (December 2007): 643–70.

56. Roy Mill, "Inequality and Discrimination in Historical and Modern Labor Markets" (Ph.D. diss., Stanford University, 2013), v.

57. Delton, *Racial Integration in Corporate America*, 283–84.

58. Glenn Eskew, *But for Birmingham: The Local and National Movements in the Civil Rights Struggle* (Chapel Hill: University of North Carolina Press, 1997), 333–37; Manning Marable, *Race, Rebellion, and Reform: The Second Reconstruction and Beyond in Black America, 1945–2006*, 3rd ed. (Oxford: University Press of Mississippi, 2007), 84–85.

59. Delton, *Racial Integration in Corporate America*, 284.

60. Wright, *Sharing the Prize*, chapter 8.

61. Jerry Grillo, "Departures and Arrivals," *Georgia Trend*, March 2011, electronic version accessed January 17, 2013, http://www.georgiatrend.com/March-2011/Departures-And-Arrivals-A-Changing-Of-The-Guard/.

Chapter 1   My father and I operated a service station on Auburn Avenue in Atlanta, Georgia, in partnership. On the second Sunday of August 1952, one of my regular customers came into the station to get gas. Bobby Kennon asked me how I would like to work for Lockheed Aircraft Corporation. He stated that Lockheed was looking for Negroes with mechanical ability and a college degree.

Well, I was not unknowledgeable of Lockheed because the first model planes that I had made during my childhood had been Lockheed models—the Orion, the Vega, and the Electra. I did not know at the time that Lockheed had opened the old Bell Bomber Plant in Marietta, Georgia, and started modification of the B-29 Bell Bombers. Bobby said that he worked for Lockheed and that he was searching for qualified African American applicants because the good government had come to the conclusion that they would not be awarding federal defense contracts unless the companies awarded same had nondiscriminatory hiring practices. Another first for democracy.

When Lockheed opened the plant they used the old philosophy of hiring a local dealing wheel to get the right community result and attitude to establish a firm base community-wise. Naturally, most of the skilled people (management that is) would come from the home base, which was the West Coast. The local fellow put in as general manager happened to be Jimmy Carmichael. Jimmy had not too long before run for governor of Georgia. He did not win the election. He was a successful businessman and well known in the political circles. His personal views on segregation were also well known. With the opening of this helluva big plant and the economic result Jimmy made the statement (according to the grapevine) that as long as he was manager of the facility no "niggers" would ever hold a higher position than that of a janitor.

This was strictly propaganda for the locals. This could not sit with the powers that be in Washington so Bobby was hired to go out and find some "super niggers" (with mechanical ability and a college degree) who had a desire to drill holes and shoot rivets in airplanes. Bobby was that lonesome one held up to say, "See, we have a Negro recruiter desperately looking for qualified Negroes."

Most Negroes were either overqualified or underqualified so poor ole

Bobby was running all over the southeastern states looking for Negroes with a college degree interested in drilling holes and shooting rivets in airplanes. The going salaries (like $54 a week) during the early 1950s do not seem as impressive now even though one was able to live fairly well with that income at the time. I was not happy with the pay I was making at the service station nor with the relationship my old man and I were having. My hours were too long and the atmosphere was becoming strained. I wanted to expand to several stations and my pappy and his banker friend could not see the advantage of having more than one station (be free of debt first was his philosophy). My family was growing and I needed more income at a faster rate than the single service station was providing.

With a degree in biology and a minor in chemistry I figured I had at least the first part of the qualification requirements. My studies and background were in the pre-med area, but I did not have the money to go to medical school. My GI Bill funds were practically exhausted. I had to realize that my livelihood would be in a different area. My surgical hands had turned out to be pretty good in the manual dexterity field (mechanical that is). Hell, it dawned suddenly on me that I had the required qualifications.

I told Bobby that I was interested and after a few days of thinking it over and talking about possible hardships, I informed him that I would fill out an application and follow through with it. Well, the old boys had to move fast to show that all effort was being made to prove that they were sincerely looking for qualified "Neegros" to fill these highly skilled positions.

I filled out an application form, which was a typical form requesting your race. At the time in the United States no one was an American, they were a race. We were all Americans but were known as races, as that information was required on all legal forms. Naturally, the number one race was Caucasian (preferably Anglo-Saxon), Italian, Irish, and on down the line to "Negro" (black) and last but not least the only American, the American Indian. This classification process was necessary because then your position and pay scale could be established. Damn the qualifications, full speed ahead.

I was instructed to report to the Lockheed employment office on the corner of Peachtree and North Avenue, Atlanta. The time was about 7:00 p.m. on the fifth of September 1952. This was the testing location for all new hires. On entering the office, I found that the testees consisted of ten Negroes and about fifty whites or Caucasians. There were no Chinese or Japanese and no Indians (natural born). We looked at them and they looked at us. They sat on one side of the room and we sat on the other. This probably was to prevent contamination, to whom I never did figure out. The ten Negroes consisted of one fellow who was six hours and a thesis short of a master's in math; five fellows with degrees ranging from English, math, sociology, physics, biology, and chemistry; and four fellows who had no more than one year to complete for their degrees. Bobby had failed to attain his goal of ten college graduates. Anyway they figured we had enough intelligence to at least get past the test. It never was determined how many degrees the white fellows had because we later heard that you automatically qualified if you were white. By the way, all the whites were white, pink, or anemic. The Negroes were from almost white to black according to the melting pot of their ancestry.

The Negroes in the original ten were indicated as the "super Negroes" with the ability to shoot rivets and drill holes in airplanes. They were J. L. Hicks, B. R. Petty, Alburt Burt, Esterest Smith, Mac McMorris, Lou Morris, Robert Gist, H. L. Hudson, G. L. Kelly, and Ike Jones. Since all of us had finished the sixth grade, we had no problems passing the qualification test. We later found out that we had very good IQs. One fellow had an IQ of 87, another was 101, and mine was very high, 113. Hell, I had an IQ of 132 according to the navy (when I was trying to play crazy and get out) before I went to college. I decided that the test examiners could not rate anyone with a higher IQ than they had. We all passed, including all the white guys, and were instructed to report to the Bomber Plant the following Monday.

If you have never seen the Georgia division of the Lockheed Aircraft Corporation, then you have missed the thirteenth wonder of the world. Until much later it was the largest aircraft manufacturing plant in the world. It is 76 acres under one roof, air conditioned, and with 27 miles of neon lights. You have to go inside to actually be impressed with this gigantic structure.

We had to proceed through what is called a "head house." This is the entrance past the guards. We all got extra-long looks because it seems none of the guards had ever seen "super Negroes" before. We were instructed to follow the yellow line. The yellow line led us through the tunnels of the dungeon to the identification office. There we were fingerprinted, photographed, and identified. We then went to the medical department for our physical examination. Having studied pre-med, I was impressed by that industrial medical center and over the years have come to recognize it as one of the best in the industrial world. We passed through the preliminaries and were found to have all the required features of the human anatomy. We were certified that we were ourselves. At last we were told to proceed to the training department and, you guessed it, to follow the yellow line.

The yellow line ended in the training department. We were shown into a room similar to an average college classrooom. We were instructed on what an airplane was (I often wondered what them noisy things floating through the air were). Orientation consisted of a tour through the plant. The biggest exhibits were the tools crated and greased, awaiting shipment to some destination. Some B-29s were in different stages of modification or repair. There were two B-47s on the line, and this was the plane that (with our skills) we were going to produce for the good old air force. The size of these aircraft was very impressive as I had been in the navy and never seen aircraft this large up close. Looking up over 64 feet to the crane rails overhead was a sight to behold. The building was over 2,000 feet long and 1,000 feet wide. One got the feeling that he was somebody. After all, one was now employed at the Bomber Plant.

We were herded into a room to meet the department manager we would have after finishing the training period. This husky fellow of about 5 feet 6 inches walked in with personality oozing from every pore. We took a liking to him immediately. He was from the California division and seemed to be honest and straightforward. We did not know that he was the only manager that would take the first colored (Negro) department to be established (skilled that is) at the good old Lockheed Georgia division. No other manager would accept the responsibility because the knowledge at the time was that no Negroes could build airplanes (and the damn fools believed it). This may not have been the attitude in California, but in Georgia it was a fact based on the average level of thinking at the time.

Our foreman's name was Lloyd DeWester. His confidence and respect for us and the respect we developed for him proved in later months helped create one of the best department teams in the history of the company. This statement was made by a number of instructors in much later classes in training and also in management development classes, and that's the truth. DeWester was known as "Dee" from then on throughout his stay at the plant.

When Dee finished his greetings, another fellow took the rostrum that everyone seemed to be apprehensive about. Of course, by "everyone," I mean the training instructors and Dee; we did not know enough to be leery of anyone. I was the first person this person shook hands with and that was the beginning of one helluva relationship. We learned that he was the superintendent of assembly. We found that this was on the hipbone of the hog as far as the level of management was concerned. This person will be found throughout this narrative as he was somebody plus being one prime SON OF BROTHERHOOD. His name was H. Lee Poore and I can only compare him to General George Patton. Both of these gentlemen had many good points, but on most of the points they were very blunt. We called H. Lee old "Blood and Guts" or BG. Naturally, never to his face.

After orientation we were sent to our classes. These classes would consist of aircraft blueprints from preliminary to advanced design, aircraft math, aircraft terminology, and NAS [National Academy of Sciences], MS [margin of safety], and AN [Army-Navy] standards. Since we would be building a Boeing-designed aircraft it would also include Boeing prints and design specifications. We would be instructed in the design and use of thousands of aircraft fasteners, some electrical and hydraulic training, and riveting and drilling of close tolerance and other types of holes. As you can see, being ignorant as hell, we were going to get some of the best training ever given to workers before actually performing the job. We were told that the overall cost was better than $10,000 per worker. It took about ten weeks and you can bet that we took full advantage of the opportunity. As everyone was segregated, the white fellows that came in with us on that training period were always interested in our progress and gave us all the advice they thought we needed to succeed because they wanted to help us in this equal but separate training. Since they had the advantage of completing the fourth and fifth grades and up to the twelfth, they had a better education.

At the time a degree from a black college was considered equal to a diploma from a white high school. Any white person that had some college education or an undergraduate degree was automatically considered as management or salaried material. We never knew what the white fellows' marks were and ours were never mentioned except as noted on the certificates that were issued. Everyone seemed to be happy as we rolled along, so now let's go into the classrooms see what fun we had in learning the essentials of building an airplane.

The best way to start an education is to progress from ignorance to knowledge. Therefore, let's start with our most brilliant instructor, that is, if we are starting from the lack of qualifications for the subject he was supposed to have been teaching. This fellow, we'll call him "Blue," gave us all the fundamentals of fractions and decimals and their relationships to measurements. By the time we had finished fourth-grade math, old Blue came to the conclusion that his eleventh-grade education was not exactly teaching us ignoramuses any aircraft math. He did not seem to understand any form of higher math and that was the level we were trying to attain in order to tie in with aircraft-building. Blue got real teed-off with us and became frustrated. After two days Blue walked out and probably told the bosses that he could not teach us anything. We had no intention of embarrassing him because it was the fault of the training management to put him into such a situation. We did not have a math teacher for two days.

On the third day in walked "Pop" Keller, a retired professor from the University of Georgia. He was one fine fellow. Pop smoked a pipe and, to demonstrate the respect we had for him, we kept cups of water handy to put him out every time he put that lit pipe into his coat pocket. His first words to us after looking at our records were, "Gentlemen, there is nothing to be taught to you on this level, so why don't we discuss the merits of math and its relationship to the manufacture of aircraft?" We really learned from Pop but he was only temporary for this assignment. We had him later on in a number of classes, as he specialized in other subjects. Math was not one of my best subjects, but under Pop I made an 87.

One of the most impressive people I met in this industry was our drilling and riveting instructor. His name was R. R. Brown, so naturally we called him "Railroad." I don't think that Lockheed ever realized the value they had in this man as an instructor. Sometimes (in later years) I wondered if Lockheed (management) recognized any of the potential of some employees. After this period of time it would be very hard to repeat verbatim the talk Railroad gave us as his initial instructions, but with the following I will try:

You people are now coming into the business of building airplanes. They may be for the military or commercial use. Remember one thing, without quality the product is not worth the effort or price put into it. If airplanes were built like automobiles, they would not fly. For the cost of an aircraft the product must last almost twenty years to realize a profitable return. No businessman can afford to invest in the cost of an airplane without a guarantee of reliability that we build into it. You must remember that people fly in our products and therefore we have to guarantee their safety. You may have a kinsman with the air force. Would you jeopardize their life with poor workmanship or quality? Could you, honestly within yourself, do a job you were not satisfied with and pass it on knowing that someone's life might be in danger because you thought that it was sufficient? No one in this company will ever criticize you for stopping a line to guarantee quality and safety. Without quality you will not get reliability. Quality and reliability are the integrity of what you produce. Engineers can design all of the factors into an airplane, but if you can't make it to meet those standards your product is worthless. If you don't get satisfaction in what you have done, don't buy it! You will have times when you will make overtime and get more money. Live within your normal pay range and save your extra money. In this business there are ups and downs. Now let's go to work and learn how to drill holes and shoot rivets.

Well, old Railroad put us through the ropes. We learned all about holedrilling and the installation of rivets. He kept up a steady stream about quality, reliability, and the integrity of the job. For the ten people who studied under him, they came out with a thorough indoctrination in the right attitude of the professional aircrafter. I never forgot the basics of quality that Railroad instilled in us, though he was promoted to supervisor and moved to the production floor about two-thirds of the way through our drilling and riveting course. Those lessons have followed me throughout my career as an aircrafter.

Railroad will show up in later episodes, but it saddens me to say that he died in his early forties from alcoholism. At least that is what we heard, for he was one helluva drinker. If you know any aircrafters quite a few of them can move the booze (not at work but on weekends). Managers and union officials are included. If you think that this is an indictment of aircrafters, think again. About 40 percent of most industrial workers do likewise. The pressures that these people work under in meeting delivery schedules and commitments are, at most, just plain stupid. The military way is that everything must be done on schedule. My experience with the military has been to hurry up and wait. This idiotic philosophy has not changed one iota since I left the service after World War II and the working pressures are a result of this intense follow-up. All old veterans and aircraft workers can certify that quite a few military officers, aircraft managers, and union officials drink like hell. They get inebriated. A hell of a lot of enlisted men and aircrafters also drink heavily, but they get drunk. Big difference. Regardless, all of them do some tremendous jobs. Railroad was one of the first people up there I met who did not seem to be bothered by racial prejudices. We respected him highly and a lot of people were really saddened by his premature death.

Two or three classes were taught each day. The next class we had was blueprint reading. All aircraft blueprints are basically the same as to interpretation but there are differences in information and the way certain aspects are governed by patents and company policies. In basic blueprint you start out with putty, mud, or crazy dough. It holds the shape you make and you can see the object you are trying to make as you work. A lot of people can't make a ball. All squares turn out to be rectangles, perspectives turn out to be perceptions. Eventually, you learn the difference between a solid line and a phantom line. Before you know it you are able to visualize the object. As *Gray's Anatomy* is the Bible of the medical student, blueprints are the same to the aircrafter. With the ability to read blueprints one can build all of the engineering requirements developed to produce the high-quality, reliable, and safe end product we know as the airplane. It takes hundreds of people in engineering (design, methods, structural, stress, electrical, electronic, hydraulic, and many others), planning, tooling, quality control, materiel handling, purchasing, plant layout, production control, scheduling, shipping and receiving, and the thousands of other necessary functions required to complete the building of an airplane. All of the above starts with an idea, then a blueprint. It ends with the most important people required, the aircraft assemblers. If the assemblers cannot glue all of the materiels together correctly the first time, then the efforts of all the preceding people are worthless.

Sealing is the method one uses to make sure an aircraft does not leak. Sealing prevents leaks in fuel, oxygen, water, air pressure, and any other damn leak that may occur. It also prevents mixtures of those elements that could be dangerous to the operation of the aircraft. Sealing compounds consist of rubber, glue, and other chemical combinations of specified compounds with resistance to the different problems arising within the areas to be sealed. The same precise methods are used to make sure that quality is attained on the first application of the sealing compounds. Engineers are responsible for the compounds and the method of application. You can always blame one of the engineering groups if the gunk does not work. In the beginning sealing was a very messy job but improvements over the years had made the application of sealants a relatively easy job. Anyway, we learned all about the different types of sealants and their application at the time.

All in all, we covered the training period, which included basic arithmetic, basic blueprint reading from primary through some advanced design, and all the other subjects listed previously in this chapter, including processes like coin-dimpling. Coin-dimpling was a method of preparing the aircraft skin and thinner understructure holes for receipt of flush rivets or screws by heating sheet metal and applying a coining die to the surface. Altogether, this was over two hundred hours of classroom and practical study. Finally the time arrived to fire us or put us to work. We went up to the production floor to see if we could build airplanes. Since it was said that it cost $10,000 per person to train us it was time to produce something. The first week in November we presented ourselves on the production floor at the grand pay of $54 a week (before taxes). The ten weeks we had spent in training was a very enlightening and, most times, a pleasant experience.

Chapter 2

The following Monday morning after finishing training we went to the floor. We had been on a floor all of the time but it was in the basement. The main floor, which was the manufacturing area, contained most of the tooling (called "jigs") arranged in an order indicating progressive assembly. One group started with the small jigs for the components to be assembled. These were passed to the next group, who assembled them to other small assemblies, resulting in a larger unit consisting of several assemblies. This was the beginning and start of that section of the airplane. In our first job we started on the nose or front end of the fuselage.

Dee brought a young fellow over to us and introduced him as our new supervisor. His name was Buck. If you have ever seen a young child on his first visit to the zoo, then that was the expression on Buck's face. All of management had followed the progress of the "super Negroes" while we were in training and there were bets made that we would never make it through the first three weeks of training. It is hard to believe that was the level of some managers' thinking at the time. All of those stupid bets were lost. What had Buck amazed was the fact that out of the 10 courses almost everyone in the group had made a 98–100 grade on at least 2 of the courses. They acted as if this had never been done before. This is a fact and anyone contradicting it I call a liar (I have the records). Just before Buck came down to meet us there was this good ole boy driving by on his tug (a motorized cart used to pull aircraft and portions of them around the factory floor). He had never seen Negroes in a skilled production area before. He stopped his tug, cut the engine, got comfortable, and stared and stared. We looked at him and found him to be an interesting specimen also. We were establishing a mutual admiration society until Buck told us it was time to go to work.

Subassembly jigs are tools anchored to the floor and calibrated to produce a part that will fit, when assembled, another part. This eventually ends up into a larger assembly constituting a major part of the aircraft. These type tools are calibrated back to a master jig and controlled to guarantee a fit down the line maintaining a 0.030-inch tolerance in most instances. Quality begins when you make the first installation of a part into your first jig. Quality cannot be bought, inspected, or corrected into an assembly if it is not right the first time. Once you have located the parts in the jig and clamped them in position you come to the meat of your being there. The inspector checks the load and authorizes you to proceed (on the aircraft numbered job sheet) with the next step. The next step is the hole-drilling part of the "drilling holes and shooting rivets," which is the reason for your being hired.

Ninety percent of small holes predrilled in the component parts are known as pilot holes. These holes tell you where to drill up to the final size or diameter, which is also the size of the rivet to be installed in that hole. For top quality the pilot holes should be in only one of the mating parts. Pilot holes are usually only ⅛ inch in diameter. After drilling the pilot holes you step up to the final size, which is inspected, and you are ready to install the rivet (fastener). What we had not been taught was that a solid rivet expands to fill a hole and the size of a rivet hole can be slightly out of tolerance by a few thousandths of an inch and still be acceptable for a quality installation.

It was during this time that we experienced our first encounter with the red grease pencil. Among other things a red grease pencil is used to indicate a squawk (minor discrepancy). If the tolerance is over the maximum size required, then engineering can give the approval to install the next size larger rivet. If the red markings had been blood our workmanship would have been dead and ready for burial before it was finished. Just about every drilled hole was redlined. We found out later that the inspector was using a micrometer to measure every damn hole. We thought he was just doing something to be sure. Our assemblies looked like blooming rose bushes in the spring. Using the old Hitler tactic of being told we were doing poor and unacceptable work, they almost had us believing that we could not do the job. Railroad had taught us to inspect our own work and we knew damn well that what we were doing was not the sorry inspection results we were getting. The new bet in management was that since we had made it through training it was not possible that we could actually do the manual work required on the manufacturing floor. This was the second losing bet.

There were always people in suits and looking important walking around observing us as we put every effort into doing a top job. Often there were members of the air force being given a tour, I guess to show the all-out effort management was making to meet the requirements of the defense contract. After two weeks the inspector called us together and told us that he had been instructed by upper management to reject everything that he could of our workmanship to prove that "niggers" were unsuited for skilled labor and could not be trained to do so. He stated that he was a moral and Christian man and his conscience would not let him go on with this farce. He asked us to please not say that he had told us this, as it could mean his job. He said that we were producing some of the best quality he had seen since becoming an inspector. He said that he would not be able to go on rejecting our workmanship under these circumstances. He said enough. From that day on our squawks and rejections were far below the plant average. By stepping up holes and installing oversize rivets the problems we were creating in the quality of the end product were greatly diminished just because some prejudiced bastards were trying to win a stupid bet. That inspector had a long and prosperous career at the Bomber Plant and eventually became a salaried employee. I would like to mention his name but he will recognize himself if he ever has the opportunity to read this and know that we kept our word.

We tried hard as hell to do a better than average job because the word was already out that if we did not do good, which is always better than anybody else, then there would be no reason to hire any more Negroes to do skilled labor. This was not the belief of most of the managers but they were not in the majority among the middle management. The simple bastards did not even consider the fact that we had not only superior ability but also a decent education. Poor Dee was catching hell from every direction. Not only was he teased about his "jigs" among the jigs, but what did he hope to accomplish with his "super niggers"? I can imagine that anyone under that type of constant criticism would have wished that he had not accepted the responsibility of that assignment. But as previously stated, Dee was a fine person and he constantly expressed his confidence in us. Our supervisor knew we were doing a good job and he was satisfied; plus he was knowledgeable about the work he was supervising.

The big lump hit the fan about the middle of November. Other new hires were in the training process and would soon be coming up to the production floor. Things had been going pretty well except for the subtle harassment from the other departments and from some of the service groups (tool cribs, etc.). Big Kelly got teed off because we were making the fine pay of $1.35 an hour and he had been doing better at the Post Office before he decided that Lockheed would give him better opportunities. With the crap we were taking he just quit and went back to the Post Office. That $10,000 training cost was blown up into a bear's backyard. He refused to come back so the powers that be informed the postmaster that he was doing critical defense work (you know, the Korean War and everything) and they could not afford to let him go after all of the extensive training he had been given. The postmaster sent him back.

Now the normal reaction by the bosses was that they had let this "boy" know what power they had over us peons. Kelly reported to the foreman's office and impolitely cussed out everyone, informing them of his service time during World War II (emphasizing his having jumped from a crashing cargo plane over Montana and spending almost two weeks in the boondocks before being found) and no one was going to tell him where to work. He informed them that he expected to be promoted to the next upgrade, general assembler, and the rest of us likewise or he would be walking out and he dared them to screw with him again. Well, since Kelly was 6 feet 5 inches and weighed 260 pounds (no fat) he was taken seriously. He and the rest of us were upgraded to structure general assemblers and got an increase in pay to $1.50 per hour. Shortly afterward the wheels would come by and say, "You boys are doing a good job." Among those was old BG himself.

There were rumbles going on about organizing the plant union-wise. The two major unions in that attempt were the AFL and the CIO. Both had organizers around the plant out in the parking lots trying to influence the employees to vote their affiliation as collective bargaining agents. These organizers were the cream of the crop when it came to influencing future members. I never saw so much screaming, blacking of eyes, busting of noses, cracking of heads, and general rioting to prove how advantageous it was to be a union member. After a few days of getting acquainted through these actions a date was given to vote. No one seemed to have given a thought to the fact that the Negroes would also be able to join the union so no attempts were made to organize us. We were able to sit back and have ringside seats to all of this scrapping without getting our heads busted. We were rushed through the voting process by departments and I think the AFL won. Now we were a unionized plant. The only difference we noted was that they took out ten cents a week for union dues. I was a charter member of the union.[1]

We moved on down the line making little assemblies into big assemblies. Quality was maintained and respect began to grow. Dee's boys were proving out to be pretty good. A few of the originals were left to work with and instruct the new hires who were coming to the floor with less training but enough basic instruction to perform in the subassembly areas. By the first week of December we moved into the major assembly jigs. These were the big babies where the larger assemblies were put together and you could see the beginning of an airplane. I, with several others, was moved into the 43 section, which was the aft end of the fuselage of the B-47 Bomber. The B-47 was a Boeing aircraft that Lockheed was subcontracting to meet the need of the Korean conflict. It was a helluva airplane and it preceded the B-52 Bomber.

My first workstation was the mating of the longerons at the 1054 stationline. The longeron is a heavy milled or extruded part mating or tying in the four main sections of the rounded body of the fuselage. This is called a monocoque design. That forms the main structural parts of the fuselage.

A stationline was the measuring distance from a given point in front of the nose, thus the location of the area was 1,054 inches from that point in front of the nose. The location in front of the nose on the B-47 is 66 inches. A buttline is the measurement from the centerline (or middle line) of the aircraft to the right or left. The waterline is the measurement from the position of the aircraft sitting on the ground in a normal position, that is, from the ground up. The exact locations were indicated on the jigs at each permanent point. All assemblies were made to coincide with these points. The jigs were calibrated to guarantee that the parts would all come together at their designated points per the blueprint. Our quality standards said that we would be within 0.030-inch tolerance of maintaining that requirement. We did as was required. Stationline 1054 is where the center section mated with the tail section of the fuselage.

At stationline 1054 the longerons mated like putting two capital U's together. That is, laying the U's down facing each other and pushing one into the other until they were mated together. The distance between the two parts inside was a little over 4 inches. Since this was the first ship being put together at Lockheed-Georgia (called GELAC within the company), no tooling had been developed to drill the finished holes to the final ½ inch-diameter. The final hold had to be 0.500 inch + 0.300 inch tolerance. The hole could not be 0.499 inch or over 0.503 inch in size. Those bolts were in the most critical stress and structural area of that assembly. The mating area had been covered with the skins on the mating assemblies so you could not drill from the outside inboard. This was found to be the case in a number of situations as we progressed with the production of the aircraft. Blame that on methods engineering. For the interest of those who might remember that was the first B-47 completely assembled at GELAC, SIS #0026. The following is for detail only and will be the only time I will go into such detail of the type of work that was not normally required.

J. L. Hicks (Buddy) and I were partners on this particular operation. It was necessary to have a 90-degree drill motor to get into the 4-inch area to drill. With the size of the drill motor, our bit (cutting edge and shank) could not be over 1¾ inches in length. The material was 1⅛ inches thick and had #40 pilot holes drilled in one section. We started with a #40 drill bit (⅛ inch in diameter) and cut the shank to the length just to get a good fit in the jaws of the chuck of the drill motor. We reduced the cutting part of the drill to 1¼ inches long just to get through the material. This was easily done with the help (I call it "bootlegging") of a tooling machinist. We had the drills re-sharpened in the tool repair shop with the proper angles called out by methods engineering to perform that particular drilling operation. The smaller drills were easy to reduce to our needs. We were able to do this up to the ⁵⁄₁₆-inch drills; then the problem really grew.

When we reached this point and the need to be able to get the final size, no drills or reamers in the lengths we needed existed for that particular job. There were drills and reamers of the proper size available, but who could put a 6-inch length drill or reamer into an area only 1½ inches long or wide and get a good hole? Everyone stood around giving off smoke and vapors, which is the evidence of deep thought and consideration being exhibited by the great engineering powers that be. To hell with that. I went over to the tool crib and checked out a carbide drill and reamer that would give us the final finished hole. I took these items over to the tooling department and got an acquaintance (I always made good acquaintances) to cut each tool to the lengths I wanted and make smaller shanks, which would enable us to tighten them into the drill motor chuck. The cutting lengths also had to be 1⅛ inches long. Some of these guys had worked during the Bell B-29 days and retained some of that expertise. Those specialists did a top job of centering the shanks of our tools and we got no wobble during the drilling and reaming operations.

Buddy L and I put "C" clamps on our air hoses to the drill motors, reducing the air pressure and thus the RPMs down to a speed that gave us good control over the drilling. We spent about 10 minutes on each hole and came up with 8 full-size holes within 0.003-inch tolerance as required. This procedure was duplicated on the other three locations of the longeron tie-ins. This was an operation of improvising, which is very common in the beginning of a new and complicated design. All of our equipment was inspected by quality control, planning, and engineering before we proceeded with any of those operations. There was nothing done here to rate the bootlegging as wrong. I imagine some of the people mentioned above knew what I had done to get those special items but I'd be damned if I was going to tell them. Since I left those two pieces of drilling equipment for the fellows that followed Buddy L and me on that operation, I guess Lockheed is still wondering what happened to those two expensive items that were never returned to the tool crib (damaged). Actually, the installation procedures were changed on the third assembly, eliminating the need and time expended to accomplish that first assembly. Methods engineering came through and cleared up that problem. Oh yeah, we maintained schedule.

That particular problem seemed to have been solved so we went to the next one. It seems that the rudder stud that we received from Temco (a Texas aircraft manufacturing firm) would not fit our aft fuselage section. The rudder stud held the rudder (the vertical stabilizer) for the tail assembly. This non-fit was probably because their jigs had lost calibration somewhere down the line. Their component parts would not fit our assemblies, period. I had been gaining a little reputation as one who was pretty good at improvising to overcome little nitpicking problems. This meant that if there was a problem I had enough sense to think about a solution. I thought that if we built the rudder stud on the fuselage to the locations per blueprint that we should come out with a good installation. Well, after the smoke and vapors cleared, it was decided that this might be possible. The support group (quality control, engineering, planners, and methods, etc.) decided that it might be better for us to go to the night shift so there would not be too many wheels wandering around guessing what the hell we were doing while we were doing it. To the swing shift we went.

The great swing shift operation started about a week or so before Christmas. We had in this qualified and distinguished group one standards engineer, one methods engineer, one senior planner, one top quality inspector, and two experienced structure general assemblers (Buddy L and myself). With all of this talent we assembled all the component parts required to build the rudder stud that would accept the vertical stabilizer (rudder). I don't think that any one of us had ever seen such an array of stringers, angles, extrusions, small forgings, skins, and cleco clamps in one pile. The blueprints were brought out and laid open and thus began Operation Rudder Stud.

We checked the component part numbers against the print locations and with a 6-inch scale we found and marked the location points with a soft lead pencil. With the Alclad (corrosion-resistant aluminum) on the skin that meant that the top 5 percent of the finish was pure aluminum and it should not be damaged (such as scratched), as this would destroy the anti-corrosion capability of the skin surface. As each part was located, each member of this famous group had the opportunity to double-check the locations; this meant everybody. You can see that this took some time. Time is nothing when it comes to building a quality aircraft. The previous sentence has been my philosophy all of these years and it was more firmly established during this time in my experience as I became an aircrafter.

Once the locations were determined to be correct by all concerned then we drilled #40 size holes and installed cleco clamps to hold the parts together. When all the holes were drilled and the clamps installed we re-measured all locations and agreed that the assembly was in its place per blueprint. Although the Skunk Works (CALAC's experimental shop) may claim first place in improvising, we had surely got second place for that beautiful metal porcupine sitting atop the fuselage. We stepped up each hole to its required size and installed rivets, pins, or bolts per blueprint. We then checked all of the dimensions to be certain that the materiel had not moved or crawled out of tolerance. Everyone agreed that we had made a good installation. The critical point now was to get the crane to bring down that massive vertical stabilizer and see if it would fit. Well, the smoke and vapors that arose then were strictly apprehension and anxiety. This was the test. Would you believe that that big sapsucker fit damn perfect and was within 0.030 inch of tolerance or better, dead on it! Unfortunately (or fortunately) there was no natural beverage of the aircrafter with which to toast the occasion so we just let out one helluva yell that shook the rafters. For you who remember, that was S/S #0026 and we accomplished the same results on SIS #0027. By the next ship GELAC was building its own good subassemblies and they mated. The first Negro group and the ones that followed were building those subassemblies that were going into the 43 section of the B-47 fuselage.

As production speeded up a night shift was started on the 43 section. One night there was a commotion down at the water fountain at the base of the big jigs. We did not have a supervisor covering our group at the time. I was not a lead man but I had to be unofficial supervisor for none was provided for about two weeks. Usually, they took a lead man from a white group and put him over a Negro group and after a few weeks he would be promoted to supervisor. Then just possibly a Negro could make lead man. I was a structure general assembler so that made me the senior person and I acted as lead man and supervisor at the same time with no official notification, just responsibility. The white quality control inspector assumed he was the supervisor and he tried to act like it. I found about fifteen whites and ten Negroes milling around the water fountain. The fountain had a sign on it that read "White Only." A lot of things said "White Only" in those days. The fountain was in our work area but the whites did not want the Negroes to drink from it as it stated "White Only." Well, the Korean War was going on at the time and a lot of the Negro vets were not for that bullshit.

We had an explosive situation building so I walked down and, not giving a damn, said, "What the hell's going on down here?" Since my complexion did not readily identify to what American race I belonged, the tone of my voice usually got respect. The supervisor of the other group (tooling) walked up and said, "Damn right, what the hell is going on here?" Both of us were speaking routine aircraft language. I said, "I'm not sure, but one thing is for certain, this is where it stops." This other supervisor told his people to go back to their work area while he talked to me. This was agreeable to me at the time, as I did not want any trouble this early in the game. I told my co-workers to go back to work while I talked with this other guy. During this time one did not have to take any crap from a subordinate so our request was obeyed. He said, "My name is Gus Hale." He was the supervisor over that group in tooling. I replied, "My name is Hap Hudson."

We went over and looked at the water coming out of the fountain. Both of us came to the conclusion that the water was clear, it had no color. I agreed with Gus that the water had no color, therefore no problem existed. Gus walked over and pulled the sign from the fountain and it was declared that anyone wanting a cool drink of water was welcome to help themselves. Gus was from West Virginia and stated that in his opinion any man had the right to go as far as his ability could take him. He established himself, in my opinion, as somebody. No further trouble occurred at that particular water fountain and the signs began to drop from the others as time went by. My relationship with Gus as a working friend continued for many years right up to his retirement.

About this time we recognized that Dan Haughton had become our president and general manager. Old Jimmy (he did not last one year) had bit the dust somewhere down the line.[2] Dan, as he requested everyone to call him, was a man of extraordinary accomplishments. Born in Alabama, a little above the hard poverty level, through hard work and study he had pulled himself up "by his bootstraps." No man has gotten ahead without the help of others, however, and he was a man who recognized this and would have been the last to deny it. Dan was a guy who seemed to understand the plight of the workingman and had the ability to communicate with him. He had no pity on the person who did not try. I don't think anyone can explain the feeling that the average employee had for "Uncle Dan" at GELAC. He was the person who could come to the floor and request an extra effort to attain a delivery or pull-ahead and get it from all the employees without a question of why. He was the only person I have known who could call at least one thousand employees by their first names. This he did every Christmas at the stairs and head houses as we went out for the holidays. We always kept a hardhat in the area that said "Uncle Dan" and it had four stars painted on it. Dan was in his middle forties but he exhibited experience beyond his years in dealing with and influencing people.

Dan Haughton was probably the most respected top boss that GELAC ever had. He worked toward meeting the requirements as specified by government contracts in employment. Most southerners were beginning to realize that one cannot advance when one has to stand in the ditch holding down another. They slowly understood if both left the ditch the path to a better future was on the level land of opportunity. Quite a few northerners and westerners thought that if they came down and made derogatory statements and acted with prejudice that they would be received with open arms. This was not the exact way they found things. Basically, as long as one stayed in his place (wherever) southerners wanted benefits for all of their people. You never could get one to admit it publicly. Anyway, this was the beginning of the growth of economic opportunity for the whole area.

It so happened that after the episode of the rudder stud there was another problem that had developed in the area of the tail cone. On removal from the major jig the tail cone would not fit the 43 section of the fuselage. The contour of the tail cone did not match the contour of the fuselage within the 0.030 inch required. Someone, possibly a methods engineer, remembered the guy who had helped with the solution to the problem of the rudder stud installation. I was told to report to the tail cone section. The problem was the same: the Temco parts would not fit the major jig. To make a long story short, using the same method of installation we built the tail cone from the skin inward on the major jig. That is, we installed the skins against the stops on the jig and added all of the components inward to the calibrated points and then drilled small holes, stepping up to full-size and installing fasteners. They pulled the tail cone out of the jig and it did not fit the fuselage or anything else. "They" said bad workmanship. I politely picked up my toolbox and proceeded to a department that had started making the nose assembly for the B-47. This assembly was a new addition to Dee's department as it grew. They were just beginning to put workers in the area. Since my time card was stamped in every day Dee knew that I was somewhere in the plant. On the third day he found me in the new section, working like mad.

DEE: "What the hell are you doing over here?"
ME: "The tail cone did not fit the 43 section and I know damn well that I am doing quality work and some bastard up and says bad workmanship while looking at me and he can go to hell."
DEE: "You can't walk off of a job like that. They meant that the tooling was not right. That's what they meant by bad workmanship."
ME: "Why didn't they look at the people who did the tooling instead of me?" (I knew that most of them assumed that I had screwed up.)
DEE: "Don't be so damn sensitive. Now go back over there and build one more assembly and you can come back to this area as this nose assembly is in our department also."

As previously indicated, we thought the world of Dee so I went back over to the tail cone and this time it came out in tolerance and that problem was eventually solved. After all the crap I had gone through during these times (in general), I would have quit at the drop of a hat. If we walked out of the immediate work area (except for brief trips to the tool or blueprint cribs), we were watched over by plant protection (PP) to be sure we did not sabotage the place. I think when a situation is past it should be counted to experience and put out of your mind. (Some of the people in PP were the dumbest bastards that ever drew a breath.) Therefore, I don't dwell in the past but at the same time my opportunity to go to medical school was very good. The good state of Georgia was sending Negroes out of state for medical training, thus eliminating the necessity of integrating the University of Georgia Medical School. This offer covered tuition, room and board, and funds to take care of your family if necessary. Thinking that I would eventually do well at GELAC, I decided to remain. I went over to the nose section as Dee had promised.

Every so often I will add a paragraph or two about some of the characters (some weird) who worked at GELAC. There was a gentleman who had control of all the keys to practically every lock at GELAC. He was known as the locksmith or lockmaster. I think that he had names for all of the locks and keys. He had a hawk nose like Dick Tracy and wore a black suit just like Freddy the friendly undertaker. He even looked like Freddy with black string tie, white shirt, and wool hat. It was always dark in the tunnels, as most of the area there had not been activated into work sections. One day I turned a corner and there sat Freddy gazing at the starter switch on his motor scooter as if he had misplaced the key. He looked like a combination of Dracula and living death. That fellow scared the living crap out of me. I did not want to give the impression that he was ugly as hell and twice as shocking but my reaction gave me away. From then on he always looked at me as if I were the nut.

In early 1953, Temco was building the forward fuselage or nose section of the B-47. This company has since merged with a larger company. It seems that the wheels that be had given consideration to the fact that since GELAC completed assembly of the B-47 and flew it away, why not build it complete in Georgia? Unless they had taken a long good look at our accomplishments, it was beyond me to understand why they came to the conclusion that the Negroes would be given the opportunity to do the job. I guess if one wants to find out if another can accomplish anything, then give them the opportunity. This has to be done to determine if a person can meet the challenge. Under Uncle Dan's regime, more Negroes had been hired but without the extensive training that we first ten had been given. We were expected to teach the others, including those that had worked with us. We were more than happy to pass on the knowledge that we had gained to the newcomers. There is a personal satisfaction that comes from doing a quality and acceptable job in any endeavor.

When I went into the nose section they had assigned a supervisor to the group. He was a young fellow in his middle twenties from Texas. Quite a number of people were hired from Texas, especially those put into supervision. The supervisor's name was Beck and the first thing I noticed was that he had about a quarter pound of "chawing" tobacco in his jaw. There were paper plates with sand in them that had been installed around the area for the tobacco chewers' convenience. Funny thing—very few Negroes chewed tobacco so no plates were in the area where Negroes worked. Beck could hit one of those sapsuckers from about 8 feet if he aimed correctly. He was a roly-poly sort of easygoing character, not exactly 5 by 5 in dimensions. He turned out to be a likable guy who did not step on your heels as you worked. After a short while quite a few of the Negroes started to chew tobacco. It got so that one had to careful not to step in the sand plates as you moved around the work area.

Beck assigned me to complete the nose ring that we had built as our first assembly when we came up from training. A fellow named Buster Jones was assigned as my partner. I had known Buster from earlier years and we hit it right off, becoming a good team in a very short period of time. We completed one assembly and the inspector bled it to death with his red grease pencil. They scrapped the assembly. I had had enough of chicken crap inspectors screwing up workmanship because of bullshit. I told Buster to go and help someone else for a while. I called the inspector over and told him to check out the jig to be sure that it was in tolerance. Since he did not seem to be too busy I asked him to stand by as I loaded the jig. There were two and a half standard hours assigned for the production of that assembly. With the inspector checking the inspection calls as I progressed, I loaded, clamped, drilled, brought the holes up to final size (this being a small assembly), riveted, and bucked the assembly complete in thirty-five minutes. I put the job up for final inspection, called the inspector, and told him, "Now dammit, scrap that!" I watched him do his inspection and came to the conclusion that he did not know what the hell he was doing. That assembly did not have a red mark on it. Beck seemed to appreciate my attitude, but he requested that I not do that again as they might lower our standard production hours on that assembly. In other words that would make our cost center budget smaller.

Initially, there were ten people in this group, but none of the original ten. I wish I could remember the names of all of them but Milton (Buster) Jones stands out. Buster seemed to have the knack of doing things right. He had a lot of confidence in himself. Two weeks after going to the group I was made lead man. They put an "L" on your hourly badge. A lead man is sort of an assistant to the supervisor. Normally, he is given about half of the crew to supervise and he keeps up with planning and methods and the changes that occur in the assemblies (including spares). A lead man is an essential part of the team. We had assemblies coming from the subassembly areas as component parts to complete the nose, which was a major assembly.

We were called together and informed that if we produced a top-quality nose within budget and on schedule that GELAC would be awarded the contract from Temco, and the unit would complete the manufacture of the fuselage of the B-47 at one location. Our first assembly had to be top quality and on schedule. We were told the on-floor delivery date to the air force. Beck took his ten structure assemblers and the lead man (structure general) and said, "Fellows, we can do it."

I had developed the theory that Beck was smarter than he seemed. He had exhibited the qualifications of a manager in my opinion. Beck was liked by all of the crew, as he recognized the fact that a manager has only his workers as his tools and keeping them well informed and on the job, kicking them in the butt, or patting them on the back as deemed necessary resulted in a close-knit team. No need to go into minute details but that crew sat that nose assembly on the floor twelve days ahead of schedule and it was accepted. All hell broke loose in celebration of a good job. We got the contract from Temco.

After confirmation of the new contract a hiring frenzy began. We got about seventy-five new people directly off the street with no internal training and were told to produce. In other words, we had to train them as we went. Who had ever heard of such a thing? I often thought, "Where was management when the brilliantine was passed out with the morning coffee?" I was asked to recommend everyone I thought capable of doing aircraft work. I gave the names of about thirty people whom I previously knew with mechanical ability and an indication of general knowledge of manual dexterity. After interviewing all were hired (damn!). At one time people thought that I was the employment agent for Lockheed. I continued to get calls for employment for the next four years.

Our biggest problem on the B-47 was the in-flight refueling system. This was a preformed, pure lead component in the front of the nose. It was made of lead so as not to create a spark on contact with the refueling nozzle from the aircraft known as the tanker. This nozzle receptacle was shaped like a triangle. The thickness was about ¾ inch. It fit against the understructure with approximately 1-inch clearance. There was no way to get to the installation from inside the assembly. All of the bolt installation had to be from the outside. This is under the skin and up that 1-inch clearance for (all around) almost 3 or 4 feet. We had what is called metal fingers. Since I may have to compare those fingers with the ones that man has, it would not be socially acceptable. That is the ability to go up holes. The lead assembly for acceptance would not hold a permanent form because of its natural softness. Therefore, it was necessary to continually form it to stay within its parameters. We had a problem.

It was decided that we bring in some people from the developmental mechanics group to come up with the procedure for the installation of the in-flight refueling system. Two gentlemen came over and I'll be damned if it wasn't two of the white guys that had gone through training with our first ten group. It had not been one year and these guys were more than four pay scales up the ladder and now developmental mechanics. Not a damn one of them had more than a high school education. How could they be just a few steps lower than an engineer? After about one week of smoking (spitting) and vaporizing they came to the conclusion that the problem would eventually be solved. This included the methods engineers and planners. The only fault was that they could not solve it. They were sent back to the development area, where they continued to develop whatever they were developing. I got a brass hammer to form the lead component (having noticed that they used a brass hammer to form the lead) and drilled the holes up to full size one at a time starting at the top, which was the length of the metal fingers. We countersunk the 1½-inch holes to seat the flush head bolts, put sealant on the washers to stick to the nuts, inserted the nuts up that 1-inch opening, and torqued to specifications hole by hole. It was hell holding those metal fingers tight enough to properly torque. Inspection was with us all the way on each hole. We solved the problem ourselves. No need to call for development mechanics ever again.

The next nose assembly was completed and set on the floor. The appearance was that of an aircraft that had flown through six hurricanes, four tornadoes, and a sandstorm. The skins looked as if we had failed to keep account of the number of hailstorms. It was scrapped. The whole damned thing. Boy, we had to do some helluva lot of training in a short period of time.

I may as well recount some of the other little incidents that happened during this time. One of the new hires was standing very still with the look of a mating lion on his face. He was sweating like hell. All of a sudden one of the guys stepped up and knocked hell out of him right upside the jaw. This is a termination offense. When the fellow got up from the floor he went over and shook the hand of the guy that had hit him with all smiles. It seems that he had been standing in a puddle of water with his electric drill in operation and a short had knocked hell out of him with about 110 volts and he could not move or speak. His co-worker recognized this and let him have one. Luckily, this saved his life. Everyone appreciated the alertness and effort of the co-worker.

One incident happened to me. The lead man would assist any structural assembler who might need help to complete a job. The operation was the completion of the opening of the escape hatch for the navigator. This was the floor of the nose assembly. I had one of the new hires backing the drilling for the installation of the frame surrounding this area. I drilled the pilot holes for the fasteners with George Fuller (bless his heart) holding a piece of phenolic block braced against the back frame to keep it in place during the drilling. Everything went well until he leaned out of the assembly and requested my permission to go to the medical department. He did not seem sick to me so I asked him why he had to go to medics. George said, "You have drilled a hole through my finger." I politely answered, "You are full of crap. I have not drilled a hole through your finger." Whereupon he held up his finger out of the opening and there was a perfect #40 hole through his index finger, including the nail. Instead of holding the phenolic block against the part he had held the bracer in the other hand while using his index finger to keep pressure on the part being drilled. The drill came through the structure and continued through his finger. Since things were becoming pretty bloody I readily gave him directions to the medical department and sent him on his way with my blessings.

I shall never forget that we only had one pressure-testing jig for the nose section. This piece of equipment was kept in the final assembly area where all the sections of the fuselage were put together, making the total B-47 fuselage complete. For some reason methods wanted to check and see if pressure-testing of the nose could be accomplished in the assembly area. Being lead man at the time, I could sign for the responsibility of such equipment. I signed for it but it was not formally released from the flight line area. It was a big bowl-like contraption and we had to use the overhead crane to move it to our area. It was returned after the check but I was charged $4,700 (to my account) for it because someone assumed that there were two of them and I had borrowed one and not returned it. I never found out how one could lose a 1-ton piece of equipment within the plant. Anyway, after fourteen years it was found that only one such animal existed and I was given credit for the $4,700. I think that most of our problems will be cleared up in time.

Things were going along fine. Quality was good, units were on schedule, and costs were under control. It was the latter part of June 1953. The schedule was picking up and more people were being hired all over the plant. It was decided to open up the graveyard shift (midnight to 6:30 a.m.). We did not have a swing shift (or second shift, from around 4:00 p.m. to midnight), but it never occurred to me to wonder why the graveyard was activated first. I was told that I would be acting supervisor with about fifteen men under my control. We reported to work at midnight the following Sunday night. There were some security people and the plant only had the security lights on. The plant was almost completely weather sealed so there was no light coming in at all. It was weird in that big place with only the overhead lights in that area turned on. This was the time when the ghosts of the past, the cats, and the rats managed the facility. You got the feeling that someone was watching constantly. The cats and the rats were about the same size and there were big fights going on all over the manufacturing floor during those hours. We settled in and things went well for about two months. It seems no one ever knew that there was an acting supervisor (Negro that is) on the graveyard shift in the plant. With the other areas closed down during this shift we had a rather free and enjoyable time. You can bet we did a damn good job.

One morning during the first week of September I had arrived home and just gone to sleep when the phone rang. My wife advised that someone from the plant wanted to speak with me. I had just gone to sleep and was in no mood to speak to anyone, plant or otherwise. The caller turned out to be none other than the superintendent of assembly, Clint Weinke, who had taken old BG's place when the latter was promoted. He asked me if I would come back to the plant as soon as possible. Clint was three levels up on the list of bosses so I considered it to be to my advantage to get my tail in his presence as soon as possible. He told me he would be waiting in the department manager's office for me. Damn if someone hadn't screwed over Dee and busted him down and he was now salaried and in the planning organization. I have never gotten any facts for this but am willing to bet that "his boys" did *too* well. The pressures put on him during the year I was under him were ridiculous. This was the first indication to keep a pound of salt in my hip pocket for all of these fine working relationships that management seemed to profess.

On my arrival Clint told me he wanted me to go and take a test, as a formality only. I asked, "What kind of test?" He replied, "Just a test to see if you have the ability to be a supervisor." This was the first I had heard of a test for promotion. I thought that they just promoted you and that was that. I said, "I guess so." We proceeded up to the test area. One of my best attributes is taking tests. This test contained no oral examination and very damn little about how to build an airplane.

In my opinion written tests can be some of the most stupid methods of determining an individual's capability to do anything. Theory goes nowhere without experience. But it can be a starting place. I always use the same system of taking a test that I developed in my educational years. There is a time limit on each section of most tests given. The method is to answer all the questions you know right away and then go back to the ones you were not sure of in the beginning. This gives you all the time left to think out the answers. If a paragraph is in proper composition the first sentence gives you the subject, the middle sentence gives you the meat, and the last sentence gives you a summary. Don't waste time trying to read the whole damn thing. The question is usually, what did the paragraph say? Multiple-choice questions are a flip of a coin; you can get better than 50 percent correct by guessing. Most English meaning is based on Latin or the Romance languages. If you can remember your Latin from high school, you can pass that part. Math is a different story. If you are testing for a position in high technology requiring a great knowledge of mathematics, you had better know your math. I passed the test with so-called flying colors.

I reported back to Clint and he told me to wait around for him to get back. About two hours later he returned and told me I had made one of the highest marks on the management selection test. He gave me a supervisor's badge (name and all) and told me to wear my hourly badge to get out of the gate. He told me to wear my new supervisor's badge in on Monday morning and turn in my hourly badge. Don't say a damn word to anyone until they notice the new badge, he advised, and then say, "Damn right, I am a supervisor now." Well, some of the faces showed a surprised expression but most knew that I had worked very hard for this moment and deserved it. This happened one year and one week after starting work at the Bomber Plant. I made $86 per week as a lead man. Now I was a salaried supervisor at the great sum of $96 per week. Back then one always got a big boost in pay on assuming greater responsibility.

Chapter 3   September 1953. I was now a supervisor. Someone seemed to think that I was the first black supervisor that Lockheed had ever had. (Since I was pure American, that is, the melting pot category, no one could tell anyway.) That is open for discussion as surely they had some other than all-white during World War II. Anyway, here it is Monday morning and I walked in with my watermelon badge on. This did not create another round of identification at the gate. I walked into the area that had been assigned as my first position of management. All of the people in the cost center (a unit of production) were black, colored, or Negro. That is, except the inspector, who had been informed that a new supervisor was taking charge. At first he did not seem to have any apprehensions until he noticed that all the people in the cost center seemed to know me and were on a more than friendly basis.

The person who had replaced Dee earlier, I can't remember his name. He had come from another area and I think he had been an assistant to someone on the next level up from department manager. He was a real quiet fellow who did not come to the manufacturing floor too often. He came down and informed the inspector that I was "the first of my race" to become a supervisor at the Bomber Plant and he was expected to work with me and help in producing a top-quality product on schedule at the lowest possible cost. Because the inspector was white and a good southerner, this indicated that he was the most knowledgeable and qualified cat in the area (psychology is potent as hell). Therefore, with his help in getting me over my ignorance and stupidity we would make a good team. That is exactly what we did, make a good team.

The inspector's name was Fisher. He was not a young man in appearance. He had experience from many years in previous aircraft jobs. If he ever put a red mark on an assembly with his red pencil, it was on the item to be corrected and not all the area around it. He usually just pointed out the item to the worker. Not only was he an inspector, he was also a teacher of quality workmanship. He proved, as most southerners, that "us southerners" could do as well as anyone in these United States when it came to doing a quality job. As this is being written it is no effort to say that directly and indirectly, whites and blacks have worked together, unknowingly, for the benefit of us all, as long as we were under the impression that he was in his place and I was in mine. In other words, I did not expect him to invite me to his house for dinner and vice versa.

It seems that Fisher was a brother of the Elks or Moose or some other great fraternity. I let him know that although I was not a member of the Masons that I had a lot of respect for groups of that nature. I did not give a damn about the Klan but he did not need to know that. Fisher expressed to me that we would have the best damn cost center in the department and we would be on schedule with a top-quality product. This I agreed with and we proceeded to make it a fact.

I had a good crew of sixteen men. The hardest thing I had to learn was the fact I could no longer work on the aircraft myself. The lead man was Frank Jones. Frank had been a brick mason in previous jobs and he had the expertise of knowing how to work with measurements and close tolerance required in this type of work. I think that he was one of the first to make lead man in a short period. Frank exhibited the leadership that granted him opportunities later on down the line. Fisher's enthusiasm was that we be a success to the extent that he regretted that he could not share in the work on the aircraft himself. The men were not as good as our original ten but they were learning fast. There were some rough times in trying to maintain schedule and quality. Eventually, at times I drilled holes and shot rivets or Fisher did. We maintained schedule and quality and were not caught by the union or management. We did not do that for too long. I did not have any trouble in performing my job requirements, as Clint had instructed all concerned that I was to get all the help from the service outfits required to do my job.

In January 1954, our department manager had a heart attack and died shortly thereafter. We got a new department manager who was comparable to BG but without the ability. This fellow came from North or South Carolina and considered himself God's chosen best. He was as ignorant about aircraft as anyone I had seen up to that time. He was a politician and all one had to prove to some of those half-assed characters from California was that he could handle "Negras" even though the government required that all would be treated equal. He came in demanding that his "boys" would do a better job than any other crew in the division or he would get rid of them and see that he did have the top crew. I never determined that this character could even read a blueprint. After the department built to capacity he was the boss of almost five hundred hourly and twenty-five supervisory personnel.

This was the beginning of the first big crisis that I experienced at the good old Bomber Plant. We called the new boss "Mr. Hal" and he rode my ass without a saddle for about five weeks. It was always that we were behind schedule, quality was bad, and we did not make the necessary standard hours to make enough realization to justify our budget. The man could not even understand our production charts. I was not discriminated against. That man gave all the other supervisors (all white) hell continually. No one was doing a mediocre job but he had to emphasize that he was in control and things would be run as he required. The man did not know what was required nor would he let anyone tell him. His own assistant foreman was scared to death of him and never said a damn word to correct or inform him.

My guts began to pain me off and on, and as I had been a pre-med student, I wondered if possibly I was developing ulcers. The climax was reached one day when Mr. Hal told me I would either produce or get fired. I snatched that watermelon badge from my shirt and hit him in the chest with it and told him to ram it up his ass, I was going back to hourly and to screw with me then. After all the money spent on me to show the government that they could produce a supervisor (black, stupid, or otherwise), they were not going to let me bust my own ass. Mr. Hal stooped down and picked up my badge; he told me to take it and cool off. The rest of the crew (including the inspector) had seen what happened and seemed ready to go down with me. This made me feel pretty good. No one had ever bucked Mr. Hal before so he cut his ass on back to the office and let the situation rest.

About three days after this incident I had been feeling woozy and wondering what might be wrong. At least I had a definite premonition that something was wrong with me. I took two days off and headed to southern Georgia. I told my wife that I would call her when I arrived wherever I was going. Naturally, this upset her to a certain degree. I could not give her any better explanation. I returned on a Tuesday. I had gone south to a half-uncle's farm, helped kill a hog, and headed back home with, of all things, fresh PORK! I did not feel any better but I went to work that Wednesday which was a week after the altercation with Mr. Hal. After lunch I grabbed a jig to keep from falling flat on my face to the floor. Some of the men helped me up and after a few minutes I felt better. I went to the tool crib for something and on the way back I felt that peculiar feeling coming on and plopped down in an Indian position (cross-legged) and passed out. I came to in that position and several people were looking at me. I slowly got up and proceeded to the cost center. I knew then that definitely something was wrong with me. All of my symptoms were indicating ulcers. Most of us doctors (bullcrap) recognize symptoms with patients but never really think that these medical problems happen to us.

I went home that evening driving with a full-face (puffy) feeling. With my body attempting to digest a belly full of blood, I did not have any appetite. I might have eaten some soup. Although not too weak, I felt sluggish when I awoke the next morning, which was Thursday, and went to the bathroom to wash and shave, etc. I noticed that my face was flushed and my eyeballs and fingernails were mighty white. I went on, shaved, and got ready for work as I usually did. There are two versions of what happened, mine and my wife's. I guess that my wife's is the factual one. I turned from the bathroom door with one of those "in love" lion's expressions on my face and, saying nothing, fell flat on my face on the kitchen floor and lay there. She pulled and pushed and lifted when possible and finally got me across the bed, whereupon I commenced to vomiting coffee grounds all over everything. When I had no more to throw up she straightened me on the bed. I did tell her to call the doctor. This she did and he told her to get me immediately to the hospital and he would meet us there. On arrival at the hospital I was able to carry on the tale of this experience.

After three pints of blood I was able to think rationally. They fed me Jell-O and half milk for two days plus the necessary medicines. By the third day I was so hungry I could eat a horse. I told my sister-in-law, bless her heart, to bring me a malted milkshake with two eggs mixed in it and to make it chocolate. She did this, plus bringing me eight hardback novels to read. Every day she brought me that milkshake and I began to improve like mad and I was not hungry anymore. She hid that milkshake in a big shoulder bag she carried. Think how much hell the hospital and doctors would have raised had they known that milkshakes were curing me of ulcers.

Meanwhile, my crew on the lower panel of the B-47 carried on without my presence and the great Mr. Hal got his production and quality. To mentally help cure myself in the hospital I had to get my head screwed on right. I decided that nothing would ever get me into a stress condition or otherwise to cause sickness again. I did not know it at the time but that was the beginning of the development of my second personality—one for home, the other for the job. Being Gemini, that came relatively easy.

I read the eight hardback novels and concentrated on getting well. In seven days I walked out of that hospital cured of ulcers with seemingly six-month-old scars. It would be forty years before I had another attack of ulcers of a different type. I learned that the mind is the greatest part of the body. Set a course and stick with it. Deviate when circumstances indicate it but keep your original plan in mind. I set deeply into my conscience that nothing—stress, bills, problems, conditions, job, or anything else—would ever cause me to have ulcers or any other stress-related condition again. This worked for a long time. After two weeks away from the job I returned. This was the latter part of February. Although no symptoms of ulcers remained my stomach seemed to gripe me constantly. My only food for a couple of months was baby food, half cream and half milk with plain biscuits. I dropped more than a few pounds. The cost center was on schedule, the quality was good, and we were running about 95 percent realization on production.

About this time in 1954 the Supreme Court came down with the decision on segregation that upset a helluva lot of people in the South and other parts of the country. Actually, all it did was to re-emphasize the guarantee of the Constitution concerning American citizens. It had to have been Mr. Hal who sent the assistant foreman down to the floor with the request that we not put on a demonstration of glee. Hell, about half the guys did not know about any attempt to get a decision from the Supreme Court on anything. But the bosses were under the impression that there would be an outbreak of demonstrations as a result of that news. The only reaction from the guys was, "It's about damn time." The assistant foreman looked and sounded like a fool. The fellow was actually embarrassed.

That section of plant protection, a few people I could identify that we called the Gestapo, was still keeping an eye on us suspected communist saboteurs. If we walked out of our work area, other than to the tool or blueprint cribs, we were often stopped and questioned as to our reasons. They knew exactly who I was so I was never questioned, just watched. One day one of my crewmembers found a micrometer in the walkway from the tool crib. He gave it to me. I told him to return it to the tool crib on his next trip. He put it in his pocket. Unfortunately, at the end of the shift he still had the blame thing in his pocket and took it home. That night an SOB who will be known as "Sam Catchem" from now on in this narrative, went to this man's home and pushed his way into the house when his knock was answered. This alone indicated to me that the micrometer was planted and watched. Sam had two of his cronies from the Atlanta Police Department with him. No warrant or any other form of authorization for a search with them, they went into this person's bedroom and found the instrument on his chest of drawers by his bed with his badge and other items. On coming to work the next morning he was fired on the spot, with no chance to say anything in his defense. By the time I heard about it, it was too late and all over. That was the way the bullshit worked at the time. I promised myself from that day on, directly and indirectly, I would fight old Sam at every chance I got. As we go along I hope to show it was not a shallow promise.

Before relating the above episodes I stated that I was eating baby food and other unseasoned crud. By Memorial Day I had enough of the stuff so

I bought and drank a whole pint of 100 proof Old Crow whiskey by myself. That made me very drunk and my brain must have taken over, for my stomach never hurt after that day.

There was a young white fellow who supervised the center section of the 43 side panels. Like I said, Mr. Hal gave everybody hell all the time. No white supervisors ever hit him in the chest with their badges. When I met this particular guy about 6 months earlier he weighed about 180 pounds. Now he was down to about 155 pounds and developing ulcers. He was having home problems because of the stresses imposed on him at work. He told me he was going to ask for a downgrade to flight line mechanic (his pre-supervisor position) and return to hourly status. That pay was equal to what he was making anyway as a supervisor. No new supervisors were paid worth a hoot except for the promise of what you might make. He followed through and that request was granted. The reflection was that he was not qualified nor did he possess supervisory ability. After he left Mr. Hal saw reason to move me to a new cost center, the one just vacated. Yeah, in June I went to a new crew and the side panels of the B-47 (mentioned above). I now was supervisor over thirty-five men.

Negroes comprised about six hundred of the total seven thousand-plus workers at the plant. More than likely, it was Mr. Hal who suggested that we should have more expert training and the experts should come from California. Whether GELAC was shorthanded on experts I don't know, damn our records up to this point. They brought in about twenty-five good people from CALAC (California Lockheed) to be sure we were properly trained. To get a sufficient number to come took a little effort to convince them that they were not coming to a backward southern-ass state (this was their way of putting it). We almost but not quite recognized them as the kooks, nuts, and flakes they were rumored to be. Their first impression of us was that we worked too hard. They had quite a bit of knowledge and experience, but they did not believe in working. They showed us all the ways to fake out a job and appear to be working hard. They advised us to do good quality work but never on time. The idea was if you performed on schedule you would never get overtime. To make money one had to have overtime. This was a big pot of bullshit and I am proud to say that none of the Georgia boys accepted that crap. We still liked an all-around good job to be done for the pay we received. I don't intend to give the impression that these characters did not know how to build an airplane, it's just that they did not give a damn about meeting schedules. I think upper management finally recognized this and sent those fellows back to CALAC with praises and appreciation.

As the supervisor of the side panels I had thirty-five people under my control. One of the original ten of us, Lou Morris, was lead man in this group. With the supervisor (who had taken the downgrade) and Lou, this was a pretty tight crew. They had the attitude that they could learn all possible from the fabulous bunch from CALAC. Those guys helped to train everybody in methods and tool use that was advantageous to a lot of our workers. The whole effort was not a waste, they just did not believe in working at the tempo that we were accustomed to doing. We had two fellows working as a shooting and bucking team. H. Longshore on the shotgun (a 10-inch-long rivet gun for ¼-inch rivets) and Joe Dill on the bucking bar. Those two dudes could fire and buck rivets at a 44–45 per minute rate. That big rivet gun sounded like a 45-caliber machine gun pumping. People from all around would come to see what and who was making that noise. These included wheels and the air force customer. There were thousands of rivets on that assembly and the quality rate was about 97 percent consistently. The new job was going nicely and no major problems were active at the time.

I had come to the conclusion that I would have to continue training to grow and perform my responsibilities. I never missed any advanced courses given by the company, even if it meant staying overnight. In April 1954, I completed supervisory development for a total of 80 hours. They graded S or U in all management courses.

Just about July, the supervisor in the cost center next to mine quit. He had been catching hell from Mr. Hal like everyone else. There were people who just couldn't take all of that crap. This guy waited until lunchtime one day, walked into Mr. Hal's office, and left a note on his desk. I went into the office for some reason and saw the secretaries giggling and got a glimpse of that note. This guy had told Mr. Hal to go to hell on a space shuttle (which had not been invented at the time) and quit. I made sure that I was not in the office when Mr. Hal returned from lunch.

With no one to fill that slot Mr. Hal gave me that cost center also. While he was in a giving mood he also gave me the coin-dimpling operation, which included the lower panel for the 42 section, which was the center fuselage for the B-47. Good gracious, here I was the supervisor over eighty-seven people and still had not completed one year as a supervisor! I wasn't supposed to know that some departments did not have eighty-seven people overall. I had responsibility of the payroll for eighty-seven people, over $3.5 million of tooling, and all the problems that went with it. Eighty-seven people equals eighty-seven different problems each day. Hell, I was somebody, with more people than any one supervisor at the time in the plant. My equitable salary was $112 per week. Did I get a raise? I had four lead men and I utilized them. I delegated authority and responsibility like mad and ended up with a real smooth operation. It got so well organized that at times during the day I just didn't have anything to do. This went on for over a year or longer but I did not get a damn thing out of it except experience.

One problem we confronted was the drag chute door on the B-47. The big problem with the drag chute door was that it was not interchangeable between aircraft. All doors, including access doors, had to be interchangeable on to other aircraft. Mr. Hal figured that anything that did not work was the fault of the production crew. Tooling had reworked that jig a number of times and still could not get it right. After smoking and vaporizing for a while, I figured that if we used a nickel, dime, or quarter on the location stops in certain places that we could produce a door that met specifications. After thinking for two or three weeks, I decided to use my method unknowingly to tooling. We were skipping along fine and caught up to schedule when some big wheel from tooling, superintendent level, came around and found out what we were doing so he raised hell and shut down the assembly. As weeks rolled around and the assembly got further and further behind schedule, old "Blood and Guts" (now the production manager) came down to check out the problem. He and I always did get along even though some heavy aircraft language was required to fully understand each other. His hell-raising did not fluster me and he developed a level of confidence in me because we could understand each other. I showed him exactly what we were doing. I took one of the doors we had completed and walked down the line installing the door on any ship serial he suggested. The door fit perfectly. BG, with his usual emphasis, told us to go on and use the change but don't get caught again. We continued to make acceptable quality assemblies with inspection buying our method after we showed them the interchangeability of each assembly. The tooling superintendent did not come back and the tooling was corrected about a month later. We were on schedule. The lead man was Tom Weaver and he had knowledge of that operation better than anyone, including the service organizations. Mr. Hal said that he knew we would solve the problem. Commendation, anyone? Don't make jokes.

In the drag chute area we also built the air intake vent at the junction of the rudder stud and the vertical stabilizer joining point. The main component was a large casting that would be covered by an aluminum skin. The casting was not a machine-finished part. The skin was preformed to fit like a sleeve over the casting with fasteners only on the bottom edge. One of the pimples on the casting created an image of a bump on the surface of the skin. This was noticeable only if you looked at a certain angle and reflected the light against the seeming discrepancy. One of the air force inspectors (civilian) present did not like the visual appearance and said that the skin would have to be removed and replaced. This would result in poorer quality than was presently indicated. I called our Lockheed inspection supervisor (quality control) and asked his opinion. He agreed with me that the removal was not necessary. The air force inspector demanded that the skin be removed and replaced. John (Big John) White, our inspection supervisor, was not buying that bull so he called for the air force quality control manager (a Mr. Rogers) from upstairs and requested that he come down, inspect the assembly, and make the decision. Meanwhile, the air force inspector had gone back to his office.

When Mr. Rogers (air force quality control manager) arrived and made his inspection, he requested that we get the air force inspector from his office. Their conversation went as follows:

ROGERS: "Do you consider this to be a discrepancy of such magnitude that it necessitates the removal of the skin?"

AIR FORCE INSPECTOR: "In my opinion this is a bad case of workmanship and quality and the skin must be removed."

ROGERS: "Well, in my opinion, this is an unacceptable decision and the skin will not be removed. The indicated discrepancy is of a visual nature and can only be ascertained by looking from a single angle. If all you have to do in making quality decisions is of this nature then it may be necessary to replace you with someone with the ability to be objective, rational, and expedite rather than hinder production of this program."

The air force inspector was only trying to show his prejudice (without being seen). No one bought it. The man remained at the plant for over twenty years and never spoke to me again. This caused me many sleepless nights like alligators still fly. I wondered why the air force quality control manager was so hard on the air force inspector, but we found that the inspector had demonstrated this attitude on a number of occasions and Mr. Rogers was fed up with him in general. Big John became a friend of mine and that respectful relationship lasted for over twenty-six years until the time he retired. You will read much more about him in later chapters.

With my eighty-seven people and four lead men I had it made. I delegated authority to the lead men and the people fulfilled their obligations. I had learned through experience and management training that only three things were necessary to have a good operation—communication, organization, and production. If honesty, principles, and integrity were not the guidelines, you did not have anything to operate from. I had developed but not recognized these qualities in my business life before Lockheed but I began to realize them more thoroughly as my responsibilities grew larger.

I will close out this chapter with a few incidences that happened during this time. On the side panels we ran into a quality problem. It seems no matter how careful we were and how hard we tried, we were getting cattails (or rattails) from our drilling operations. The engineers and inspectors could not understand or determine the causes and everything was attributed to bad workmanship (according to Mr. Hal). Mr. Hal could not tolerate any situations that he could not understand. There was just so much Mr. Hal could understand anyway. Therefore, he up and issued thirteen "boomsheets" (poor performance notices) for bad workmanship to my men. The next step would be three days on the street (suspension). There happened to be a union shop steward working for me by the name of J. B. Mabry, who had an undergraduate degree and continued his education through further classes and self-education. He had a command of written English that was commendable. Well, J. B. was ready to file a grievance to fight the boomsheets. This was one time that I thought that management (Mr. Hal especially) had made a drastic mistake. Hell, you could not tell Mr. Hal a damn thing about him making an error.

In the meantime, I found that the tooling department was re-sharpening drills and we were using them in a cost savings effort. I personally tried to drill holes with those drills and found that I got the same poor quality results. I went down to the tool repair area and discovered that whoever had re-sharpened those drills had done so at an angle that was several degrees off the specified angle required. Thus, when an attempt was made to use those drills they jumped out of the pilot hole and created the cattail effect on the skin. The supervisor immediately corrected the problem and the discrepancies ended. Funny how all those drills showed up in my work area. Since Mr. Hal would not lift the boomsheets even after we proved my crew not guilty of bad workmanship, I take great pleasure in stating that I as a supervisor (member of management) got together with J. B. (union steward) and came up with one of the best grievances ever written against a company. Mr. Hal had to eat every one of those performance notices and we went back to quality workmanship. No engineer, methods or otherwise, or inspector solved that problem. It seems that J. B. and I had to honor the company-union contract according to the preamble to that contract. If it was ever found that I had helped to write that grievance, it was never mentioned. However, upper management would have understood anyway. My interactions with the union seemed to be better after that incident. I was never bluffed with grievances against me as often as the other guys were and I never lost one grievance.

During this time I became a recruiter for the Red Cross blood program. I had given a pint every six weeks up to the time I had my ulcers and as soon as

I was able I continued to donate. Our department gave a tremendous amount of blood during the years 1952–56. Since we were over 500 employees by the third year we averaged about 100 pints each time the blood bank visited. I will always remember the blood I received during my ulcer attack and will support that program as long as I am able.

One day the assistant department manager (Richie) came down and told us that Mr. Hal's wife was in the hospital. To show our love and respect for him it was requested that all the supervisors contribute a dollar, all lead men would donate fifty cents, and all employees of the department would give twenty-five cents each so that her hospital room would be filled and covered with flowers. There were about 25 supervisors, 30 lead men, and 525 employees in the department. No hospital room would hold all of those flowers. Having to put up with him I figured she should have an engraved plaque. The supervisors donated their dollar, the lead men told the assistant foreman to go to hell, and the employees threatened to file a grievance. Anyway, Mrs. Hal got several bunches of beautiful flowers in her hospital room. If you get the impression that we despised our department manager, you are wrong. We just understood him.

One day a fairly young guy came into the drag chute area and asked if we had been missing rivet gun sets. Hell, every assembler was issued the necessary tools with his toolbox when coming to work for the Bomber Plant. It seems he was from plant protection and making a routine check on some missing items. Who the hell would want a rivet headset except an aircrafter with his own assembly plant and rivet guns? We did not have any missing items to report so he and I got into a conversation on general status, etc. Shortly after this meeting we came in one morning and our latest assembly, ready for final inspection, was missing. After notifying Mr. Hal that we had this unit missing, we called up plant protection. This same young fellow came up and we gave him all the details and identification of the part. How in hell could this $4,000 (or more) unit disappear within a plant with all the security we possessed? It happened during the night when no shift (or Negroes, therefore no plant protection watching the Negroes) was on duty in that particular part of the plant. I don't remember if this was on a weekend or not, anyway the damn part was gone. Those great Sherlocks got busy finding the drag chute door. They were not looking for rivet headsets this time. After four months the part (door), which the stolen door had replaced, showed up in a trash can out on the flight line. It seems someone had run a tug or forklift into the door on an aircraft out there and severely damaged it. What the hell, no point in making a big issue out of it. Go into the manufacturing area, steal a completed door, and re-serialize it to go on this plane and trash the original by hiding it where it would not be found for a long time. Even with the help of the Gestapo unit no one in plant protection found that unit.

The young agent told me later that no one was qualified in plant protection to lift, identify, classify, or prepare fingerprints to send off to the FBI. He said that 80 percent of them had come from jobs as deputy sheriffs out of the most northern counties of the state. This was before it was necessary that they have training that is required to hold that position now. Quite a few of these fellows were upgraded as the need came about for more and better-trained people since they had seniority. The young agent told me he had finished law school and was holding this job until he could set up a law practice. We talked about my eighteen months of criminal and investigative training, including fingerprints, and some civil law and court ethics. Although this was supposed to be in my records (I found out later it had been eliminated), I was never questioned or considered for a position with plant protection. Anyway, my buddy quit and went into the practice of law and finally was elected to a judgeship later. He said he was never given consideration for his training in law either.

Things went along pretty well. I added dimpling to my area of supervision, with Robert Grist (one of the original ten) serving as my lead man in this area. Dimpling is the process where the understructure is countersunk to receive flush rivets. The skins have full-size holes drilled and then go to a piece of equipment known as the coin-dimpling machine. This machine has a head (different diameters) that is heated to a temperature according to the hardness of the material you are working with and punched to dimple a countersunk hole into the skin the same size as the rivet to be installed. This retains the thickness of the skin plus seating the flush rivet. You do not lose any strength by lost material from the skin. This is a highly skilled job requiring knowledge of all the different heat controls for the different alloys of aluminum and gives a perfect fit to the rivets on the outside of the airflow of the plane. This will increase the speed of an aircraft up to a possible 15 miles per hour.

If I tried to cover most of the things happening during this period I probably would never get on with this narrative. But I must tell you the following. This happens in most jobs that I found out about in my dealings all around the country and experiences with suppliers, et al. Some of the supervisors were professionals when it came to brown-nosing (the method of kissing ass without making contact). This was accomplished by supplying the clay pigeons when the boss was taken on trap shoots. The boss did all the shooting. There were the fishing trips and the boss did not pay anything. The guys would tell me what great times they had with the boss on weekends. I never participated because I was never invited. I would not have gone because he had never invited me to dinner either. There were about three more Negro supervisors by then and they did not get invitations either. We felt terrible for being left out of all of this activity. You can believe that too.

The time is 1956 and the B-47 is phasing out. I think we had built 272 B-47s and the last few were near the end of the line to be delivered to our customer, the air force. There were now approximately four or five Negro supervisors—a nice gain out of the several hundred Negro employees now in the total plant over the four years. Mr. Hal told me he had tried everywhere to find me a position in a new area. This was the same bull that he gave most of the other supervisors (white and Negro). If I had depended on him to find me a job I would probably have ended up digging ditches. I found my own position based on my record and actually needed help from no one, especially Mr. Hal. One of the main brown-nosers was left in the cold and swore out loud the he would never kiss another ass as long as he worked with Lockheed. Big deal! By the way, he did not have a high school diploma.

Now we will move on over to the most exceptional cargo aircraft ever produced since the Douglas C-47 (World War II-era transport plane) by any other aircraft company—the C-130 Hercules.

My supervisors gave me good reviews in this period, but seemed reluctant to give high marks. And in a pattern that would mark my career, it seemed that my greatest problem was getting experience.

Chapter 3.1

Before we move to chapter 4 and the beginning of the work on the C-130 I must tell about my major encounter with agent Sam Catchem. It seems that the two girls in the office (a secretary and a stenographer) had been going to one of the real popular nightclubs in Atlanta where the most well-known black musicians and entertainers were playing at the time. All the music lovers felt no compunction about associating with Negroes when it came to good music. The men did not want the white women to go unless properly escorted by white men. Who gave a damn because the reason for their being there was to enjoy good music and entertainment.

In the 1950s everything was black or white and not gray in between. These two gals had decided that since their men did not seem to indicate a preference for jazz (which was still considered "nigger music" at the time by many whites), then they would slip down to Atlanta and take in the shows. Naturally, they ran into some of the workers from the plant enjoying the same entertainment. One fellow, after commenting on their presence and asking their opinion of the show, suggested that they had better have escorts on their next visit because single white women would be looked on by the community (and Lockheed) as being out of place and "loose women." One of the women was married and she became upset and told her husband that a "nigger" had approached her for a date on her next visit or something of that nature. I imagine, after beating hell out of her for going there in the first place, it behooved him to inform plant protection that his wife had been propositioned. (As if the Gestapo would go down and close the club.) I got wind of the situation and took it on myself and advised the girls to just stay away from the club. This was relayed to her husband or the Gestapo and I was called down for an interview with the great Sam. I will try to give the conference as verbatim as possible:

SAM: "I understand that you have been advising some white ladies about their visits to some of the Negro nightclubs in Atlanta?"
ME: "So?"
SAM: "Where do you take it on yourself to advise anybody about their private lives?"
ME: "I thought that I would tell them to stay away when they did not have escorts because 'the company' would look disapprovingly on their presence under those circumstances."
SAM: "Did you know that we were investigating the situation and who gave you the authority to advise them?"
ME: "In the first place, who gave you the authority to investigate the private lives of any employees and under what circumstances was that investigation instigated?"
SAM: "That is none of your goddamn business and you have no authority to interfere in our methods." (Note that Sam had used the first word of what I consider real profanity. He had a secretary taking notes of this conversation. Taking the cue from him, I took for granted that I could use the same language to be emphatic when necessary.)
ME: "Since this ain't Russia, where do you get the authority to investigate the private lives of our employees?"
SAM: "You could lose your job if you are not careful."
ME: "Would you repeat that?"
SAM: "Repeat what? You heard me the first time."
ME: "I damn sure did, but I want to make sure that the steno did also and recorded it correctly."
SAM: "Why?"

ME: "You have just made a personal threat against me and I want to make damn sure that it is recorded."

SAM: "Well, forget that for the time being. Who told you about the ladies being at these clubs?"

ME: "Forget hell, if you make a threat against me I want to be sure it is recorded."

SAM: "Okay, now who told you these ladies were at the club?"

ME: "The grapevine."

SAM: "What do you mean, the grapevine?"

ME: "As I said, the grapevine, and I can't point out any one person as the source and you know damn well that I can't with impunity." (I think the word "impunity" flipped him but be damned if he was going to admit it. I was sure he knew who had mentioned it to me and he was sure I knew but if he had any interrogation experience he also knew that I was not going to tell him a damn thing.)

SAM: "Well, we are going to get to the bottom of this and when we do some heads will roll."

ME: "I think that you are going to leave this as it is because this is the USA and people don't stand for this crap. One thing is for sure if anything results from this that will hurt anybody, I will testify in a court of law."

SAM: "I want you to sign this statement and stay the hell out of this department's business."

ME: "Sign what?"

SAM: "This statement that you have made."

ME: "I haven't made any statement, all I have done is had a conversation with you."

I read over what the secretary had recorded and found it to be factual and to the last statement correct to my conversation. Therefore, I signed the piece of paper and noted that any changes made subsequently would void my signature. Overall, the other units of plant protection did an exceptional job.

Nothing more was ever heard of this great escapade. Seriously, wasn't that stupid.

Chapter 4

I moved down to the C-130 area. I thought that I had seen a big airplane during the manufacturing of the B-47. This C-130 had a belly that was twice the size of the B-47's. The side panels were made on 2 levels (about 12 feet high). This was called the upper deck of the assembly. You needed a crew on the lower level and one on the upper level. Also included in this area was the top panel. The day shift was already in place so I went to the night shift as supervisor. The day shift supervisor was a guy named Jack Rochester. Since we always assigned nicknames to people we called him "Roc." I told Roc that I would back him on the night shift. The day shift supervisor was supposed to be the senior supervisor. We got a good understanding on what we were going to do and took off.

Roc was a regular fellow, as he had had to hustle practically all of his life in growing up to make ends meet. Bootlegging (moonshine that is) was an acceptable method of earning a livelihood in those times as long as the law did not catch you. Roc admitted that he had had experience. Quite a few of the mountain boys and some of the city boys also had experience in that type of endeavor and it resulted in a high degree of independence and a sense of capability. In other words, they had confidence in themselves. As said, both whites and Negroes had experience in similar endeavors and it turned out that great teams were in the making. There were still all-white and all-Negro crews in the separate cost centers; there were no Negro supervisors in the white centers but many white supervisors in the Negro centers.

BG was now the production manager, which meant he was over about three superintendents under his management. BG was off the hog's hipbone and halfway up his backbone as far as the level of management was concerned. All the department managers and supervisors were always apprehensive whenever he was in the area because he cussed out and raised hell with them all if he thought anything was out of place. He would check all the status data on the areas he was going to visit so he would be informed on how much hell he was going to raise. Some of the other supervisors would wonder how that man knew so many details about their particular areas. BG had started with Lockheed in 1939 as an assembler. He made manager during World War II and he told me that to hold a job he was reduced back to hourly assembler after the war. When the Cold War broke out and then the Korean conflict he was reinstated in management. When the Georgia division was opened he was offered superintendent of assembly if he would transfer to the new plant. I don't know if he had a high school diploma in the beginning but he did not let any opportunities for further training and education slip by.

BG was aggressive and expected the people under him to be the same. He thought more of the people who demonstrated their knowledge and ability and who stood up to him (naturally, man to man in private) whenever he was bulldozing and you knew better. As long as you did not forget and beef back in the presence of others you got away with it. So you can see the man was not stupid even though most times overbearing in his contacts with his subordinates. Luckily for me, I read his characteristics almost perfectly from the beginning.

Whenever he would come into my area I would greet him with a smile. I kept good records of our position on quality, schedule, and realization daily. Hell, I knew where we stood. He would say something like, "What the hell are you grinning about?" I would reply, "I feel good, Mr. BG." Damn if BG began to call me "Lad," and that was the way he addressed me the rest of our time at GELAC. He was about ten years older than I was. I think that his harshness and mean-acting attitude came from the fact his back must have hurt continually; he often limped. Well, BG and I established a good working relationship. I began to respect him as time went by and even though he probably cut my throat a few times there developed a good working combination, me on the hog's toenail and him up on the hog's backbone. We understood each other and were working toward a common goal. By the way, BG could move his share of the aircrafter's beverage in his off hours also.

After a while I noticed that the day shift was making a number of mistakes and looking for us to clean up by rework at night. I told Roc that this crap had to stop because the night shift could not make any realization or man-hours because we were doing mostly the cleanup from the day shift. I began to keep records of the amount of cleanup we had to do and proved that we could not accomplish any work for this reason. I flat told Roc to clean up his act. I am proud of the fact that I have never been diplomatic. State the situation for what it is and go on. Don't beat around the bush about anything, come straight to the point and say so. This atmosphere created a situation where the night crew came in looking for the day shift mistakes. After much cussing between the crews and a couple pushing and shoving incidents we knew some real fighting might start. This situation was occurring in other areas of the plant also. The attitude of wanting to do a good job on schedule and cost was great but the competitive spirit was heading in the wrong direction.

Eventually, someone was going to get fired for fighting. BG appreciated the production being accomplished but was highly concerned about the hell-raising going on during the change of shifts. Some of the other supervisors and I suggested to BG that if the swing shift was held back from the work area until the day shift had ended, then the two crews could not mingle in the work area. Believe it or not, the day shift ended at 3:30 p.m. and the night shift could not enter and go to work until 3:45 p.m. This arrangement ended the problem. The shift changes were made and the squabbles were eliminated.

Previously, we had used a number of gimmicks to provide incentive for production. There had been the white elephant and the eight-ball. The white elephant went to the cost center that had been the highest producer (quality, schedule, and realization) and the eight-ball to the lowest cost center over the past month. Gimmicks are only good for a short period of time. We needed something new to keep the competitive attitude going so as to keep down squabbles. Since standard hours were assigned to jobs according to the level of difficulty involved it was possible to chart the results of tempo in production. I came up with a chart showing the number of standard hours produced by the day shift in comparison to those produced by the swing shift. This was a humdinger, no person on the night shift would let their counterpart on the day shift outperform them in hours produced and quality achieved. If an error was made and there was not enough time to correct it, then the following shift had to clean it up (rework, etc.). Since the crews never met between shifts anymore it was necessary that the supervisors settle it. With the results we were getting the supervisors were as happy as blind dogs in a meathouse. BG felt so good that he started other areas using our methods. This was one of the good periods for a few months.

Everyone was very quality conscious during these times, the work was going well, and our area was ahead of schedule. The union and management were getting along fine and no major problems in our area were in effect. Normally, some "willie" had a problem and maybe a grievance was in process but no major problems that could not be solved satisfactorily were occurring. Let's look at some of the serious accidents we had during this span.

I had a fellow in my crew drilling holes in a couple of small angles. He had them clamped in a vice attached to a workbench. He was standing pretty close to the work and using a #40 12-inch drill bit. If he had taken the time to use a 6-inch drill it would have been the correct drill for the job. The drill slipped and drilled a hole straight through the head of his "pistol." Now every man knows that his "pistol" is loaded with thousands of small blood vessels and nerve ends. When damaged (especially having a hole drilled through it), it explodes with a scattering of blood and much pain. The fellow grabbed a shop cloth and covered his damaged part, took off for the medical department smoking like a B-47 (which he had helped build). No nurse could help him because he had to see a doctor (male that is) without fail, immediately. Although bloody as hell he would not let a nurse touch him. Given a tetanus shot and two Band aids with a sedative he was allowed to remain there until the end of the shift. It was painful, funny as hell, bloody as all get out, but fortunately not fatal. He learned a lesson on safety the hard way.

When large skins were installed to the frames in the big jigs it was necessary to use shock or bungee cord to maintain tension and mate locations as you drilled the pilot holes from the frames through the skins and installed clecos (brand name for fasteners that held sheets together for drilling) until time to rivet or bolt them together. One night a diligent aircrafter was stretching the shock cord around the assembly when for some reason the cord broke. The backlash caught him squarely in the mouth. Within thirty seconds or less his face was better looking than that of Mr. Willie B., the Atlanta zoo's most valuable gorilla. (Come to think of it, Willie B. wasn't even born then.) Although very painful for him it was one helluva sight for the rest of us. He spent the balance of the shift down with the medics with ice packs against his face. These were two accidents that were not too serious and no lost workdays were recorded.

Unfortunately, all accidents did not turn out with a happy ending. I had a Pentecostal preacher in my crew. The company always gave leeway to our employees in their religious beliefs. This fellow had prayer meetings on Wednesday nights and requested short-time on that day to hold his church services. His absence was not conducive to producing quality aircraft at a low cost and on schedule. Shortly before this became a problem he was involved in a bad automobile accident and his neck was broken. After a number of weeks he returned to work and was admitted to work with the restriction of wearing his neck brace while in the production area. He still had his problem with his Wednesday night church service. I found him a much safer position plus work schedule on the graveyard shift out on the flight line where they were doing modification on some B-47s. For some reason, maybe the heat, he removed his neck brace. His job was aligning wire harnesses for reinstallation in the fuselage of the B-47. He backed into the landing gear door on the plane and the jar snapped his spinal cord. He was dead by the time he hit the ground. This was a bad time for all of us. Even though he was supposed to have had that brace on in the production area the company gave his family compensation equal to his accidental insurance coverage. His family was especially appreciative, for he had five young kids. The company always at one time or another proved appreciation of its employees whether they were liable or not.

The emphasis is still on the use of all safety precautions when working around aircraft. Them damn things can kill you.

I was always satisfied with the emphasis I put on quality. The first priority on any job during production was that quality was built into it from the start, for you could never add it to the finish. There were times when decisions had to be made concerning quality to expedite the movement of an assembly from one position to another. Usually, this would be near the end of the shift, allowing the next shift to continue on schedule. I had a pretty good inspector and normally we worked together really well. He realized that I would not do anything to jeopardize the safety or quality of the aircraft. He was one of the first Negroes to make inspector and I knew that he was working under the gun. He also knew that I was purchasing a ticket myself. His name was Sampson and he knew his job responsibility.

This particular night we were running a little late in moving a major assembly from the jig and putting it into the next position. I checked it thoroughly and came to the conclusion that it could be moved. One thing must be remembered—that I always had to check out all possibilities before I made a decision. Sampson had his tail plate on his shoulder that night and came to the conclusion that the assembly would not be moved. No inspection supervision was available that night so I had to make a decision. The service organizations followed my request and not others. I called the overhead crane to make the move. The crane operator hooked onto the assembly and proceeded to raise the assembly over the overhead platform to go to the next position. Sampson held on to the panel and was raised about 6 feet from the floor. The crane operator stopped the lift and Sampson decided that he did not want to take a 20-foot ride through the air so he dropped off. The assembly was moved to the next position.

The next day I spoke to my old friend, Big John, now a department manager, and he approved my decision. Plop went another inspector, not intentionally. Everyone knew that I would not mar my integrity by making a stupid move. I told Sampson in front of his top boss that I respected his decision but my experience exceeded his under the circumstances. My emphasis was always to get along with the people I worked with and gain their respect while acquiring respect for their ability and integrity at the same time. Everything works so much better that way. All in all, people are pretty wonderful animals.

I remained on the night shift about one year. That plant was one of the darkest places in the world when the lights were all out except the ones directly over the bay in which you were working. The same old melody of the cats and rats fighting over food scraps at night continued until the night shift increased. Mainly, there were fewer than two hundred people working in the main plant at night and most of the lights were out. One Sunday morning (about three o'clock) we were working overtime to seal a unit for movement down the line Monday morning and the only lights on again were the ones directly overhead. I almost hit a guard with a bucking bar as he made his clock rounds because I could not see him and I'd be damned if some ghost was going to walk up on me in the dark. Luckily, he did not pull his gun. Would the bullet or the bucking bar be the fastest? That question was never answered.

We had a boss at night who was one of the best garbage can inspectors I have ever encountered. He was known as the night manufacturing manager. It seems that he had owned and operated a small plane repair shop at the Atlanta airport. I think he must have been hired during the reign of the great Jimmy [Carmichael]. Probably because of political contributions he was given the position because of his expertise in servicing small plane requirements. He was in charge of the plant at night (graveyard shift) and had the whole plant to manage (cats and rats included). He always made his first tour about midnight. His chore was to lift every garbage can lid to determine if they had been emptied. It was impressive to see this distinguished, well-dressed fellow walking about looking very stern at the employees and opening garbage can lids. You have never seen such a frustrated man, during the holidays, when we would find every empty whiskey bottle in the plant, put them in a can a long way from our area, and listen for him to lift that lid. He would explode and raise a thousand dollars worth of hell while we looked real concerned and shocked that such a thing was happening in our plant. He always exhibited an air of accomplishment after such an occasion.

Time was moving on and in this business you move with it. I was instructed to come in on the day shift and take over another cost center. You always hate to leave a good crew that you have worked with and have such good rapport with but usually you come together again somewhere down the road.

I went on the day shift into the section known as the cargo ramp assembly. There were about twenty-six people working in this area. Among a number of the people I already knew was my old buddy J. B., who had written the grievance against Mr. Hal and whipped his butt with common sense. Our paths would cross many times during our careers at GELAC. I had developed my method of maintaining accountability records on each employee's performance. I took every opportunity to take classes that were offered by the training department to increase my knowledge of the manufacturing process and the management of people. Some of these were mandatory and the others were offered on your own time. I took classes in time study, the foundations of human behavior as related to the industrial complex, tooling, methods, and improving work attitudes. I learned quite a bit about the different chemical and physical reactions one might experience from working with metal and other components in the manufacture of aircraft. My main point was that I intended to learn everything possible about my job. If I did not know what I was talking about, then I should keep my mouth shut. I knew I had to be a qualified supervisor.

We ran into a problem that was different from the cattails on the skins of the side panels of the B-47. There were pit holes in the floor plates of the cargo ramp showing up during the drilling and countersinking for the installation of the floor plates to the assembly. This turned out to be another time when the engineers and the methods people were called out so we might have smoke and vapors rising, which resulted from the fact that somebody was doing some deep thinking. It turned out that we were using magnesium drill plates on the aluminum floor plates and the roof was leaking whenever it rained. This combination created a helluva condition. We only got the pit holes when it rained. One of my crew (I'm sure it was Lee Monroe) who had a BS in chemistry, asked if the water was acting as a catalyst between the magnesium and the aluminum, creating what is known as an electro-galvanic reaction. Well, I'll be damned if it wasn't doing just that. The pits were the result of this chemical reaction. A few years later, Monroe ended up in methods engineering, no joke.

Monroe might have made it into methods sooner but he had to accumulate the necessary qualifying experience. They rigged a big canvas cover when it rained for a while to catch the rainwater leaking through the roof. We had to watch that cover to be sure it had been emptied before the whole thing came down on us and the assembly. Later it cost $6 million to replace the roof. This was a good investment, but unfortunately, one life was lost when a contract roofing company worker fell from the ceiling to the floor.

One of the men in the ramp crew I recognized as a fellow student at college with me. I had the impression that Ted Ramsey was a pretty smart fellow at school. He had a master's degree in psychology and was six hours and a dissertation short of his doctorate in clinical psychology. Do you know that those stupid bastards at Lockheed had that man drilling holes and shooting rivets because they were too prejudiced to recognize the fact at the time that he would have made one of the best human factor scientists at the plant? The only top scientists we had were so wrapped up in their own importance that they would not have recognized talent if they were drowning in it. Ramsey was not a veteran so because of short funds he had to leave school and work to try and get enough money to finish his requirements. I got him a six-month leave of absence to continue his education at the University of Chicago. Even then he did not complete the requirements. He came back to dear old Lockheed. At a later time Lockheed would regret that he was not given the opportunity he deserved. A lot of talent was lost to both Negroes and poor whites because they were keeping Negroes in their place by sitting on them. They had a good time until they realized that they were in the ditch also. A lot of things in general should have been accomplished for the people and the plant if middle management hadn't been continually telling upper management that everything was going fine. Well, if you stand before or behind the fan long enough something is going to splatter you.

The cargo ramp cost center was doing fine. Having kept records on the entire crew I took the top thirteen and awarded them commendations for performance. That stuff that usually hits the fan splattered. About fourteen filed grievances against me. Their main cause was that they had been performing equally as well. As often as a pat on the back is due, it is just a few times less than a kick in the ass is required. They were informed that their performance had been average but that it did not deserve a commendation. So down comes the union steward. The men did not know that I had known the union steward for over fifteen years before we came to Lockheed. This would have no effect on the outcome of the problem except that we conversed with the most emphatic language of the aircraft industry. There was no room for doubt of the meaning of our discussion. He told the whole crew to go to work as he would handle the situation. Very few people who had the pleasure of meeting "Tup" Holmes could never forget him.[1] He was voracious as hell and twice as blunt. I told him to cut the bluff and took him over to my records.

Tup studied the record of each man. He just said okay and told me to call everybody together. I never heard another union or company man explain the situation in more precise terms. He told the whole crew what a union and company contract meant as to the agreement to produce together a quality product at the lowest cost and deliver on schedule. He said that the contract had been negotiated by both sides agreeing to the pay scales and other benefits and then signed as binding. He had looked over the performance of each employee and he knew that they knew what was recorded as they had furnished the information to the supervisor. He stated that the records indicated that the tempo of each individual had been noted and the varying job difficulties were described. He also stated what standard hours had been reduced (acceptable to the worker) when experience and workmanship dictated that the time requirements should be reduced. He asked if anyone had any comments. There were none.

Tup told them in no uncertain terms, when they got off of their asses and performed to the letter of the contract, upholding the union's agreement, then he would bust his ass and see that they got all they deserved under the contract. With those words he took the grievances and tore them in half and threw them into the trash barrel, then walked away. The men and I both knew that Tup would go all the way to arbitration with a case if there were grounds. Over a period of six months every man in the cost center had won a commendation on an individual basis for above average workmanship. There was no animosity held by anyone.

Everyone in the cost center was concerned and always looking for ways to reduce the cost of production. We laid 2,400 rivet holes and 1,200 for the installation of the nut plates and then the floor boards. Trying to figure a way to cut the time involved one of the crew suggested we use nut plate gang channels for this installation. We determined that if this could be done we could save about 20 man-hours and approximately $800 to $1,000 in cost reduction. We suggested this to our assigned engineer and he thought it would be a good idea. He took it to his manager, who responded as if we were trying to tell engineering how to design the damn airplane. The manager's decision was based, without doubt, strictly on the theory that no "nigger" was going to tell him what was best for the job. This was the attitude, not of the people working alongside us, but of some upper levels of management. It seems hard to believe but that was the way it was.

I decided to fight that rejection because I did not give a damn about anyone's attitude when it came to the type of job I performed, as long as I was right. I went down to the field service group and asked for all the correspondence from our customers, military and commercial, concerning the installation of nut plates and quality fasteners in the floor areas of their aircraft purchased from Lockheed. I explained to these good people why I needed that information and what I intended to do with it. After a few weeks these guys were kind enough to furnish us with the records going all the way back to the P-38 and the Lockheed-Hudson (boy howdy!) Bomber of World War II British fame. The information indicated that our customers left it up to Lockheed to determine which fastener was best for their requirements. I called the office of the chief industrial engineer and requested a conference. I explained to him what we had in mind and that I would bring all the records to back our request. He told me to come on up and bring the information.

It took a small hand truck to deliver the info but we went through all that was necessary for his decision. It is always refreshing to see that the respect paid to ideas by people who know that they know what they know but realize that they don't know it all is still available out there in the world of reality. It takes a pure damn fool not to recognize a question or suggestion as being relevant to something of significance. Without any announcement or fanfare, the method of floor installation was changed. Crew members working that job and involved with that suggestion all got cost reduction certificates. I really suffered moments of grief for those two engineers who never spoke to me again (like water freezing in hell). We would overcome any obstacles that arose in the path of the production of the C-130 as it progressed toward becoming the historic aircraft that it was destined to be.

Chapter 5

Believe it or not, this was bound to happen one day. BG called me into his office (a real sharp layout) and told me that he had an experiment he wanted to make. He did not think that a Negro could supervise a mixed crew in the South without friction. BG's theories when dealing with aircraft were great but not worth a damn when it came to people. I got the impression that he thought he was a top bird when it came to labor relations. I told him that this would cause no problem. I did not realize that he had an ulterior motive in mind. Then I have to give him credit if he was actually trying to prove something. At first I thought he was putting up a situation to prove that although we had passed all the other "couldn't dos" it was now time to prove that a southern white man would not work for a Negro. In the South at the time not too many whites and Negroes had dinner together but damn if there wasn't a lot of Negroes cooking dinner for whites. But if you wanted a decent cuss-out, make a disparaging remark to a southern white about his ability to work with Negroes and he would tell you, "We've been working with them boys for years and nobody is gonna tell us to work or not."

I told BG, "Let's go," and put the experiment into motion. The rough looks and derogatory remarks that came from the whites who surrounded our work area were ignored and they got tired of being ignored and stopped. I would not doubt that a few might have been offered transfers to settle any complaints of where and whom they worked with or who the supervisor was.

I remember that I requested from BG that I preferred to have the older guys (in age) and the ones who were dissatisfied with their present area along with any that might seem to be misfits. My theory was that if a person was dissatisfied and not happy at work that a different atmosphere and surroundings might change his attitude. I knew that every man needed and wanted to support his wife and family in the best manner he could. If he had a job where he felt needed and had full responsibility for his work and also had respect he would be happy not only in his work but at home also. In other words I wanted mature people in my crew. A few whites told me, "I ain't never worked for a colored fellow before." My answer was standard: "Me neither, both of us work for Lockheed." I had seventeen whites and fifteen Negroes in my crew. That bunch developed into one of the best teams at Lockheed. If you think I'm making a habit of saying my crews were great, dammit, the fact is we had some of the best quality, cost reductions, scheduled deliveries, and performance rates around and I kept records to prove it. When you are right or good, then toot your own trumpet because I can say positively no one else will.

When I had eighty-seven people in my crew during the B-47 days I mentioned the fact that I had eighty-seven different human problems every day. One can't help but develop a sense of human relations in such a situation. It is the best hands-on training a manager can get. I was fortunate to have had a long history of dealing with people. I was president of the Atlanta School Safety Patrol (Negro that is) for five years as a youngster. As a petty officer in the navy I had twenty-seven men in my crew and as a business owner I had eight employees. I learned from the school of hard knocks how to keep people like a good mechanic keeps his tools. That is, well-cleaned (informed), in their place (a specific job with responsibility), and ready when needed (performance with authority when required). I never met a man who did not respect those conditions. Therefore I am going to devote some time to the people who worked with me during this time. I intend to leave race identification more and more as we go along.

I can't remember his first name but Mr. Brown was a fellow from a small town right outside the city limits of Atlanta. He was a veteran of World War II and was satisfied to have made it home with no major injuries. Since he owned about 10 acres and was free and over 21 there was no reason for him to have any worries about making a living and having a happy life. The only thing that bothered him was the fact that they had dropped an atomic bomb and killed a lot of people. He could not reconcile to the fact that it was considered to be right at the time. Therefore he decided that he would not own a radio or television, take a newspaper, or have anything in the house that would influence his children. He taught them tolerance toward other people and to maintain their ways as Christian people. He raised everything on his land except sugar and flour. He did not drink coffee. Every summer he took his old school bus, loaded his family, and went to the Florida coast for vacation on the beaches. Two times I had to give him an extension to his vacation while he got the dingdong bus fixed as to make it back to work and get his kids back to school. He was not interested in discussing current events, desegregation, or anything about what was going on in the world. He said that as long as he knew nothing about what was happening then nothing would bother him.

That was a helluva attitude but the guy was happy and I respected his right to that opinion. He always had a nice wad of money in his pocket; this was good security.

While he was a member of the crew, it was decided that rather than desegregate the cafeterias it would be better to close the whole bunch and replace them with mobile food carts. Everybody could go to the "roach coaches" in their respective work areas. As it was part of the job to maintain clean work areas then they could also serve as eating areas. Since the bosses still had a dining room in the main office building there was no harm of the workers eating on their workbenches. A few metal shavings and other crud did not make it necessarily unsanitary. This was not the decision of the workers but the ruling of the powers that be, who seemed to know it all. Some of the whites decided that they would rather eat that way than mix at the lunch table. I brown-bagged just about the whole time at Lockheed. My generous pay did not allow me to feed my kids and eat store-bought lunches. This did not bother me at all.

Brown got mad one day after listening to all of their crud, jumped up in the middle of a workbench, threw $300 on the dirty table, and told everybody that the first SOB who picked it up he would beat hell out of them because it was not necessary that he eat off of a dusty table or workbench. I quieted him down by asking him to eat with me at my highboy (desk). This did not solve a damn thing but I liked Brown and had a lot of respect for him as a man. He expressed himself in this manner. The last time I saw him in later years, he still had no radio or television and did not take a newspaper. He continued to raise his own food. His children were finishing school and doing well in their endeavors but still maintained a lot of respect for their "Pa" and his ways. Brown was also a damn good aircrafter.

We found out that we had a dope-head in our group. This character was one who kept to himself and never participated in any activities with the crew. When there was a death or illness within the crew (or their families) he never donated for flowers or anything else. He was absent just about every Monday. I had to say something every week about his attendance. He came to work with a suit or other nice outfit on and would wear a leather apron. He built the forward end of the wheel fairing assembly (protective, aerodynamic covering for wheels) by himself. The only time he required help was when he could not reach around the assembly to shoot and buck rivets at the same time. His quality was tops and he consistently produced 100 percent realization. He never got dirty on the job nor had a dirty work area. I cut the standard hours on his job to the bone (asking his concurrence at the same time) and he still produced five days' work in the four days that he was present. How do you criticize someone like that except for his attendance? We did find out that he went to Detroit, Michigan, every fourth Saturday and picked up a cigar box full of pot. I was told that he always returned by Sunday night. He would go into his room and go out of this world until Tuesday morning. He would report to the job Tuesday and was never absent or late any other days.

One Friday the straw broke the camel's back and I told him if he did not come to work Monday that, since I had already given him verbal warnings, I was going to give him three days on the street (suspension) for absenteeism. He used up his vocabulary of profane words and added a few, including an invitation out to the parking lot. I guess I had grown a little more mature or mellowed out for nothing would have pleased me more than to accommodate him in the old days. I was glad that I did not see him on the weekend for I was not quite as mature on weekends. Anyway, I told him to meet me at the foreman's office with his toolbox Monday morning and we would get the situation squared away. The foreman knew about his attendance record because he had been on my back to do something about it. I gave him to the foreman and the foreman gave him to Roc and after about three weeks Roc fired him. I guess that one could say that I indirectly fired the man but I never had to fire anyone directly. Nor did I have another experience like that. I still believe that we lost a good man, as everybody has problems. The company developed methods to handle these types of situations as we moved on down the road.

Another big bunch of bull I experienced was the day the foreman called me in and told me that we were getting a new man who was bumping back from the flight line. Bumping happened when layoffs were necessary and the senior workers bumped the less senior ones for the positions that they had formally held. This was covered by the labor contract. The foreman told me that this man had worked for him on the flight line and was a natural-born bastard. He wanted me to keep a close check on the man and as soon as we had enough information gathered he would fire him. I did not mind receiving help in developing my own opinions but I'd be damned if I was going to be issued one like in the military. I just said okay and the man came in the following Monday morning. Remember that I already had an integrated cost center so I was not worried about any repercussions along that line.

The fellow reported to the office and I was introduced to him. He seemed pretty sullen. I took him down to the work area. We will call him J. C. (actually his first initials). I showed him the assembly he would be making and the production record of the man that he was replacing. I told him I expected him to be able, after adjustments, to accomplish the task in the same number of hours as the last worker. I found out he had a wife and two little girls and wanted to support them in an acceptable manner. I told him about my little boys and my hopes for them and the ice began to melt. I told him I never looked over a man's back and I was there not only as a supervisor but a tool for his benefit. Any problems he may incur were my responsibility. He was expected to carry his share of the load and keep the cost center on schedule with 100 percent realization. He thought that was fair and expected that he would do his best to maintain that record. He went to work and I got the impression that he felt a little better.

After about three weeks the foreman came down and stated that we had had enough time to set this character up to fire him and wanted to know that the hell he was doing. I took him up on the high rail and asked him if he could pick out the man down on the floor. After looking he said "no," and assumed that J. C. was in the restroom screwing off. It gave me great pleasure to give the foreman the answer I did. I asked the foreman if he recognized the elbows and asshole that I was pointing out to him. Naturally, he did not. I told him that that was the guy he was looking for and he was doing one helluva job and maintaining the record of that assembly from the start. From that time on I would make the decisions pertaining to the character of the people who worked in my crew.

J. C. came to me one day and told me his stomach did not hurt anymore. He said that he had ulcers and they hurt all the time (boy, could I understand that). He said that they had not hurt in over three weeks and he did not drink Maalox anymore. He also said that he had never worked for a colored fellow before but I was the best supervisor he had ever had. He said that I understood the workingman and he had high respect for me. Well, I'll be damned. A few years later J. C. was elected to the position of business agent for the union and was re-elected again and again until he retired. It was always a pleasure to run into him occasionally and have a good talk. I don't remember if he was retired but twenty-seven years later J. C. showed up at my retirement party to wish me a happy retirement.

There were incidents with people other than the ones who worked under my supervision. There was this quiet fellow, a civilian air force inspector, who wandered around checking on the work and asking questions here and there. We had the jet assist take-off (JATO) door in the cost center. The JATO had a dual purpose; it served as the parachute jump door and it held the jet assist take-off bottles. There were four bottles on each door. These bottles were actually solid fuel jet engines. The doors were installed on both sides of the aircraft. These solid fuel types kicked off about 14,000 pounds of thrust each for assisted takeoff when the plane was fully loaded. It was one tough assembly. The biggest problem was that it was a compound contour design. From the front to the back it had to mate with at least four different contours of the fuselage to maintain the airflow. There was always trouble fitting the parts to the jig stops during assembly. Based on the experience we had gained from similar doors on the B-47 we did a lot of improvising with methods that won't be explained here. All were acceptable.

One day the air force inspector (we will call him KC) came down and wanted to see us pull a door from the jig. We were just about ready with a little improvising to do before removing the door. We could not pull the door for him because it did not fit the jig. We told him it was not quite ready for removal. The assembly was laying on the jig but not clamped into position. He decided to wait until it was ready and put up for Lockheed inspection approval. This created a problem because we could not pull it and prove that it was a good assembly in that manner. I told the men to leave it alone and we would get to it later. KC demanded that we pull the assembly and put it up for inspection. At the time the understanding with the customer was that he could monitor the performance but not tell us how to build the product. As diplomatically as possible I told him to leave the area and I would call him when it was ready and he could inspect the final assembly as much as he wished. He refused so I pulled the workers from the assembly and put them on other jobs. When he realized that I would do no work on the door he asked me what I intended for him to do. I told him to go back to his office and we would call him when the door was ready for removal. He finally agreed to this and left. I assigned a couple of men to watch for him and make sure he was not peeping. We finished our operation and sent for him.

He checked back to the jig for contour specifications and the assembly was perfect. He did not believe this was possible. I suspected that someone had informed him that we were having major problems with the door. I took two men and the door and requested that he follow us. We attached the door to four aircraft down the line and proved interchangeability by a perfect fit to prove the door met all specifications of the blueprint. He never found out how we assembled it and that remains one of the aircrafter's secrets. I had a few friends flying our birds and you can bet your life that I wasn't going to jeopardize their lives or any crew members' for lack of quality or reliability. KC was a knowledgeable and congenial man (not like that first character). We had him for a few months as our air force inspector and had respect for each other. KC showed up twenty-seven years later to wish me a happy retirement.

We had a new company inspector assigned to the group. This character carried a large amount of money all the time. That is like $150 to $200, which was a large wad at that time. According to him he had been rich all of his life. His folks had money and he only worked because he wanted to keep himself busy. This is the BS he told us. He said that when the company decided to open a credit union they called him down and asked him to make an initial deposit of $10,000 to help get the credit union off to a good start. If any of the men ever needed a substantial loan from the credit union, he told us to let him know and he would see that there would be no delay in getting a loan without all the necessities required. It was nice to know that we had people working with us having such power and to meet another lying braggart who believed his own lies.

There was another fellow who claimed that he had finished law school and therefore he was a lawyer. If the "boys" would each give him five dollars a month he would be available to get them out of jail every weekend that they were locked up for fighting or getting drunk. This fool actually believed that all Negroes did was get drunk and get locked up every weekend so he would make a personal sacrifice and help them with their problems. The dumbass seemed to know that as a fact. Can you imagine trying to keep a straight face listening to some sincere character telling you something like that? I thanked him for his concern and interest while wishing him a merry trip with his one-way ticket to hell. Some of the guys went to him with a straight face and told him that they intended to get drunk and raise hell this weekend and if he would loan them five dollars, just in case they got locked up, they would gladly pay him back the following payday. He said that he could not do this as it was not good legal practice. He didn't get any clients nor did he establish a law practice. This was probably because he did not have a license to practice or know the difference between an oath, being sworn in, and perjury. About the only time he had seen the inside of a courtroom was when he was caught running moonshine.

I had an older gent in the crew who was the best tool controller, parts preparation specialist, cleaner upper, and all around handyman for maintaining the order of the workplace. He could hold his own in the assembly operation but we needed someone with the knowledge to be sure everything was in order for the rest of the crew. He maintained the small miscellaneous parts (rivets, bolts, screws, and other required fasteners for the assembly). This was what we called MSP. He also maintained the tool cabinet and kept the area cleaned of shavings and other crud that accumulated around the work area (known as housekeeping). With our schedule and work tempo his presence was needed and appreciated. I took a week off for vacation. Instead of making my lead man acting supervisor, the foreman sent another supervisor (we will call him "Bill") over to run my cost center while I was out. In his stupid attempt to show my people how a real cost center should be run, not only did he disrupt the operation but he took it on himself to fire Pop Jones (our cost center organizer) the Friday before I returned to work. That old man called me at home crying and all upset over the loss of his job. He could not give a reason for this action except he was told that he was inefficient in his duties. I blew my stack and then regained my cool. I told him to be at the head house Monday morning and remain outside until he was sent for. Actually, it took the whole weekend for me to settle down and plan my Monday morning actions.

I knew that with the time constraints from Friday to Monday no formal paperwork had been generated to process Pop's termination. I walked into the foreman's office Monday morning looking, as I was, mad as hell. He asked what the problem was. I told him to call Bill's ass into the office and we would find out. He knew some hell was going to be raised. Bill came in and I started right off.

ME: "What the hell do you mean by firing one of my men while I was on vacation?"

BILL: "That man was incompetent and I did you a favor by getting rid of him."

ME: "You don't know a goddamn thing about the people who work in my crew and if there was a problem you should have waited and informed me on my return."

BILL: "I recognized a sorry worker and I took action and I don't appreciate your tone of voice or your language."

ME: "You can go to hell because I'm about two seconds off your tall ass!"

FOREMAN: "Now hold it just a second, we are not going to be making any personal threats over this situation."

ME TO THE FOREMAN: "You call whomever is necessary and tell them that I will be at the head house in about ten minutes to pick up Pop and bring him back to work and Bill, you keep out of my operation from here on out."

With all the standard hours we were putting back into the department to keep the realization up, I think the foreman decided that Bill had screwed up.

I went to the head house and got Pop. Everyone in the group was happy and satisfied and stated that they knew they had a supervisor who would stand behind them. I let the foreman know that from now on when I graded a man on his review that it was my opinion and I would not downgrade anyone to fit into a pattern. I had and maintained the records on all of my people and it would not be the first time if I had to buck management to prove a point.

I had another member of my crew who was up in age, about 62 or 63 years old, who lived in Cedartown, Georgia. My crew averaged about 45–50 years in age. We had younger members but most were mature people with a sense of responsibility. I was about 34 at the time. I'll say again that I had a damn good crew. They were very low on absenteeism and high on quality, schedule, and reliability. We had one rough snowstorm and this fellow, Mr. Knight (I can't remember his first name), was involved in a bad car wreck on his way to work. He rode in a car pool. In those days there was no 911. He got a ride with some other guys and they brought him to work. His head had a bad 4-inch cut above the left ear. He went to the medics first and they told him he should have gone to the hospital. He explained that the ride he caught would only bring him to work because of the bad weather. They did not give him first aid or anything but sent him up to his work area to try and find a ride to the hospital. I would not have believed this if I had not walked in on him setting in the cost center bleeding like a stuck hog. The man was covered with blood from his wound, down the side of his face, over the neck, and onto his clothes. I sent him with an escort back to medics and I be damned if they did not send him back up into the area with the same message. I called medics and told them who I was and that I was sending him back down for first aid until we found a way to get him to the hospital. He sat there until noon and they put some gauze around his head. We found someone to get him to the hospital and he finally got treatment. By that time he was pretty well screwed up. I never could understand why he was not given emergency treatment by the company medics. We had ambulances available and he should have been taken to the hospital since it was necessary.

After a few days at Kennestone hospital in Marietta he was transferred to the hospital in Cedartown. He had pictures taken of himself in the hospital and then sued the hell out of Lockheed. Since I was his supervisor and had seen his condition here again I was seemingly in opposition to Lockheed management, as I received a subpoena to appear as a witness in the court. Fortunately, his pictures and other records seemed sufficient and they did not call me to testify. If they had called me I could only have told the truth as I saw it. Anyway, the settlement was substantial and he retired a few years later.

One day a distinguished-looking gentleman walked into our area. I had seen him before but was not sure of his position. He introduced himself as Bill Rienke, vice president of the Lockheed-Georgia division. He had been observing for a few minutes and he asked me how things were going. I told him quality was good, realization was close to 100 percent, and we were one ship ahead of schedule. He observed, "It seems to me that things are going pretty slow. Are your people really working at top performance?" I replied, "Yes, sir, these guys are working at a tempo that is comfortable for them to maintain quality work and schedule; they know what they are doing." He seemed concerned that he didn't see "sweat flowing due to their efforts." I responded by informing him that I had "daily records to prove that what I say about production is a fact." I took him over to the highboy and pulled my books. I rolled back six months and proceeded to show him the record of each employee. He picked out two or three individuals and asked to see their records. This was easily done. He stated that we must be mighty fat on standard hours per job. I showed him six months of records, indicating how many hours had been cut out of each assembly. These hours had been given back to the department to facilitate those areas that needed some more standards. He looked around again and told me to leave the information out and he would be back shortly. I had no idea what he had in mind.

Rienke returned in about thirty minutes with, of all people, the chief industrial engineer, Mr. Wilton himself. Wilton remembered me from the cargo ramp and gang channels. Rienke told me to give him my records and go on back to work. They stayed at my highboy for thirty minutes or so going over all the records of the previous six months. Finally, they thanked me and left. I never heard a damn thing, except that I was doing a good job, for about a year. I'll get to that later.

The year 1959 rolled around and we were building top-quality aircraft on schedule and at a reasonable cost. We had family days, Easter egg hunts, and Christmas parties. Everything was separate for the races but the activities were the same and we had the same prizes for participation in the events. We paid double for everything, separate but equal. Eventually, someone thought of the cost factors, I guess, and before too long these activities were combined. 1959 [the strike actually occurred in May 1958] was also the year for the union contract to be negotiated. Up to this point the relationship between the union and the company had been pretty good. This was the time for the union to let the company know that we had labor and management. Regardless of any effort to reach an agreement, union leaders believed it was necessary to strike to prove there was a union. We had a new contract for modification of the B-47 Bomber and therefore it was the best time to strike for everybody. One does not strike when there is no work available (well, back then anyway). The majority of employees at GELAC had never been involved in a strike. We would learn the hard way.

Chapter 6

The union and the company had started negotiations a few months before the current contract expired. This was the checkout and consideration time to be given to the changes to be requested by each side. In contract negotiations the union is the "seller" and the company is the "buyer." The seller wants the highest value for its labor. The buyer wants the lowest price possible with all the requirements of the product being guaranteed. With all of the benefits to be discussed one would think that these would be the first things to try and conclude before getting to the nitty gritty, the wage increases. Instead, in this case the two wiggled and waggled right up to the expiration date of the contract. The union did not have a strike fund and did not believe the company would allow a strike. The union was under the impression that the sister union at CALAC (California), who did have a strike fund, would back them financially if they went on strike. They found that expecting that help was like blowing bubbles into a hurricane. The company gave the impression that the strike would last a week and be settled and that time would not affect the delivery of those four hundred B-47s for which we had just won a contract for modification. I would not say that the people giving these impressions were attempting to sabotage the negotiations, but their actions sure appeared stupid.

When one sees a union and company officials come together to negotiate a new contract the impression is that you have people of high principles, morals, and integrity. Those people think that of themselves and most of them do have those characteristics, but you find that bunch of hardheads from both sides attempting to gain every benefit possible, seemingly without regard for the people (both union and salaried) who are actually the company (have you ever seen a company without people?). They butt heads until a strike is called. The union people are out on the street, the salaried people are trying to come through the picket lines suffering all the derogatory catcalls and personal insults as expressed by the striking members. In our situation, both had no control of their situation as the almighty negotiators had created the conditions. A lot of respect was lost to individuals across those lines. Long-standing friendships were broken. A state of distrust was created. It took several years to regain the atmosphere and fellowship that had existed before the strike. Let's get into the strike and some of the happenings.

The union lined all of the entrances to the plant and blocked them. Salaried workers had to stop and have their vehicles checked to be sure no scabs (the name for non-strikers) were slipping into the plant. The orders to the salaried workers were that no hourly workers would be brought into the plant. This slowed up the ability for the salaried workers to be on time. This was recognized by management so none were docked for being tardy. The local cops (both city and county) and the state patrol were supposedly preserving the peace. All three of these organizations sided with their constituents (the strikers being in the majority) and the company people did not stand a chance. The strikers cut and punctured tires, scratched car bodies with nails, insulted human beings (formerly co-workers), and intimidated company workers' families, and the local businesses cut off credit at the local grocery stores, service stations, and other local facilities to the extent that a company worker was unsafe (or felt that way) in any situation. The characters with the busted heads, scars, and missing teeth from the northern unions were in control of the activities. This went on for the first week. The poor dupes out there doing all of the damage were under the impression that this was the way a strike was carried out.

The local union had given each registered striker on the line a big check of $10 for the first week of the strike from the underfunded strike fund. All the wives of the striking members were real happy over this big amount of money received, for surely this took care of all the current bills. Lo and behold, the second week of the strike it was discovered that no more money was in the strike fund. The California sister union stated that they had no money to send. Well, Mama had put her foot down on the Thursday payroll change and won so she decided to tell Papa that he couldn't saddle his horse anymore until he brought a decent paycheck home, strike or no strike. All Papas like to saddle their horses several times a week (the younger ones anyway) and this was certainly a blow to their recreational activities. Children like to see their mamas happy and mamas are not happy when little children's tummies are empty.

We heard that Uncle Dan had informed the city fathers that he did not appreciate the actions of the local constabulary and the county cops in their treatment of the salaried workers. If they continued their discriminatory actions he would possibly close down the whole operation and to hell with the local economy. He called on the governor to advise the state patrol of their duties as covered by law. This action turned out to be not exactly necessary.

The Wednesday of the second week the biggest Negro (in size, mentioned in an earlier chapter) at the plant at the time pulled up to the picket line and was blocked. He had three people in the car with him. Each had a baseball bat or one of those Buford Pusser Peace Sticks (a 3-inch diameter, 4-foot-long oak pole with the bark shaved off). He informed the picket line that his wife had told him either bring a check, food, or some form of paying bills or don't come back home, therefore he was going to work. On being informed that he was not going to break the picket line, he quietly replied that he would kill the first bastard that stood in his way. This was occurring 50 feet inside company property. One of the city's finest was standing in the crowd and informed him that he would not carry out such an act. This officer was invited to be the first to die. The officer deemed this unnecessary and stepped back mainly because he did not have room to pull his gun and fire before his brain would have been splattered over the landscape. The worker got back into his car and sped through the line as the strikers stood and looked astonished. While they were immobile, about five more cars pulled through and that was the beginning of the end of the strike. By the following Friday about 80 percent or better were back to work. I knew the people involved and I saw a lot of the action. I give less than a damn about what the official releases may say.

The union lost everything and the company lost over 50 percent of the B-47 modification contract. No one gained a damn thing. At the next election the union had a slate of new officers and these people proved to be more considerate of the desires and needs of the employees. The attitude of the company officials changed accordingly.

There is a lot to be said about the strike. I think that a lot was learned concerning labor and management. One cannot run over the other. There must be cooperation and respect engendered by each for the other. Only by working together can any mutual goal be achieved. If that sounds like malarkey then so be it, but it's a fact. At this time in our history neither the company (GELAC) nor the union (local) had any major experience in the art of striking. Both had been overly influenced by so-called experienced people from other areas of the country. Both learned and it would be a long time before another strike would occur at good old Lockheed-Georgia. It was at least three years before the level of confidence between management and labor was regained to the extent that existed prior to the strike. We went back to our areas and resumed building good aircraft. Maybe to emphasize a point some of the other incidents that happened during the strike should be related.

GELAC had received a contract to modify the wings and other areas of the B-47 Bomber. Our contract called for four hundred aircraft. The strike occurred just as we were getting into full swing. From the top down to the supervisors, in the manufacturing branch, hit the modification line to keep those planes rolling. We found that about 40 percent of management couldn't build a chicken coop. This is not to say that they could not manage, just that they had no manual dexterity ability. They held up their end because they made some of the best knowledgeable "gofers" ever needed.

The first job I had was the installation of the wing drag angles. The B-47 was a long-range bomber that could carry conventional bombs and had atom bomb capabilities. The grapevine said that some genius decided that it could be used as a skip type or possibly a flip type bomber. It was not possible to be used as a skip type as that required low-level flight and skipping the bomb into the target as the British did with the mosquito bombers. Flip-bombing was to pull straight up over the target and release the bomb from that position and it would flip over and fall directly on the target. Don't ask, for I told you this info came off the grapevine. This had to have been considered and attempted because the wing joints were cracking at the point of attachment to the fuselage. It probably was found that this condition happened because of the stress created by the weight of the engines and the fuel load in the wings.

To gain access to this area you proceeded through an access door on the lower side of the wing. Each compartment of the wing was a fuel tank. The entrance was three tanks from the fuselage and the wing attachment joint. Thus, you had to remove three more access doors to get into that area. Once inside and against the belly, if you squatted and bent over you could at least be on your feet. This was summertime and the temperature inside that wing was about 150 degrees. There was a big fan blowing refrigerated air into the wing. If you raised up and touched the skin of the topside of the wing, your skin remained on the wing and you had a nice third-degree burn. With the fan it was cool enough to stay inside for up to an hour at a time. It was very close, tedious work. Drilling close tolerance holes (0.005 inch) through the steel drag angle and the adjacent main framing of the fuselage was difficult and slow going.

After I got out of the navy I began to notice that I would get uncomfortable whenever I was in a crowd, elevator, or at games, etc. I thought that this was a slight case of claustrophobia and it seemed minor. I found out better in a rather dramatic way. About the third day in that hellhole all of a sudden I could not breathe. I felt as if I were suffocating and going blind. The cool air was blowing in my face and common sense was telling me that everything was okay. That's crap! My mind told me that I was dying. Those access doors were about 15 by 24 inches exit space. I went through the three doors and fell head first onto the platform, which was 6 feet from the bottom of the wing. Fortunately, I did not break my neck or damage the platform. I was forever impressed with the fact that it was not to my advantage to fall on my head under those circumstances again and made the promise to myself never to lift over 25 pounds or get in a close place again. Since medics had to disinfect and bandage the places where I had lost skin (upper arms, elbows, hips, and knees) coming out of that wing it was confirmed that I could not work under those conditions again.

I went to the area on top of the fuselage where the wing joined the body. This was where the drag angle was installed. There was an area about 6–7 inches wide and approximately 3–4 feet long. No one had come up with a workable method of installing the 1-inch diameter bolts in 20 or more locations and maintaining that 0.005 tolerance. The depth through this opening to the angle was 2.5 feet. This was too deep for the arm and hand to reach and have control of the drills and reamers. Most of the holes were oversize and wobbly as a result of the method being used and a call had to be made to Boeing Aircraft for an engineering fix every time we broke wind into the wind. This took many hours of waiting for them to give us a disposition or repair method. Even with the experts (management and engineering, both companies) doing the negotiation we had to sit around for hours awaiting the answers to proceed with the rework. I sat around looking down that hole one day and got an idea. I went down to the manager of the tooling and tool repair unit and told him what I had in mind. We took a ¾-inch steel rod and machined one end to fit a ⁵⁄₁₆ drill chuck. We put a universal joint on the other end and attached another 2-foot steel rod to it. On the other end of the second rod we welded a ⁵⁄₁₆ drill motor chuck. The drag angles had ³⁄₁₆-inch pilot holes already located. Taking a ¼-inch drill with a ³⁄₁₆ pilot to start the operation we inserted this drill into our drilling rig which now consisted of the ¼-inch drill, the chuck on the 4-foot-long extension with the universal at the 2-foot location, and inserted the extension into the last of the three ⁵⁄₁₆ chucks we had put in random on the drill motor. You will have to ask an engineer how this contraption slowed the revolutions down to about 35–40 a minute but that was the speed we had.

We drilled the ³⁄₁₆ hole to ¼ inch, put a ¼ pilot on a ¾ drill, and stepped that hole up to ¾ inch. We then put a ¾-inch pilot on a ⅞-inch drill and stepped that hole to ⅞ inch diameter. Next we put a ⅞-inch pilot on a 1-inch reamer and very carefully reamed that hole to the final size of 1 inch and it was within the tolerance specified. All of this was accomplished by standing (in the sun, 100+ degrees) bent over on top of the wing joint with the 6-inch opening. As one can see this was time consuming but we got quality holes for the bolts and did not have to verify with the Boeing engineers. Unfortunately, the superintendent (acting as foreman) instructed me to take the tool and show the guy on the next shift the method. After going through the procedure that bastard screwed up sixteen holes and told the super that I did it. I was in the process of wrapping the tool around that fellow's head when the super told me to instruct another fellow. This fellow listened and learned and the modification of the B-47 continued. Later on methods came up with a way that simplified the operation. If you ever wonder what those two-story outhouses opposite the "A" frame building near the South Cobb fence are, those are the modification covers for the B-47 nose work. After the strike we went back to our old areas in the plant.

Chapter 7

Early in 1960 we had a new bird in research and development. This was Lockheed's follow-up plane to the C-130. It would become known as the C-141. Where the C-130 was a turbojet, jet and propeller driven type, the C-141 was the transition plane to pure jet and it would be designated as a fan jet. We were already in production of a little fast two-engine passenger type called the Jetstar (civilian) and the C-140 (military). That aircraft was another brainchild of Kelly Johnson and the R&D section of CALAC better known as the Skunk Works. Some of the people in my old crews were working on the Jetstar (Buster Jones was lead man on this program) and we were in negotiation for the contract for the C-141. GELAC was in good shape as far as work was concerned and everyone seemed to be back in the groove. We had lost a big chunk of the B-47 modification program, but we were recovering in other areas and the B-47 was just about completed.

The United States had a number of sections within the country that were designated as poverty areas because of lack of work and the overall economic conditions. The government decided that Lockheed-Georgia should establish feeder plants in some of those areas so as to improve their economic status. The southeastern states being some of the poorest it was our prerogative to put feeder plants in Clarksburg, West Virginia; Charleston, South Carolina; and Meridian, Mississippi. These would be production shops. We had other areas specializing in engineering and development. A number of the smaller assemblies were initially transferred to these outside plants as they started their production buildup. Assemblies for other Lockheed aircraft were eventually placed with them, including some major sections for the L-1011 commercial aircraft (CALAC). Although quite a few of those assemblies were from the Negro cost centers no Negroes were requested to go to Clarksburg or Charleston for the six months or so required to help kick off production. Remember, this is still the South (or East, or West, or North). Believe it or not, one Negro, a fellow named Wilder, was sent to Meridian. He liked it there and they liked him so he moved there and spent a number of years. I visited Meridian and found it to be a real aircrafter's paradise. When you start a crew from scratch and train them properly you end up with a damn good team. Those feeder plants did a good job.

During the early part of 1961 things were running well and we were doing a good job. All of us were expecting a decent raise so I decided to get an appointment with BG. The main reason was to feel him out on that possibility. He told me to come on up to his office. I told him that I and three other supervisors had busted our butts as proven by the performance records and we wanted a decent raise. We had been getting about five to six dollars a week raise (every six or seven months) for a long period of time. He thought that was a reasonable request and would give it positive consideration. I decided to drop the bomb. I told him that I figured that there was a need for an assistant department manager and I had been working and taking training on my own time and company time along those lines to qualify for the position. That sapsucker dropped an atom bomb on me. He told me in no uncertain terms that as long as he was production manager that no Negro (pronounced "Nigra") would ever be a foreman in his production crews. Being stupid and not giving a damn, I demanded to know why! He said he could not see a Negro being boss over six hundred people, including at least four hundred white people. There was no point in me giving in to the urgent desire to kick his butt as I needed the job. I reminded him that he was the person who requested me to take the first integrated crew in 1959. After that had been successful he must have been also one that lost his bet that it could not be done. As previously indicated, BG was hell.

Our department manager told us that he had put us in for an eight dollars a week raise, hoping to get at least seven dollars. Believe it or not, I got an eleven-dollar raise; the other three got nine dollars, and the rest of the supervisors got eight dollars. Every once in a while BG was generous. The foreman knew I had talked to BG, but he did not know what the conversation was about. Damn if I was going to tell him. I heard that there was an opening for an assistant foreman. No more was heard of that. We got the little raise and that took care of that. The relationship between BG and me kind of cooled after that and actually was never regained. (All alligators stopped flying.) I never developed confidence in anyone else exhibiting his characteristics—as if I would ever meet someone like him again. Meanwhile, who else gave a damn—let's build airplanes!

The Lockheed National Management Association club chapter had finally invited the Negro supervisors to join. This was eight years since they told me I would not be expected to apply for membership. I hope you can understand how I suffered during those years that I could not join and become a member of the team. I suffered as much as a house cat being denied application to the local gaggle of polecats association. I don't think I ever considered myself the weak link in the anchor chain. I accepted the invitation and fell in with the crowd. The NMA was a fine organization, screw some of the local chapters.

During the late part of 1961, the NMA had a meeting at one of the private clubs in Atlanta. All of the big wheels from corporate headquarters were present. Dan Haughton was now the president of the Lockheed Corporation. I had not seen Uncle Dan for quite a while but he walked up to the bar with Carl Kotchian, who was VP and general manager of GELAC at the time, and another distinguished character whom he introduced as Burt Monosmith, the corporation VP of manufacturing. E. (Slowfreight) Smith, who was with me, and I were introduced by Dan to Burt. All three of the wheels were very congenial and offered us what we were drinking (beer). We were carrying on a conversation when Mr. Hal (being president of the local NMA) walked up and informed the bosses that he had taught us boys everything we knew about our jobs. This impressed the hell out of the bosses and they turned back to us to continue the conversation. Mr. Monosmith asked me to have dinner at his table and I became the one known as the character that ate in high grass that night. We talked about fishing (he owned a boat) and then got around to the job at Lockheed and how I was doing and if I had any further ambitions with the company. After telling him about my eight years as a supervisor and how I had pursued further training, I bluntly stated that I thought I had reached a ceiling and in the foreseeable future saw no opportunity for advancement. We had about two hours to talk and I just answered his questions. He told me if I ever came to California we might get a chance to go fishing. I thanked him for the invitation and the meeting was over. It shocked me to find out a few years later that Mr. Monosmith was killed in an automobile accident in Arizona.

The second week in August the foreman told me I was requested to go over to an adjacent building for an interview with the materiel department. What the heck was this for and what did they do in materiel? The foremen told me to go and find out for myself. No one could give me a reason for this interview so I went over. I met a gentleman named Owen Malcolm who was on the staff of the director of materiel. He informed me that there was an opening for the position of buyer. He said that it was similar to what I had done when purchasing materiel for my service station business but more complicated. He said that I had been recommended for the job. We talked for about an hour and I told him I would think about it. Interview over. Negroes were spreading out into several of the other divisions by this time.

The next day Bill Rienke came down to the area and after greetings asked me what I thought of the interview for purchasing. I told him that I had not decided yet. He told me that he had come up through purchasing and that was the way if I wanted to really learn the ropes of the aircraft business. He talked about all the different people and companies I would be dealing with and the variety of items I would eventually procure. (I would learn how to become a procurer.) I would have to deal with every organization within the company in satisfying the needs of the whole Georgia division. What he did not mention was the fact that he was a vice president and my chances of ever reaching that position were about as possible as two grains of sand raising the ocean levels a foot. I had apprehensions about the job for a reason that I would discover later on. I talked to several other people and most thought that it was an opportunity not to be passed up. I finally decided to take the job and so notified those concerned. I told the foreman that I was leaving and he wished me good luck. The balance of the time before leaving I spent in closing my association with the manufacturing branch and the people I had worked with for nine years. I saw BG walking down the street past the work area and I told him I was leaving. His words, verbatim, I will never forget were, "I don't give a goddamn where you go!" One thing was a fact—I didn't have to work for that bastard anymore. He walked off before I could respond.

It seems to me the checking of my records of the work crew led to a discussion with someone further up the line and possibly finally got to Dan himself. Maybe Dan's introducing Burt to me started the ball rolling. It was not too long after these incidents that I was offered the new job. I was told that this would be a lateral job movement. How can one call a move from management to a salaried position a lateral move was a little much for me to comprehend, having been in management for eight years. Is every one supposed to be dumb and stupid? The actual fact was that I would retain my pay level and assume one helluva lot of responsibility with no authority. Whenever you assume anything (literally) you make an ASS out of U and ME. Don't get into the habit of assuming anything. Always check it out.

As I prepared to leave manufacturing I remember two fellows who were exceptional under the circumstances at the time. George Mitchell was working the Drivmatic riveting machines, drilling holes for nut plate installation. This was a precision tool that located and drilled them precisely. You then took a nut plate jig and inserted the pilot into the hole to drill the nut plate rivet holes to attach the nut plate with rivets to the understructure. Since this fitted to another part of the assembly in a flush manner the nut plate attaching rivet holes had to be countersunk. It was at this point that you riveted the nut plates to the part. After doing some smoking and vaporizing on his own (that is, deep thinking), Mitch came up with an idea that he could design a system that would combine and perform all of these operations into one. After consulting with some tooling people they came up with a gizmo and fitted it to the Drivmatic and the thing worked. The smoking and vaporization really started then. It seems as the talk commenced with the tool manufacturer, a patent was obtained. Mitch seemed to move further and further into the shadows. Not too long afterward the gizmo was added to the machine and much time was saved and quality installations were attained. Mitch was told that the tooling people and the manufacturer were already working on that theory (they just had not discovered it at that point). I don't know if Mitch ever got a commendation or his 5 percent royalty from the patent or not. If so, he had never mentioned it to me. One thing I can proudly say is when he retired with forty-two years of service to Lockheed he had been acting director of labor relations for about one year and his retirement position was manager of the labor relations department. It took a long time but that is still a helluva achievement to go from structural assembler to branch-level management. As he learns to slow down Mitch is enjoying his retirement. His experiences would be a book.

The other fellow I remember well was J. B. Mabry. Remember, he was the shop steward who formulated, after much research, the grievance against Mr. Hal on the side panels of the B-47. Well, he eventually moved into the quality control department and proceeded to work himself up the ladder. He filled in as acting quality control division manager on a few occasions and retired as manager of the tool inspection and offsite plants department. J. B. traveled around the States and into overseas countries where we had offsite locations. He had one nice (full of crap at times) career and his experiences would make an interesting book. He retired with almost forty years of service and is enjoying his retirement also.

I won't comment on the grades I received on evaluations in this period, except to note that my attitude, potential, and job knowledge sure did vary according to who was grading me. One thing that never appeared on my reviews (except one time later) was the potential of upgrade.

Chapter 8

On September 5, 1961, or so, I reported to the T-400 building, which was west of the main head house. It was exactly nine years since I had been hired into the Bomber Plant. I bought a ticket but my journey on that ticket expired before I reached what I thought would be my destination. It never occurred to me that I would have to buy another damn ticket and go over practically the same track. It seemed that no one in the new job knew where I was coming from or what my previous jobs had been. The only other Negroes in that two-story old barracks-type building were one janitor and one maid. No one had heard of a Negro buyer in any other division of Lockheed Aircraft Corporation. Breaking up red Georgia clay for planting the first crop ain't no easy job.

I was taken to the office of Jack Stewart (Jack S. from here on out). Jack S. was the purchasing agent (supervisor) for the group known mainly as raw materiel buyers. He explained that these items consisted of sheet metal, forgings, castings, extrusions, and other materiels necessary for the construction of the plane, including 1,001 different fasteners of all metals and alloys. Ninety percent of this material would be machined or milled to the required specifications except the fasteners. This work was performed in the shop, resulting in one helluva number of finished parts. Jack S. seemed to have been the only one at the time who had even partially read my employment record. He emphasized the fact that with my enormous weekly salary of $156 I would be the highest-paid buyer in the group. I told him that if he had looked closely at my employment record that he would find that I had been a member of management for eight years with as many as eighty-seven employees under my supervision at one time. I asked him how many employees he had in his group. He said fifteen, as if this was a large number. I stifled a "Ha." Actually, he did not count the hourly employees, of whom there were about ten.

The hourly people were all women and were known as schedulers, handling all of the paperwork requirements for the buyers to release purchase orders. Jack S. told me that the highest-paid buyer in the group made about $120 per week. I got the impression that he was saying there would be a rainstorm in the Sahara desert before I got a raise, as the others had to catch up. I was not getting a good impression of Jack S. (that first impression proved to be right).

I believe that Jack S. was from Pennsylvania. He tore his britches (nice word) with me when he told me I would be expected to inform him of any irregularities I may see the other buyers doing in their work. I did not know but I wondered who in hell he thought he was talking with to make a request like that. I told him that my interest would be in learning my job and working as a team member. If I was to know what I'm getting paid for, then I would not have time to be looking over my co-worker's shoulder (I wouldn't know what the hell he was doing anyway); therefore, you have the wrong man to be overseer for the group. I told him politely that I would do the best job I could to help the department and make him look good. In other words, if my efforts make you look good, then I expect the equivalent in compensation. He thought that over and said that I was one of the frankest people that he had met. He said that he could appreciate my candor. There was no doubt as to my personality and character and I think I read him pretty well also. I let Jack S. know that I did not get a lateral transfer and not to mention it to the extent that I had received some sort of promotion. After all, Bill (the VIP) had said that this was the way to learn the whole picture of the manufacturing field of building aircraft. I think I believed him and as the years rolled by I found it to be true. Even in my own opinion it didn't get me anywhere as far as upgrades.

Jack S. took me into the office area and introduced me to Paul Hale. Paul was the forging buyer and his desk covered the forging requirements for all of the planes we had in production. He purchased the heavy press forgings that were used in the wing and wheel well areas of the aircraft. There were hundreds of smaller forgings used throughout the plane. I was no stranger to forgings. Paul was becoming heavily overloaded with the C-141 going into production and needed help. Jack S. told Paul to introduce me to the others in the group. From the curious stares I received I felt for the second time at GELAC that I was better looking than Willie B. Everybody was pleasant but I only got about two "welcome to the group" expressions. After the first train ride this was to be expected so I considered it normal and started unpacking. If I had been a rabbit and was being thrown into a briar patch, like the rabbit, nothing could have been better.

Paul gave me the small forgings (five dollars to several hundred in value) and he kept the large ones (five hundred dollars to several thousands). The two of us bought every forging that went into the C-141, the C-130, and the Jetstar aircraft, plus what was needed for R&D. If you are familiar with forgings and the variety that we purchased, you may think that it would take more than the two of us to maintain schedule. Fortunately, they had put the cake and the ice cream together to accomplish this task. Paul respected my overall knowledge of the aircraft and I respected his unequaled knowledge of forgings and their manufacturing process. I shared mine and he taught me his. Ours was the best team in the department, or so we thought from our performance.

Three weeks after I was transferred to purchasing Roc was made assistant foreman!!! If I made any comment at this time the next fifteen pages would be red and it wouldn't be from a red grease pencil.

Paul helped me to get textbooks, manuals, and production method information from those vendors or suppliers that I would be dealing with. The suppliers were more than generous in helping me once they knew my manufacturing background and the above average knowledge of their products. I let it be known from the beginning that the only influence they could offer me was top quality, delivery as required and committed, then all pricing could be negotiated acceptable to the two of us. I still brought my lunch and with our workload there was very little time to go to lunch with the salesmen (even though permitted on certain occasions). I determined right off that I would develop a rapport of confidence and trust with my sources. By having all written information available on the forging manufacturing processes, I became familiar with each source and their capabilities. Paul was a very good teacher. I found out through our association that my old buddy from the machine shop (the supervisor during the water fountain days), Gus Hale, was Paul's father. Paul's personality and character indicated that he was a chip off the old block. Thus began a friendship that would last twenty-seven years. As we worked together with the same group or within the same department during that time I can say that Paul got to know me, as I did him, as well if not better than any other person at GELAC. He never used the standard aircraft language and by association I began to upgrade my method of emphasis as time went on. (Example: Paul would say "horse feathers!" and I would say "horseshit!")

The ladies began to treat me with more friendliness. They were our schedulers (purchase order processors). Their gazes turned to good morning, then "Hello," and finally "Hi." Things were smoothing out. I had no problem with the men. I remained myself and they remained themselves. After a while everything worked out as far as attitudes and friendly association. It was about three months later that my scheduler told me that her father was a drunkard who beat her mother, her husband was not much of a provider, and her son was one of those new juvenile delinquents. I realized that my presence was finally acceptable. They accepted my apologies, when under certain circumstances my aircraft language burst through, and I learned to control those normal outbursts. They all began to help me through my ignorance of the purchase order procedures and we soon had a good group going 100 percent.

I had no problems conversing with salesmen and vendors' representatives. Most of my life had been spent dealing with people (especially politicians). Most of the initial conferences were held with Paul, the salesmen, and myself until I determined who was who and felt that I knew them pretty well. The forgings purchased from my desk represented about 85 percent of all the forgings procured for the total programs at GELAC. I had quite a number of suppliers, whereas Paul was practically limited to two major suppliers who were Alcoa and Wyman-Gordon because they had the only available big heavy press equipment at the time. Each had a 50-ton press. To show its size a picture was made showing a World War II P-40 fighter plane sitting in its daylight space (the forming space between the upper and lower dies). You can imagine what I mean by big presses. There were a number of companies with large equipment but these were the only two with this capability in the United States at the time. Paul had his hands full because we were using quite a few of those big forgings.

Figuratively speaking, I had always carried about a half-pound of salt in my hip pocket to season out any overdevelopment of confidence and trust I might feel toward some of the people I had worked with in the manufacturing branch. I decided to add another half-pound for good measure in the new job. At least, I would try not to be any more stupid than the cat that learned not to sit on the hot stove twice. In other words I did not intend to put complete trust in anyone. Actions would have to speak louder than words from now on. I met many fine people over the years but complete trust never developed and I found that actually I only had full confidence and trust in about 10 percent of all the people I've worked with over the many years.

We won the C-141 contract and things really began to hum. We had the C-130, the Jetstar, and the C-141 going full blast and everyone was busy and we were hiring again. Jack S. was promoted to general purchasing agent (department manager) and I guess everybody got a raise except me (as I did not have enough experience). There was an employee morale builder from the president's staff running around with a lot of whoop-de-do about writing out your experiences that reflected on the overall welfare of your fellow employees and the company. These items were to be sent to him and the most interesting would be published in the company paper. It just happens that I had an experience about this time that I was pretty sure fell into the category he requested.

The C-141 was ready for taxi test and everyone was very excited, for this was to be our first delivery and the baby was on schedule. All effort is put into getting the first delivery on a new contract out on time, which means the second delivery may not be as close to schedule. Early one Monday morning, the first C-141 rolled out. Believe it or not, the nose landing gear collapsed. There was very little damage done to any other areas. It was a stress problem; therefore, none of the other struts back up the line could be used as a replacement. There would have to be a new design immediately requiring a new alloy per engineering. My department was notified to start checking all sources for that particular alloy and have information available ASAP. That strut forging happened to be one that I had purchased. The machining was done in-plant on our equipment. With the help of Paul and Gilly (the castings buyer) we started calling all known sources having the capability of producing the special high-strength alloy in the size that we needed. That meant every company indicating the possibility of having raw stock. Nothing was found at the big or small ones, best possible deliveries were four to eight weeks. All morning the engineers were preparing new prints and specifications, we were busy on the phones. We found nothing that would meet our critical need. The deep atmosphere of smoke and vapors this time meant that everybody was hustling.

As I was taking a break and eating a sandwich I noticed a business card on my desk that I had not filed. It was the card of the president of Shultz Steel Co. out on the West Coast. This was a small company specializing in rough forgings of practically all alloys. Noontime in Georgia was just right for California. I snatched that phone up and dialed the number, asking for the president. Since he had been in our plant the preceding Wednesday, he was surprised to hear from us so soon. I gave him the rough dimensions and thickness of the alloy we needed and asked if it was possible that he had any stock. After checking his stock he came back and floored me with, "Yes, we have an order running now for a customer but since he does not need the complete order right away I am sure that we can spare a part of it for you." Boy howdy! He said that our dimensions were smaller than what he had but saw no problem in cutting down to our specs. I told him to stay by his phone because I would have several engineers in conference with him in a few minutes. I called our engineers and got them hooked up and stayed on the line myself. I intended to know what was going on.

As he and our people talked I was busy figuring out how to get the written information to Mr. Shultz the quickest way. After all the verbal information was given he promised to hold his people on hand to start immediate production. I committed all the overtime he might require and would have a formal purchase order to him right away. Meanwhile I gave the purchase order to him verbally and the go ahead to proceed. Engineering jumped on the new prints and I made arrangements for the prints to go by special air shipment. The prints were in San Francisco by 8:00 p.m. and in his plant at 10:00 p.m. He called back on Tuesday about 3:00 p.m. our time and stated that he was having a few problems. I got engineering on the line and it seemed that those prints had errors. I told Mr. Shultz to stand by for a few hours until I could advise him if he needed to work that night. I rode engineering without a saddle for the rest of that day. Finally, I advised Mr. Shultz that I would have to get back with him first thing Wednesday morning. At 2:00 p.m. our time Wednesday afternoon engineering told me that the prints were ready. This time there could be no errors.

I called our transportation man (who happened to be a good friend of Delta Airlines' founder from the old days) and told him the situation. He found that Delta had a flight to San Francisco leaving at 5:30 p.m. (it was still Wednesday). I told the transportation gent to get a car immediately with a good driver (with instructions to be at that plane) and meet me at the gate as he left the plant and I would give him the prints. Delta advised that they would have a jeep at the entrance to the runway to expedite the package to the plane just in case it was on the runway. They would not be able to delay takeoff. I didn't know that car driver but he hit the gate rolling and I dropped the package in the front seat and told him to outrun everybody and GELAC would get him out of jail. He laughed and almost did a wheel stand. It was 18 miles to Atlanta and 7 or 8 more miles to the airport. If you have never driven through traffic around Atlanta during that time of day even then, don't do it now. The driver had about forty-five minutes to make it. We did not have 1–75 at the time and he had to go almost through the heart of town. He got to the airport and the jeep was standing at the gate with the lights flashing. The driver signaled our man to jump into the back of the jeep and took off for the runway. The plane was sitting at the end of the runway awaiting clearance for takeoff. The jeep skidded up to the forward passenger door and the co-pilot leaned out. The driver pitched the package to the co-pilot and got the hell out of there as the pilot gave that baby (a Boeing 707) the gun. I remained at the plant until the driver returned and told me the prints were on the plane. I called Mr. Shultz and gave him the pertinent information. He sent a man to the airport and the co-pilot placed the package in his hands as instructed. By 10:00 p.m., the people at Shultz Steel were going full blast around the clock to produce those parts.

The cost of that shipment was one first-class seat ticket to San Francisco and it was worth every cent. The story does not end there as we forgot one thing. There is a law almost as strong as the law of gravity. It is known as Murphy's Law. In essence it says, "If anything can go wrong, it will." Murphy's Law happened.

The materiel was cut to specs and we were going to get four of the rough parts. The forging company worked around the clock and was able to ship those parts by late Friday evening. The parts weighed 270 pounds each and that did not include packaging. The plane bringing the parts had one stop in Dallas, Texas. At Dallas it was necessary to offload as much weight as possible because a hurricane coming up through Mississippi required that the plane fly out into the Gulf of Mexico to avoid this weather. That meant that it would need extra fuel. They offloaded three of our units and we received the remaining one Friday night. Our machining department was standing by prepared to work twenty-four hours a day to complete the part and be ready for installation. I went back to the plant Saturday morning to check the progress (on my own time) and damned if they hadn't screwed it up. I called the transportation man at his home and told him we had to have those other parts immediately even if it meant chartering a plane to get them out of Texas. He hopped on the phone with Delta and they promised that the units would be on the next plane out of Dallas. The parts arrived at the plant about 6:00 p.m. Saturday evening.

I had been at the plant all day making arrangements necessary for expediting those units into the plant. I left and went home starved.

The machine shop worked like hell all night and all day Sunday. Late Sunday night they sent that baby to the flight line. The flight line worked like hell also and at 9:00 a.m. on Monday our bird was ready for taxi test. The first C-141 airplane passed its taxi test, went on to flight test, and was finally delivered to the air force on schedule.

With all the effort put forth by the supplier, the engineers, quality control, transportation (especially that driver), Delta, the Lockheed machine shop group, the flight line mechanics, and, last but not least, the purchasing department—all in six days—it damn sure wasn't routine. It just proves what can be done to override Murphy's Law by top-notch teamwork. I thought that this would be a good example of what can be done for the good of the employees and company according to the morale booster's request. After I had written it up and sent to him, he replied that it was not considered to be personal enough. The hell with morale boosters, from now on I would do all possible to continue doing my job in the best manner for the company and me. Jack S. said we did a good job—verbally but not in writing. Period.

The raw materiel group moved to another wing of the T-400 building that had been recently redecorated. There were new blinds and the brightest yellow paint imaginable on the walls. This was the theory of some nice person to cheer up the work area and thus increase production. After about three weeks or so a high number of the group began to develop headaches, nausea, and other funny types of discomfort. The women were really at each other's throats. The men were edgy and short tempered. I would get a headache every day. I thought the whole situation was psychological. When the scrapping got to the point that quality of workmanship was beginning to fall apart, an industrial psychologist was brought in to investigate the problem. The psychologist talked with the people and just sat around and watched for a week. A week later here came the painters and paperhangers and the whole decor was changed. The lower walls were papered with a brown cloth-type covering and the upper walls and the ceiling was painted beige. Within two days the attitudes and the whole atmosphere changed back to the smoothly working, congenial condition that previously existed. I recalled that in my class in the foundations of human behavior, we had learned about the effect that lighting, colors, and temperature could have on workers. Lockheed had hit the nail on the head and we continued merrily on our way. (Yellow?)

A salesman came down from New Jersey. His company manufactured forgings. We went through that routine of his sales talk, presentation of brochures, and discussion of quality control, including housekeeping (the cleanliness and order of the plant). He did all right until he got down to housekeeping. He stated that the plant was located in a "nigger" neighborhood, therefore housekeeping could not be as effective under the circumstances. This is the fallacy of quite a few people from other areas of the United States coming into the South and expecting better acceptance by being derogatory, in other words prejudiced. I told him to hold it as we did not use that terminology in this office. If that excuse was the best he could use for the housekeeping and cleanliness of his plant, what the hell would his excuse be in case his quality was not what he proclaimed it to be? As far as I was concerned his interview was over. He had been calling on Paul so he went over to see him. Paul probably told him that he had been talking to a Dutch, Cajun, Negro, Creek, Georgia Cracker, unborn and reborn gentleman of the South (me) who qualified as a full blown red-blooded American. We never heard from that gentleman again.

There were a number of salesmen who came in with a high-pressure sales technique and also assumed that a new buyer was dumb as hell. I may have bought a few sticks in my time but damn if I ever bought a full load of poles. Out of all the buyers I worked with over the years there were only a few who would refuse to come to the aid of a younger or new buyer. I recognized that buyers were under a lot of pressure most of the time. Getting into the habit of doing exactly what you were told by some of the bosses was not the best way as experience developed. It was almost impossible for a boss to know all the details of each operation. The point was to learn how to inform him without insinuating that he was stupid. This was necessary more than seldom.

Chapter 9

There was a special committee formed by the president to go out and check our defense plants to confirm that they were adhering to defense contract specifications that no discrimination was being practiced in the hiring and upgrading of American minorities working in the plants with those contracts. This committee made at least one trip to Lockheed each year. They called in certain Negroes (and some managers) and got affidavits indicating that progress was being made and only time would determine how soon before all of these progressive moves could be made. I was never called to testify before this committee. Since progress was so slow it must have been that Negroes just did not gain experience and knowledge at what was considered a normal rate. Next year would always show improvement. There was a slow improvement made every year. This was mainly because the requirement for ability was becoming necessary.

Finally, however, it seemed the time for my interview had arrived. The department manager, Jack S., told me to go to the office and talk to the gentlemen from Washington. I had no desire to talk to these people. From all I heard they were given the same BS each year and they went back and probably told the powers that be what they wanted to hear also (everything is going fine, minorities are progressing and advancing as fast as experience and ability will allow, etc.). I could never see any improvement that could be traced as a result of any of their visits. Sure, there was a move now and then but any promotion received was just enough to satisfy this group and the promotions by qualification and ability lagged far behind what should have been accomplished.

There were four gentlemen present, three whites and one Negro. Their questions started with the routine. How do you like your job? Fine. Do you feel that you are getting the sufficient training required for advancement? Have you read my employee record? It seems that you have been promoted to buyer not too long ago. If you knew my record you would find that I have been demoted from manager to buyer, a salaried position, not as a disciplinary measure but to make way for an individual whom I respect but qualification-wise was second in line. Don't you earn an acceptable salary? In comparison to some of the buyers, yes, but as a manager my salary was higher and at least they did not lower it. Nor do buyers get what, with their responsibilities, can be considered a decent pay raise when due. Do you ever get to travel in your job? No, I am still gaining experience. Although it's been almost three years, I have still not acquired the proper experience, whatever the hell that is.

This fact of not traveling did not bother me because my suppliers had given me manuals and books of terminology, procedures, and methods in their manufacturing processes that surpass the impressions made by a visit. I don't seem to have had a situation that was of the extent that a visit was necessary to solve it. There will come a time when this will be necessary and I will probably have the "experience" to fulfill the mission. Are you satisfied with the job you have? I can say yes to that question. My satisfaction is gained from what I do in an effort to be better than average. The knowledge gained through this particular job, purchasing, is hard to come by in practically every other branch of the aircraft manufacturing business. I know that eventually I will move into other areas of procurement. Other than salaries and benefits the purchasing division is responsible for 95 percent of all expenditures made for the manufacturing of aircraft. I'm glad I work in the purchasing branch.

Gentlemen, I think that I have indicated that I do not have much confidence in your committee and you have not given me any reasons to believe that you have checked available records to prove that any changes from last year have been made. I have a lot of work to do and would like to get back to it. I thanked them, got up, and left. Actually, the above is the nicest way I could write about that meeting. Things got hot at times because I thought from the beginning that they were full of crap and "politicking" most of the time. I didn't know what they told management and gave less than a damn. I heard nothing from anyone about the meeting or any results of the meeting. Surely, they interviewed more people than me, but I don't think I gave them the answers they were looking for. Situations like these were probably the reason that I felt I was blacklisted at times. Anyway, I always slept well at night for I never ate cheese.

The forgings and the castings and the other materiel the raw materiels group was buying were on schedule and of good quality. Everything was running well and I think even Jack S. was happy. Raise time came and passed and nobody made too much of a gripe. I later learned that the director and assistant director had brainwashed them to the degree that they were showing their cost consciousness and company loyalty to the extent that they did not want raises. Sounds stupid, you had better believe it. After the bosses got their average of about 10 percent each buyer was given something like 3–5 percent. The buyer's pay was $90 to $120 per week. (They were responsible for millions in procurement.) Since I had come over making $156 per week I was making as much or more than the average supervisor. I had not received a raise but surprisingly enough at this time I got a big $4 a week increase.

I walked into Jack S's office and closed the door. I told him in the most emphatic aircraft language that if the company could only afford that type of raise after the thousands I had saved through competitive and negotiated procurement, then kindly don't give me anything like that and call it an increase in pay. Just ram it up somebody's butt. All Jack S. could say was he had a low budget. To be able to cuss your boss out is to always be done in private, never, never in the presence of others. Never embarrass him. State that the conversation is man to man, then cut loose with everything except bodily injury. Nine times out of ten the boss will realize that he needs a little friendly advice and appreciates it if you are right. If not, then that's number ten so be ready to look for another job if necessary. By the way, the materiel division always had the lowest budget for many years, according to the bosses.

The average buyer has a burden. That burden is the temptation to accept gifts or gratuities of any nature. This burden is heaviest when the buyer is employed by the federal, state, county, or city governments. You can pick up a newspaper on any day and see where some character has gotten a big lump for awarding a government contract to some supplier other than the low bid (without a documented reason like quality and delivery without a low bid). If your parents, teachers, and preachers did not install the respect of principles, honesty, and integrity and you did not absorb them, then you ain't gonna damn find them as a buyer. The temptations are too great and a weak person will fall into the pit of what is called white-collar crime. Two buyers did just that. They were caught and immediately fired the same day. Most times one may get jail time according to the amount of the kickback.

As soon as I found out about it Jack S. called me into his office. These two people were also in Jack S's department. Jack S's voice was dripping with grandma's goose grease as he told me, "We have a problem upstairs, So & So and So & So have been fired for cause. Your desk is in top condition and can be handled with a minimum amount of follow-up and we need you upstairs for the time it takes to get new people into those jobs." That salt that I had increased to 2 pounds in my hip pocket said, "Hold it!" I am either being put into a position to prove what I can do or get my butt fired. Challenge me and I will take you on (sometimes stupidly). I told him okay and he took me up to the supervisor. The supervisor, Johnny, took me to a desk that looked like a garbage dump with paper crumpled in all directions (remember the condition of that desk for later). Jack S. and Johnny told me to see if I could clean that desk up and left.

Not only was the top of the desk covered but every drawer was stuffed full (no order to anything, just stuffed). It took me almost three days to get that stuff separated. Since I said I'm trying to drop some of the aircraft language I will just say I found from (expletive) to (expletive) on that desk. I would be buying from A to Z, aspirin for the hospital right on down to zippers for tarpaulins (including the tarpaulins). It would take two full pages to list all of the items and that is no BS. I bought materiel for the flight line, the hospital, the qualitative and quantitative laboratories, the scientific research department, the janitorial supplies, the repair of the tug engines (including automotive requirements), rags, uniforms, safety equipment, and, would you believe, chickens, turkeys, pecans, walnuts, peanuts, small rocks by the size, lumber of certain types, microscopes, lab wall tile, narcotics (no joke!) weight measurement scales, and just about everything that did not go on the aircraft. Now imagine anything else and I bought that too. When I finally got things straightened out I had almost a thousand un-bid or unplaced requests on the desk.

I did not realize what was going on so I hit that stack of work like a tornado and took off. Fortunately, these items fell into categories that had a number of suppliers each. Most of them were local. I did not have to mail out the quotations and await replies. I would collate the items and call the vendors. Being right-handed I held the phone to my left ear. Today I am completely deaf in that ear. (The ear had begun to lose its function from the nine years in the shop.) I was still receiving about 300–350 new order requests each week. I told Johnny that the desk was overloaded and it would take more than me to catch up. He told me to give it a good try and see if I couldn't clear it and catch up. I decided to try. I worked ten hours a day and eight hours on each Saturday for six weeks (at forty hours a week pay). That phone stuck in my left ear for an average of nine hours a day. Suddenly, I pulled my headbone from the ceiling and stomped into Johnny's office and told him to screw this crap for they had not replaced the second buyer at all but dumped the two desks on me. No other buyer had a weekly desk load of 1,200 to 1,500 open purchase orders on his desk. I told him and Jack S. that I was not donating any more time attempting to handle a desk load like that and they could ram it. I had spent 108 hours overtime with no pay and it just ended. They took about one-third of the desk and assigned it to another new buyer. I was asked (with a straight face) to give him as much help as possible. No comment at all for the work that I had done. The desk was on schedule but it took ten hours a day to maintain that position. I got even (in a way).

We had an assistant division manager named Jack M. How in hell he got the position I don't know. I had about 1,115 open purchase orders and 11 of them were behind schedule. There were no shortages in the plant, our stock situation was good. Jack M. called me and told me (in an un-nice manner) that my "behind schedule" position was terrible. It did not reflect that my desk was under control. One damn percent behind schedule and the desk is out of control. I wonder how some dumbasses assume that there are many other people as stupid as they are. Like I have to believe that my desk is out of control because he said so. (Mama, somebody is picking on me!) I went down to clerical and pulled ten of those orders and changed the delivery to show that they were due in thirty days. Now I only had one PO behind schedule. The very next day I received an ANVO (accept no verbal orders) from Jack M. stating that he knew that I could get my desk in order and he congratulated me on my effort. (I have to say it—Horseshit!!) Can any buyer having worked at Lockheed say that in their history they knew of any other buyer having only one order out of 1,100 being behind schedule?

Among the items I bought were moon shots made by our rockets and sent back to earth. These were purchased from Stanford University and were highly classified. All one had to do was buy the latest copy of *Life* magazine and see the whole outlay for the cost of the magazine. The photos had to be wrapped four times and sealed with my name and department number being on the fourth wrapper. I would remove this and the secretary would remove the third wrapper and send the double-wrapped package to the scientific research lab. Once, the lab got some picture packages that had been opened and resealed. Damn if they didn't insinuate that I had opened the package for the purpose of sabotage. What the hell, with all of the work I had before me, would be a reason to look at some moon shots? After all I was the buyer procuring that information. This time the great security force decided that they had better investigate before outright accusing me of such an act. It seems the secretary was real curious to see what all the big deal was over the moon. She opened the package and viewed the surface of the moon with something looking like plus signs (these must have been the highly classified reason) on it, resealed it, and sent it on to the lab. Well, surely a secretary could not be a spy and the so-called ghost hunt was canceled. The pictures came as ordered but no more were tampered with.

Because of the nondiscrimination clauses in the defense contracts, the local suppliers and vendors were beginning to hire Negroes as salesmen and sending them to call on Lockheed. We were being pressed to develop small and minority businesses as suppliers. The word seemed to have been passed around that if a salesman (minority) had not made an appointment then you could be too busy to see him. I have seen these guys sit in the lobby for several hours waiting to see some buyer they did not know who did not have the courtesy to go down and talk to them. Some of the salesmen I knew from my business and school days. They would ask me why. I just thought that they were smart enough to guess why. I could not tell them at the time that it was pure old prejudice and not a damn thing else.

Finally, a couple of salesmen came in representing small minority businesses handling chemicals and industrial cleaning supplies. The one with the industrial cleaning supplies business had supplied my service station before I hired on at Lockheed. Both of them owned the businesses they represented. I gave them the necessary forms to be filled out and sent in paperwork requesting financial and quality inspection approval to participate in the defense requirements as a supplier. After about three weeks the reports came back that both had been approved by the financial department and the quality control divisions. I told them to send me a complete listing and specifications of their line of products.

Since I purchased everything, including toilet tissue, I felt pretty sure that there would be some items that I could request quotations for in competitive bidding against the sources I already had. They were approved as sources for these product lines and I began to call them for bid requests. They knew the market pretty well so one began to receive a few purchase orders.

The minority supplier with the small distributing company had a well-established small business serving schools, hospitals, and other facilities of that type for a number of years. He was an ex-air force pilot and a reservist (at Dobbins Air Force Base) and had a good reputation. I don't remember him doing a dollar's worth of business with Lockheed as I left that desk shortly after. Most of the kinds of products he sold were bought on six-month supply contracts anyway. He later informed me that he never received one quote request from the buyer that had replaced me. This was an indication of the blatant prejudice practiced by the materiel department at the time. This attitude continued even though the word had come down from topside to develop small and minority businesses. Not one manager questioned why this minority company was not winning bids. I know that this fellow would not mind me mentioning his name because he had the principles of the good businessman. His name was George Prather and his company was Standard Chemical Supply. His products were up to high standards and he and the company had integrity. I regret that I didn't remain on the buying desk for those supplies. He was eliminated by the same old prejudiced bullshit that existed prior to my having him qualified. The subsequent buyers just refused (or were instructed not to) to bid him. Lockheed lost a good minority small business supplier as a result.

The cleaning supplies firm became the first minority (other than a few white women) firm to fulfill orders at Lockheed-Georgia. I need not emphasize the critical inspection that this one received on the delivery of his products. (This was normal.) None of these items went on an aircraft. I felt pretty good because the products were meeting all qualification requirements. This was the Arawak Chemical Company. The founder had developed a solid business with about ten employees. He was doing business with other government facilities like Leavenworth and Redstone. He had been in business also for a number of years and developed some expertise in dealing with government contracts. He also had experience in learning the ropes of supply and demand made by certain government buyers. (Kickbacks?) In other words he had become knowledgeable and slick.

My dealings where this character was concerned were some of the most morale depressing I had experienced up to this time, in part because of the way my peers reacted and treated me. I had known him only vaguely before because he was a sometime customer when I was in the business prior to coming to Lockheed. He found that his products were scrutinized much more on receipt than those of the other established sources. This was understandable on deliveries from new sources. The cost of the type of stuff we bought only varied in pennies per unit, therefore, competition was tight. After six months he had delivered about $10,000 worth of materiel and everything had met specifications. Without a doubt I knew that there were instructions to someone to inspect every delivery from this source because it was not only the first Negro-owned and -operated small business to be a supplier but also because I was the first Negro buyer the company had. It only then stood to reason that he and I must be in collusion.

When I had moved over to purchasing I had maintained contact with the many people I had previously worked with on the manufacturing floor. I told them whenever they had a shortage problem on any item that I purchased they should call me and I would bust my tail plate to see if I could help in expediting the shortage. One of those people happened to be a fellow in the Q&Q lab where a lot of these chemicals were being used. On many occasions I had expedited materiel for him. He was a technician and did the testing on the purity of the chemicals used. I also think that some of the old suppliers may have indicated that the new source was watering down the quality of the products. There was tolerance for less than 100 percent purity of certain chemicals and sometimes the vendor could go to the minimums and still meet requirements. It seems that the source that I had developed was taking advantage of this tolerance, as were others. Since the new supplier's products were being inspected precisely on every delivery, it was found that he was pushing the limit.

Did my friend advise me that he was finding discrepancies in the deliveries? Did he write up any rejection slips on the quality? Hell no, he went to plant protection with the assumption that I must be in collusion with the seller and getting some kind of kickback. Now I had failed to see what that 2 pounds of salt in my hip pocket was there for. I had fallen into the mud of team workmanship and was getting screwed again. If that particular gentleman has passed over, I hope his wings have holes in them.

I was asked to go down to plant protection for an interview. I wondered what the issue could possibly be. I had experience with plant protection on previous occasions and I never liked the results. I considered most of these characters (being nice) a bunch of stupid bastards and I had no respect for them. On my arrival I was ushered into a small room and introduced to an investigator I will call IG. If I make any errors in the following (best of my memory) I am sure that the recording is still available in their great files of critical issues.

IG: "I understand that you have made some purchases from a certain company known as X Co.?"
ME: "Yes, I know of that company and they are an established Lockheed source."
IG: "Do you know that they have not been approved financially as a source?" (This was his first error. No purchase orders can be processed without the approvals completed. I had been doing business with this company for over six months.)
ME: "All sources are approved before an order can be formally placed."
IG: "Were these orders I have in my hand formally placed?"
ME: (I did not even bother to look at them.) "They had to be approved otherwise they would not have been placed and recorded."
IG: "What do you purchase from this company?"
ME: "Mainly chemicals."
IG: "On a competitive basis?"
ME: (If he had looked on the back of the purchase request he would have seen the documentation indicating the number of sources bid plus their individual quotes. I'm beginning to get a little pissed off.) "Most of the requirements of that nature have several sources, therefore normally two or more sources are always quoted."
IG: "Was this source competitive on the orders awarded to him?"
ME: "Normally, the orders are placed with the most competitive source but not necessarily so. At times delivery and quality are the primary considerations."

IG: "I understand that you knew this particular person, who owns the business, in previous years?"

ME: "Not exactly, I knew his mother-in-law." (You should have seen his eyes light up on that bit of information.)

IG: "In what capacity?"

ME: "Previous to my employment at Lockheed, I operated a service station in partnership with my father (as if he did not know). Her employer was a credit customer of ours and I always presented the weekly bill to her, as manager of his hotel, for payment."

IG: "Did you know her personally?"

ME: "Only when I saw her to collect the bill and being damn sure to be courteous."

IG: "Was she attractive?"

ME: "You would say so." (Now the crap is hitting the fan that I am writing about.)

IG: "Did you ever date her?"

ME: "Hell no!"

IG: "Did you ever consider asking her for a date?" (I now know exactly in what direction he is headed.)

ME: "The woman was old enough to be my mother-in-law."

IG: "Well, to get back to your dealings with her son-in-law, why did you pay different prices for the same product on different occasions?"

ME: "What the hell are you talking about?"

IG: "I have three different purchase orders that give three different prices for the same product."

ME: "Can you give me the number of any one of those purchase orders?"

IG: "Sure, the first is PO #14456." (With a know-it-all smile.)

ME: (Bless my memory, the only number I could not remember at Lockheed was my own Social Security number.) "That order is for a commercial grade of pyrethrum (he couldn't pronounce it) mixed with sawdust (diluted), the lowest grade, and used as an insecticide."

IG: "I have two others."

ME: "Yes, I know, the other order is PO #320223 for a technical grade of a higher strength and usage and sells for $11 per pound. The other grade you have on PO #232465 is the U.S. pure grade and is the most expensive at $22.30 per pound. The technical grade sells for $0.77 per pound." (I had every PO correct he held in his hand.)

IG: "Well, why did you pay this big difference in price for the same product?"

ME: "Goddamn! You don't know what the hell you are talking about!"

IG: "We don't need any of your sarcastic crap!"
ME: "The hell with you, you don't know what you are asking about!"
IG: "What about your relationship with this man's mother-in-law?"
ME: "Have you taken the time to read my personnel folder?"
IG: "No! What has that got to do with this?"
ME: "Then you would have found out that I have had training in criminal investigation and interrogation and I have had a belly full of this ten cent detective book bullshit and I don't intend to answer another question of yours and you can go straight to hell!" (The temperature in the room was way beyond hot.)

Just then the door burst open and the great and mighty director of the plant protection department rushed in and immediately inquired if his assistance was needed. This immediately alerted me to the fact that our conversation had been recorded. Naturally, IG told him that his assistance was not needed. If he had I would have, in a polite manner, told him to KMA on the way out. (I can understand a little better nowadays why employees are blowing their managers' brains out.)

I did not like the connotation of this conference. I decided that somehow I was in the process of being shafted again. Similar to the string I had reaching up to BG's office in the manufacturing branch I also had one that reached all the way to the area of the top of the air force. I won't go into specifics but if it had been necessary to use that access I would have without reservations. I called long-distance from home that night and discussed the whole barrel of worms and the diversions being made from the contracts and their specifications. After about one hour I was told certain procedures to take if I decided to sue and be sure to go to federal. I was instructed on the quality of evidence to gather and the type of lawyer to obtain. Once these procedures were met, I was told to send this information to my contact. If and when the case came up in federal court, he would see that two air force people would be sent as observers to monitor the proceedings. If the results indicated air force follow-up was needed, then such action would be taken. I did not want to get into any embroilment with Lockheed because then I would have to reveal all the dope on all the bastards I knew. I know one thing: the rule of self-preservation would prevail as far as I was concerned.

A few days later the "Bigfoot" assistant director of materiel marched me over to mahogany row to the office of the director of materiel. I was given a lecture equivalent to the dressing down of a fifth-grade student on all of the errors I had made in dealing with this particular vendor. No mention was made of the fact that the director of finance and the chief of quality control had approved this vendor prior to any purchase orders being placed. I guess some wheels think they can tell an employee anything and it is acceptable because of their position. I just looked from one to the other as they tried to make sense out of nothing. Finally, they gave me a performance notice indicating all of that garbage with a promise it would be lifted within a year if my workmanship improved and warranted the removal from my record. The wording and errors on that boomsheet were enough to win any labor case but I was not a union member. I was a salaried member of management (they normally get screwed or fired). I signed it with the notation that it was an acknowledgment of receipt but not agreement. Bless his heart, Bigfoot never kept his word about lifting the performance notice within a year or any other time. He died a few years later. The director of materiel at the time will show up later. Think about what you have just read and see if you can see where the level of intelligence can be located.

I decided to drop any idea of a suit against certain individuals in the company because there were too many people in higher levels for whom I had a lot of respect. On top of that I liked my company and its past history of accomplishments in the aero industry. Then after all, I was putting my two cents worth into that history whether it was recognized or not. I went back to the "buy it all" desk and grabbed the rat race by the tail. Before I could sit down here came Jack S. with information that I should report somewhere else the next morning.

The next Monday Jack S. told me to report over to the T-401 building and check in with Tom, the department manager, for a new assignment. Tom was the manager of the government furnished parts (GFP) department. These are parts that are used on many different aircraft in the military inventory. They fall under this control because the government can buy higher volumes at lower cost. All of these parts come from government stock and are returned for repair to government-specified sources. As GELAC was a big producer of military aircraft our volume in the use of this equipment necessitated a separate group to handle this procurement.

I was assigned to a congenial old character as a materiel handling specialist. I had never heard of that classification nor had anyone else. It seems that I was not a buyer any longer. What I found out later was that I could not handle any more finances dealing with procurement, negotiations, or anything.

After learning my contacts at the different locations and the repair shops, I placed all of the purchase orders, processed them through the system, and did all of the follow-up on deliveries. My new partner signed the purchase orders since I was not to deal with or be responsible for any finances at all. I never did find out what his classification was. I went to all of the shortage meetings (generally weekly) and advised on the status of all open purchase orders. I wrote up all documentation for the orders. I had the ability in playing checkers to keep the red disk in the red squares and the black disk in the black squares. This qualified me as a materiel handling specialist. I got the same ear bone aches, dialing finger, and writing cramps as I did as a buyer. Since all my buddy had to do was to sign his name (which he was used to doing) he never developed writer's cramp.

After a few months our supervisor called me into the office to discuss my attendance record. He noted that I had been absent twelve days during the past year. He said that this did not reflect any great effort to maintain a good attendance record. I asked him if that was my file in his hand. He said it was. I asked him did he notice that eleven of those days were in sequence. He had not. I informed him that those eleven days I was in the hospital. I reminded him that salaried employees got six sick days a year. If they were not taken then you were not paid for them but fortunately the company let them build for a time when you might need them. I had well over a hundred days in the kitty when I was in the hospital. Other than those days why did I need a lecture on attendance? In my years at Lockheed I had a damn good attendance record and knew it. That conference ended as full of it as it started. Later I had some dollar value orders that required the department manager's signature. He looked at them and asked me if they were correct and if I was sure that they were ready for his signature. I told him yes. He told me he watched his people work and made an effort to know them. He developed his confidence and trust of his employees through that method. He emphasized that I should never bring anything to him for approval until I felt it was ready. Again, I said it was ready. He signed off every one without checking and handed them back to me. He said I was doing a good job. (Well, I'll be doggoned!) From then on everything I took to him I assured him that it was ready. He signed it and then my buddy signed it. I did everything a senior buyer was supposed to do except I couldn't sign a damn thing. It was that old deal about the rabbit being in the briar patch, except my briars didn't have any patch.

I guess the biggest trouble I almost got into was at a division-level shortage meeting. The big wheels and their assistants would be sitting at the table along with my boss as they went down the list of items that were short on the aircraft and causing work stoppages. One of those assistants was known for his lack of knowledge, specifically the details, as the people working under him recognized. His questions were usually gruff and arrogant, seemingly in an attempt to embarrass the person he was asking. At one meeting, I had just given the status of a shortage item when he turned to me and said, "Do you know that for a fact, or are you just outright lying to try and impress these people?" Whoops! I raised halfway out of my chair and grabbed the back of the chair and damn if I wasn't going to knock hell out of him (I even scared myself). The soon-to-be director of materiel yelled, "Hold it!" He turned and suggested in a very stern voice to this character that it would be to his advantage to apologize to me for his insult. He stated that he had known me from manufacturing days and always respected me for my honesty and straightforwardness. His experience with me was that if I said it was so, then that was good enough for him. Having stepped into a hole that was not his Mr. Big ripened like a tomato and apologized. The funny part was that gent had never attended a shortage meeting to my knowledge and the impression he had hoped to make fizzled. There are some people in this narrative I just won't name. They are like the pebble you stumped your toe on and never looked back. My time in GFP group is growing short so I may as well finish it up in this chapter.

I had a problem with one of our suppliers who happened to be just about (at that time) the largest producer of electronic equipment in the world. His product was one of the most important items for directional guidance and other functions used on the C-130. If we ever received one of these units and it was nonfunctional, thus being rejected, we had to send them a return check for $1,100 plus shipping and handling. I did not make myself a materiel handling specialist (which was never found listed anywhere as a job classification) so I considered that this was a part of my job. As previously stated, in GFP the government placed all orders for this equipment and we just accepted deliveries when we requested. Why should we have to pay a vendor for a return fee for his equipment when it did not function as required? I went over to see my old buddy Big John, manager of the receiving inspection department (John had moved up since the skin squawks earlier) and asked him if he could give me any reason that we should be paying this cost for no good junk. John jumped a few feet up and said, "Who the hell authorized a payment like that?" I did not know. We agreed that no more payments would be paid.

I told him to remember that this was GFP equipment and maybe prior agreements had been made. He told me to check it out and bring him something in writing approving such an agreement. I found that no one knew why we made payments and passed this on to John. I told John that we had another shipment of three units due in the following week. This company's contract was with the Defense Department so they only shipped once a month the number of units required by the original schedule at the time of the contract initiation. Damn the increase in deliveries or spare parts required by Lockheed. No increase in schedule could be included until a new contract was negotiated, which meant new pricing. Our government purchasing agencies always make real tight types of contracts to screw themselves later. We were making almost eight deliveries a month to the air force and they were supplying us with four units per month per the original contract from the DOD. How did this affect our customer deliveries (guess)? John told me that he would advise me on receipt and we would get a conference call with the vendor and his engineering, quality, and finance people and get the situation cleared up.

I called and told John the shipment had been made and to call me on its arrival. We got our conference call going and John talked to the head of quality control at the vendor's facility. He stated that we were getting deliveries and a high percentage of their shipments were nonfunctional. He said that we were behind schedule because of the last rejections and we wanted them to send management-level people from the engineering, quality control, and finance groups as soon as possible. We would hold their latest shipments as received and open them on their arrival. The people requested were here by 10:00 a.m. the next morning.

After a congenial meeting on their entrance to the receiving section, John introduced his functional test inspectors and with the vendor-supplied functional test manual in hand, we proceeded to open the boxes. The first unit went through the procedure and tested out perfectly. Everyone smiled, especially us because we needed a good unit to close a shortage. The second unit did not function. The vendor's representatives went through the procedure twice, but the unit did not function. John turned near the color of a half ripe tomato. Our people ran the test on the third unit. It did not function. They tested it and it did not function. John looked as if he might burst a blood vessel. These are almost exactly the words John used:

Gentlemen, we have received three units and only one is functional. For the cost of these items that is a helluva quality record. For some reason this has been occurring too frequently without having corrections made at your facility. The buyer (hell, I ain't no buyer, I am a materiel handling specialist) informs me that there is a return charge when your product is not acceptable quality-wise. Since you are furnishing this equipment under a direct government contract I see no reason that Lockheed should be held responsible for the return cost of a nonfunctional unit. We are repackaging this materiel and shipping it back to you this date. There will be no return charges paid for nonfunctional equipment from this time on and if the crating indicates any damage on receipt it will be returned also. If this happens again it will be necessary to take it to a higher level (DOD).

In essence the above is acceptable in any report. John is a full-blown aircrafter and if you think that is exactly how he said it give another thought.

When he finished John returned to his natural old hospitable self and said, "Gentlemen, let's go have some lunch on me." That included me. We did not get nonfunctional units again. If there was a malfunction one of our people could fix it. I like to think that John and I had similar personalities. Both of us had our own struggles with certain members of our upper management but we made sure that we knew what we were talking about. I know that he was an asset to Lockheed. So was I.

The GFP group moved out of the main plant to an area on Butler Street in Marietta and became almost a separate unit. Our main job was to get that GFP into the plant on schedule, which we did, and things ran along smoothly. One day Tom got a call and told me I would be loaned to my old buying group for a period of time because of some problems they were having. Hell, from all previous experience, I thought that I was the only problem they had. Let's move on down and see what in heaven was wrong with the old group.

Chapter 10

I returned to the building T-400. Jack S. greeted me warmly and stated that they needed me to help out on the bring-back operation for the C-5A. Johnny (my last supervisor in purchasing) had been transferred to CALAC temporarily to facilitate shipment of component parts and raw materiels that had been purchased at CALAC for the initial startup of the C-5A program there as we prepared for production at GELAC. I wonder who in hell considered me qualified for that responsibility. I knew I was wrong but I considered anyone who would kick my butt and pat me on the shoulder at the same time had to be short on marbles.

Johnny worked with Morgy (a CALAC department manager) in the shipment of these components to GELAC. They wanted me to coordinate the program of receipt and acceptance of the materiel and total up the cost (hell, I thought that I was never to handle finance again). As the materiel began to arrive I found some items in surplus at a level that seemed unnecessary. The cost of this materiel was expensive. Of all the high costs I found one that was ridiculous. Some buyer had made a large purchase of 4,000 pounds of 0.034 thickness aluminum sheets. This was an odd thickness and had to be a special production run. The sheets were for the manufacture of one single part per aircraft, a 1-inch square to be used on the wing. This made me wonder about CALAC's purchasing ability but it probably reflected DOD's demand that its contractors buy what was needed, damn the cost.

Otherwise, things went well and after several weeks the bring-back program was completed on schedule and within the estimated cost of the program. The department manager, Morgy, sent a letter of commendation to Jack S. acknowledging my efforts in making the program a success. Morgy sent me a copy. I haven't been able to find it but if you think that Jack S. mentioned it or put it in my personnel file then you still believe that alligators fly. Jack S. was hell.

Now that the bring-back program was over I just knew that I would be going back to my position as the only materiel handling specialist known at Lockheed, which included processing all the purchase orders on the desk for my co-worker's signature. I also noted that sometime during my stay in GFP I had been promoted (?) to materiel scheduling analyst (never heard of that one either, no increase in pay). The good things I was accomplishing necessitated the creation of two completely new job classifications, which were eliminated on my leaving the department. But no, there was another problem that required my help.

There were a lot of new buyers in the raw materiel group by this time, as the C-5A was really rolling in production. One young fellow was smoking and vaporizing like mad—from frustration. I never found out how long he had been on the desk but it was one of the toughest in the group. He had the extrusion desk. There are hundreds of extrusion designs and a helluva bunch of them were used on our aircraft. He had energetically attacked the job, placing purchase orders verbally and processing nothing. He had over six hundred unwritten POs on his desk requiring completion, including documentation and processing into the system so as to be mailed to the vendors. He was a prime candidate for a case of ulcers. I stayed and spent six weeks writing up the young fellow's orders and completing the price analysis, including the documentation required. Documentation was the most crap I found in placing orders and satisfying the DOD (or so I was told). It hardly matters what you say as long as it is two or three paragraphs long since no one reads it if it looks long enough. There are items that require a lot of documentation because of the level of difficulty and complication for the purchased component. A purchase order request must state all information required for the buyer or anyone else looking at the order. If your handwriting is pretty bad you could say all cows are brown but some have white spots. If the gobbledygook is a paragraph or two, the reviewer will glance at it and say documentation is sufficient. Anyway, I finally got the fellow pretty well caught up to date. He nonchalantly informed me that now I could do his follow-up and deliveries on the same orders. I politely informed him in my most emphatic aircraft language that I was not his goddamn helper. Being much younger than me he was real shook up by my statement. He had been led to believe that I was now a buyer's helper (never had that ever been a job classification either) and was strictly assigned to take his orders. I had no right to take my anger out on him but I was mad as hell and stomped into the supervisor's office. We'll call him Tom, recently transferred from CALAC, and this is almost verbatim:

ME: "Tom, what the hell do you mean telling that buyer that I have been assigned to him as a helper?"
TOM: "Hell, Hap, Jack S. told me that that was your classification and you were here to assist anyone requiring your help."
ME: "Tom, in all of your time at CALAC and now at GELAC have you ever had knowledge of such a classification?"

TOM: "No, I haven't but I don't know what classifications you have at GELAC."
ME: "Have you ever accepted a man into your crew without doing a background check on his qualifications?"
TOM: "Well, not as yet, but Jack S. said that you have been transferred to our group and that is your classification."
ME: "Tom, I don't know a damn thing about a transfer. I was told that I had a request to help on the C-5A bring-back program and then I go back to my job in GFP."
TOM: "Here are your transfer papers and you now work for me."
ME: "I don't know anything about that but I'm going to walk out of this office. You go pull my personnel folder and when you have finished reading it call me back. Jack S. is still the prime SOB I recognized when I first came into this department!"

Four hours later Tom called me into his office and apologized for not having read my file. He said no one had given him any information about me except I was a buyer's helper and he would utilize me as such (that was Jack S.'s crap). The period of time I worked with Tom had been very relaxed and congenial. In other words, I liked the guy. Tom was about 5 feet 5 inches with real light gray eyes. He told me that he would like to appoint me as the troubleshooter for the whole group. Where there was a problem, I would go in and help that particular buyer solve his problem and get on schedule. Just about every one of Tom's buyers had less than one year seniority. He had problems. I'm glad to say that I was able to help him. By the way, my job classification had never been changed. I was still a buyer. Although I did not know this at the time now I can understand why I was able to perform the buyer's duties without question. With that information, my respect for some of upper management had no bounds. I continued to work for Tom for about one year. Tom Carver turned out to be a fine gentleman, straightforward with a very high level of integrity.

We were now manufacturing the C-130, the C-141, the C-140 (Jetstar), and the C-5A. We had a whole lot of new buyers, including some Negroes. The department had just about doubled in the number of people they had when I first went over. I had been in purchasing a little over five years. One of the young fellows I had helped train for a little over two years was now a senior buyer (two levels above me and the same position as Paul). He still bought the same items he was buying when he began. No point in stating who his Pa was. I was still a buyer as Jack S. determined I was still in the process of learning and gaining experience. One or two of the older buyers had made purchasing agent but most remained in their jobs because no one had proven ability to learn those jobs in this length of time. Paul and Gilly were held in their positions as senior buyers because of their expertise in the procurement of forgings and castings. I had worked all over the damn place. Believe it or not, I was the one gaining all the experience but just did not have enough to be considered for an upgrade. Everything was good—attitude, workmanship, ambition—but the lack of experience disqualified me for advancement. I guess that I was too honest and frank in my expressions. I was never accused of crawling past the brown-nosing and the hand-kissing that helped a few others to gain promotions without knowing too much about anything. After all, I was still available to assist where needed.

We had a couple of new purchasing agents brought in and the job requirements were more evenly spread. I was placed with one of these guys and since he knew that he was well liked by everyone in his crew, we will call him by the name given him by the group, "Renrut," believe it or not. Renrut was a good manager. He had the ability to make you feel as if you were a member of the team even though he was the boss. The two old men in the group were a fellow named Ross and me. The others were known as Renrut's Turks. They were young and wild but eager to learn. We had a good time together. I was assigned to the miscellaneous small parts (MSP) procurement desk. These were the items that would give me recognition after about fifteen years as an expert on fasteners.

MSP consist of all the fasteners that tie the aircraft together. We are talking about thousands of rivets, screws, pins, nuts, washers, blind bolts, tapered pins and bolts, and Dzus fasteners. If you attempted to name them all it would take more than a page even when eliminating the different sizes and lengths. The prices ranged from 12 cents to $525 (specials) each. All prices were based on the type of materiel called for in the blueprint. I was on this assignment for fifteen years and other than those fastener engineers (stress and structural) I had more knowledge of aircraft fasteners than practically anyone else in the plant. At times I could push some of those engineers to the wall.

Several things happened during this time period that I might as well mention to try and keep things in sequence.

The National Management Association club meetings were held offsite. That way whoever wanted to could get as stoned as they pleased without endangering their job unless they did not make it to work the next day. Once we had a speaker who was supposed to be a memory expert. Since I had taken his class about six months previous to the meeting, I thought that I would make him look good. He told me then that all he had to do to remember my name was to think of an old obsolete automobile and he could recall my name at any time in the future. Hell, it was not my fault that I believed him, I honestly thought that he could. I stood up and asked him my name. He kept pausing so I told him, "an old obsolete automobile." He couldn't remember my name. I sat down.

After his speech I went to the bar and got a bottle of beer. Damn if old BG didn't walk up to me and say as loud as he pleased, "You SOB, what the hell do you mean insulting our speaker tonight?" Boy, that shook me for about two seconds and I shot back, "Don't you ever call me that again. It is not my fault that the dumb bastard couldn't do what he had taught us that he could." I tried to tell BG that I had no intention to embarrass the man (his course had been well taught and the training was a success according to the individual's capacity) but to help him be more impressive. BG kept raising hell and cursing me in front of everyone until I had enough. I had one beer bottle in my hand. I picked up another with my other hand and told him unless he stopped insulting me I would put those bottles up alongside his head. One of his assistants stepped up and told me I could not talk to Mr. BG like that. I told him to get back into line for he would be next. BG was already loaded so he turned real red, wheeled around, and stomped out with his retinue following. I knew my butt was ripped open then. I couldn't get to sleep that night worrying about being fired the next day. Suddenly, I realized that we were not at work and there wasn't a damn thing he could do about what happened away from work. We were both free to break heads if necessary. To hell with it, I went to sleep and even the next morning gave it little thought. BG and I never spoke again to each other for over four years. I can say that caused me to be very sad for that length of time (alligators must still fly).

There was a group upstairs who were supposed to be analysts reviewing some of our purchase orders. I often wondered why someone figured we needed to be analyzed. Usually one man and one woman took special interest in analyzing my orders. She didn't know too much and he was a perfectionist (like taking all the pain in doing things and giving it to you in the neck). I put up with this for a while but finally began to be bothered by it. My desk was close to the next desk and when we had visitors we had to pull chairs in close to the desk. This made it pretty tight if more than one person was visiting. The buyer next to me had the president and vice president of one of his suppliers at his desk this day. Our desks were about three desks from Renrut's office. This character (the male analyst) came down from upstairs and threw a PO on my desk and said loudly, "If you call this quality, then you need some more training!" All of this was done and said for the benefit of the visitors. Adrenalin shot from my ears and I rose up from my chair to about level with the two visitors. I caught myself and stopped. I told that character to get the hell out of my sight and don't come down again. He had turned and broken to run and stumbled over another buyer's desk and almost fell. He got the hell out of there. I apologized to the two visitors and the buyer and told them that this was a prime example of some of the bastards we had to work with. Renrut came to his office door and looked around, then went back and sat down at his desk. After the visitors left, Mr. Upstairs came down and looked into Renrut's office and said, "Did you hear what he just called me?" Renrut looked at him and said, "So-o-o-o-o-o-o?" The analyst did not know that Renrut heard what he had said in front of our guests. That ended that relationship of analytical review because Renrut did not see the need to have his people's work reviewed by any outsiders anyway.

Naturally, this got back to Jack S. and I don't know what Renrut told him but Renrut's stock value and respect went off the scale among his crew (two old buzzards and the young Turks).

I had a bad experience during this span of time. On August 19, 1967, I was in a boating accident and was severely burned. From the waist down both legs, from the shoulder down both arms, and the left side of my face and neck with first-, second-, and third-degree burns. One of the fellows in the boat (another Lockheed employee) was killed. He was the one who had poured about one gallon of gasoline over my head. The other fellow (he owned the boat) was burned everywhere but his beltline area. The boat (a beautiful 23-foot cabin cruiser) had run out of gas and we were refueling. The boat had a big (for the time) 80 horsepower outboard motor. The boat was a 1966 Olympia and practically new. We had lost the pouring neck for those gas cans and were using a modified plastic milk jug for a funnel. We were 150 feet from the lakeshore and the water had 1-foot chops. When the motor ran out of gas it stopped, but the switch was still on (automatic starter). I was holding the milk jug and the fellow who was killed was pouring the gas. We had the tank about 7 feet from the motor well. Any gas fumes follow the contour of the boat to the lowest point, which was the motor well. The guy who owned the boat noticed that the switch was still on. Without saying anything to anyone he reached over and, inadvertently, turned the switch to "start" instead of "off" (this I learned from him later). All I knew was that all of a sudden there was a flash explosion and I was being splattered with gasoline.

I had on a cowboy type hat, a pair of wraparound sunglasses, two T-shirts (inside closed neck, outside was open neck type)—this probably saved my chest area because of the vacuum created—a pair of jeans, a pair of ankle-length boots, and my underwear shorts. I seemed to know exactly that I was on fire. I squeezed my eyes and mouth as tight as I could as I felt the liquid gas pouring over me. I was kneeling right next to the side of the boat, which was waist high. I raised up to jump out and my feet went out from under me and I went to my knees. If you have experienced a drop of fat popping out from a frying pan when cooking chicken and know what pain that little drop will create, then consider the pain coming from your whole body covered with burning gasoline. Time stopped and I had an experience (I have crossed the burning sands). It was spiritual and I won't attempt to explain it.

I could see nothing but fire that looked like the inside of an atomic explosion to my right. To my left was a scene that can be described but I will not. There was a conversation carried on that changed quite a bit of my outlook on life and people. I asked to return and was told that I would suffer as I had never experienced before. Go! Boom! I was back on fire. I felt for the side of the boat and pulled with my last strength until I fell over into the water. The first thing that came to my mind was the old navy instructions, go deep and long. I went so deep that it was purple and I felt no need to breathe but my arms felt as if they had rubber bands on them. Finally, I knew I had to come up and I saw the brighter water and swam for it. I broke the surface about 40 feet from the burning boat. I could see but it was blurry.

The flames from the boat were leaping into the air over 50 feet. The wind was rushing across the water toward the boat like a hurricane. I felt peaceful but concerned for the others. I felt stunned but no pain. I swam around the back of the boat and on the right side I saw the owner holding a rope that had fallen out of the fire but was still attached to the bow. He was holding the hand of the wife of the other fellow. Her head was under water and she was patting the water like a child. I started for them and I went under. I remembered that I still had on my boots and I pulled one off and something hit me in the head like a boxing glove and said plain as day, "You are drowning!" I kicked back to the surface but I realized that I had had it, no more strength. It had to be silently but I remember saying that I was sorry but there was nothing I could do to help. As I learned in the navy that in saltwater you lay back flat with your arms outspread and the front of your face would stay high enough out of the water for you to survive. This I did and I floated until some guys in another boat picked me up. That burning boat of ours made a helluva fire and other boats were coming from every direction. It looked like all the skin on my palms came off as they tried to pull me into the boat.

I was carried to a boat landing. Fortunately, there was a doctor there. No one could touch me as skin was off in all areas and there was no place to get a grip. The doctor asked me if I could get up. I could not move. He told me that he was going to grip my hair (saved by my hat) and my belt and snatch me up. I would have to lean against him and swing myself as he walked to get me inside the dock club. We made it and he had me packed in towels dipped into the drink box as I was already contaminated. Finally, an ambulance arrived (naturally, from a funeral home). The next thing I remembered was being carried into the hospital in Marietta. Everything was dark even though it was about 6:00 p.m. on a summer day. I saw my friend, the boat owner, lying on another gurney and he looked like a well-done lobster. I told him what he looked like and he told me to look at myself. Shock sometimes takes away all pain.

Since the hospital was a long way from home I asked to be sent to Grady Hospital in Atlanta, rated as one of the best burn centers in the Southeast. The doctor told me I would not make it. I told him that was one of my least worries. He and the ambulance driver agreed to take me to Grady. I arrived at 9:30 p.m. and had two doctors, two nurses, and two orderlies working on me until 3:45 a.m. the next morning. I was taken to the private hospital section of Grady known as Hughes-Spaulding Pavilion. The narcotic painkillers went to work and within thirty-six hours I was a full-blown addict. They built a tent over me for nothing could touch my body. The accident happened on a Saturday and the following Wednesday at 7:00 a.m. they started the cleanup surgery required to get all of the burned skin removed. I woke up the following Saturday at 7:30 p.m. still under the tent that covered me. My burn specialist told me that they had to keep me on the edge of death for that time because the pain would have killed me even if I regained semi-consciousness. I was getting morphine or Demerol every hour. I could see the pain like heat waves. If I saw the heat waves get above the level of the bed I needed a shot.

I had dropped from 170 pounds down to 148 pounds in 10 days. I had the one major operation, a plastic surgery job, many pain shots, plenty of grease (or lard), many gauze bandages (no pajamas or gowns), 21 gallons of saline solution, and much good food (specially prepared). I give my thanks to God for I still believe that I talked to Him, then to the doctors, nurses, and orderlies (bless their little scared hearts) for the way they took care of me. My only regret was that after a while I was not able to contact the doctor from the dock at the lake and properly show my appreciation for his help. One thing they could not understand was the fact that I never cried out in pain. I never cried out in pain because I knew that I would suffer and I expected it. After 12 weeks, I returned to work at 186 pounds and just a little blotchy.

The fellow who owned the boat lost all of his life functions twice on the operating table that Saturday night. He came back on his own without any resuscitation each time as the doctors were leaving the operating room. They made bets that he would not last through Monday. He was 54 years old and burned over 80 percent of his body. His mother (84 years old) came in on Monday evening and talked the fire out of him. He regained all normal functions in less than an hour. He was discharged on the thirty-second day after the accident. The doctors didn't believe it themselves even though they witnessed the whole thing (except the procedure). They had prepared to have him in the hospital for six to nine months if he survived. He was back to work four weeks before I began what could be called healing. The body of the fellow that was killed was recovered from the bottom of the lake. His wife had jumped overboard from the bow of the boat, he dived down, found her and brought her back to the surface, gave her hand to the owner holding the rope, and said, "Take care of her, I'm not going to make it," and sank out of sight. She was not injured. I wonder what all these good people have to say when they profess a belief yet act otherwise.

When I suffered the accident my desk was in good order. When I returned I picked up and caught it up and rolled on. Renrut and the crew had watched over it real well and it was still in good shape. I don't know as yet but my life was spared for some reason. I was 42 years old when it happened and the only thing I've noticed is that my attitude began to change slowly to be a better person. Most of my aircrafter's habits remained at a lower level. I found that I had a belief in God that transcended all religious denominations. I know that there is only one. I know that I will hear His voice again.

I had to relate that experience because it is important to the story of my life during the thirty-six years that I am writing about.

Chapter 11

All of our products were moving along and we were hiring left and right. About one-third of the way through the C-5A program we would peak at about 33,000 employees working out of the GELAC division. Five thousand of those employees were engineers. The purchasing crew (actual buyers) ranged between 200 and 300 people.

My desk reached the stage where it was covering every fastener used on every aircraft being manufactured at the time. I'm talking about volume buying. Because of their different functions, all aircraft did not use the same type of fastener across the board. Not only was I getting all the information I could on fasteners already in production but also early releases on what was on the planning boards at the suppliers. In the interest of standardizing fastener output to required needs and still having interchangeable parts for aircraft in general, especially military types, the government and the manufacturers got together and formed a group known as the Handbook Five Committee that would set standards for all the fasteners. These norms would control the yield, stress, and shear capabilities of the fasteners regardless of design and materiel metallurgy. Thus the field of competition was left intact. GELAC as well as the other aircraft manufacturers with the DOD and the civilian government had representatives on this committee. Our representative was a stress and structures engineer specializing in fasteners by the name of Eddie Bateh. Eddie remained on the committee for many years and several times held the one-year position of chairman. He knew as much or more than any other engineer at GELAC when it came to fasteners and the manufacturing suppliers of fasteners. Naturally, my first prerogative was to know Eddie and for him to know me. We developed a working relationship that lasted for over twenty years and I can say with pride, we were hell. I think that he enjoyed the chance of having someone to work with, through procurement, to show an equal interest in fasteners as much as I enjoyed working with him. Between the two of us we saved Lockheed a helluva lot of money in cost reductions.

There was a fastener known as the Taper-Lok pin that had been on the market before I began to learn about fasteners (other than the general knowledge of using them as an assembler). A company called Briles Manufacturing held the patent on the pins and the drills, including the tools for the installation of this fastener. Two brothers, Frank and Paul Briles, along with their engineer, Larry Salter, had conceived and produced this fastener. The Taper-Lok was accepted as almost phenomenal in its range of uses over the entire aircraft. It had a capability of exceeding the yield, stress, and shear functions required. At the time it was a sole source item. There was no competition because it had never been licensed to be produced by any other manufacturer. It was being used by many aircraft manufacturers; therefore stock was seldom readily available. I know that other customers were requesting that they establish a licensee or two to give better lead times on deliveries. Our usage was high and we often had shortages, so I added my suggestion that they license other sources.

Because I got to know the brothers very well I can afford to say that those two rascals had a falling out and separated. The result was that Frank would hold the patent and Paul would be the only licensee for a specified length of time. It was now time to get Paul approved, having organized and opened PB Fasteners Inc., qualified, producing, and selling Taper-Loks. I got a lot of negative reactions from some of the engineers (and a few materiel people) about approving PB Fasteners as a source. The brothers had great personalities and were well liked in the industry. I needed parts. The only way to guarantee supply was to have two sources immediately supplying the units to meet schedule. I went to the manager of that engineering group for the engineering division handling fasteners and explained the situation. I told him (and it was true) that we had some personality conflicts between these brothers and some members of engineering and procurement. I named names for him. I told him I did not give a damn about personalities and I needed parts and his help in getting same. By the way, I had known this manager since the good old manufacturing days. He asked me since the need seemed to be so critical how soon could I have the vendor here to qualify. This was a Friday so I told him I could have the people at 8:00 a.m. the following Monday morning. He said that was good and he would have the necessary engineering, quality control, and production people available in his office. I called Paul and told him to bring all the materiel required plus his sales manager, engineer, and quality control manager with him and be in my office by 7:00 a.m. Monday morning. Hopefully, we would have him qualified before the day was over.

Paul was in my office that Monday and we went over to Hal Gilpin's office and met with two engineers (one I had named who had opposed the source), one quality control supervisor, and a production manager. The PB Fasteners people made their presentation. Hal asked a few questions. There were a few questions from the others on routine things. Hal asked if there were any specifics that would not allow PB Fasteners to be approved other than the need of onsite QC and engineering approval. There were no objections. Since QC had a man on the West Coast and Eddie was at a Handbook Five Committee meeting in the area, these two could make those checkouts and report and the approval given to me, who in turn would inform PB Fasteners, who in turn could begin to make deliveries where on receipt would also be given first article inspection. PB Fasteners was approved. All of the above is known as proper expediting without the bull. Whatever personality problems existed disappeared and after the customary rumblings nothing more was heard from that direction. We began to receive quantities of Taper-Loks and shortage problems on that item were solved. All of the other customers for military usage were happy also. Other situations similar to this one will show up now and then in this narrative but I eventually reached that point where at least people would listen to my suggestions before giving me the brushoff. I worked for GELAC, not just people.

I don't remember getting a promotion to semi-senior buyer. I must have gotten one for I had the classification sometime between 1968 and 1969. I guess this was at a very busy time. Renrut had to have given it because I was working for him at the time. Belatedly, thanks buddy, for I know Jack S. didn't do a damn thing. It would not be too long before Renrut would be leaving for an assignment with the corporation (in California). I probably got on Renrut's nerves at times but I think he understood that I was working for the benefit of good old GELAC and us, too. I saw no need to travel for my rapport with my sources was good and we had confidence in each other. I never cried wolf. I looked forward to it for within the next six or seven years I would have enough experience to start visiting vendor plants.

About this time, maybe a little earlier, the corporation (CALAC) had set up an organization called the Central Procurement Agency (CPA). Dale Harris, CPA's manager, procured most of the common items through this agency for the divisions of the corporation. All of the buyers in the divisions placed their orders directly with the suppliers holding CPA contracts. The result was a great savings based on the total quantities required to fill the CPA contracts. I noticed after a while that GELAC was using more fasteners (especially of a certain type) than the other three divisions put together. I brought this to Renrut's attention and got with Eddie and the three of us came to the conclusion that if we convinced Dale to do a little negotiating with certain vendors, especially the Taper-Lok people, we should get lower prices on volumes beyond that of the CPA contracts. Dale considered our idea to be a good one. He wanted to make sure any cost reduction gained would be reflected in the overall CPA contract. Hell, that was right up our alley.

We had competitive sources for the torque-off collars that went with Taper-

Lok pins. Naturally, we went after cost reductions on those sapsuckers also. Since we had a firm contract for the total quantity of C-5As, even though they would be released in increments, I decided to go out and bid the next increment totally. This would eliminate bimonthly purchase orders. After much negotiating one of the sources came in with a very attractive bid. With approvals from Renrut and Jack S., we placed the order on a competitive bid and the savings for that series of deliveries was $987,000 (you are damn right, that is pretty close to $1 million). I don't even remember if I got a cost reduction certificate for that one. One thing I did get was a good performance review and that was from Renrut. One of his greatest marks was my job knowledge. Renrut knew that was right. Now was the time for Bigfoot to remove that so-called performance report (boomsheet) from my record. In his mind it probably was so insignificant that he had forgotten his promise. I imagine most of my supervisory performance graders recognized that my patience was such that possibly I would not make a good purchasing agent (BS). That could be the reason that my potential grades got above satisfactory only a few times over all the years. My performance for nine years on the production floor cancels that impression. That salt is still in my hip pocket. By the end of this narrative you will be able to calculate that not only did I save Lockheed my total salary, but also my benefits and retirement costs.

I understood that Renrut had a degree in airport management and he had confidence in himself. Renrut was a human being; therefore, he had some faults but his balance was in the upper level. He could be considered a good manager in the tightest situations. I remember having to tell my boss in the manufacturing area that my review of my employees was my opinion and nothing could change it.

We had been buying patented fasteners from a single source as per standards engineering. The different sizes and quantities were procured on an individual basis. Having acquired more explicit usage requirements through contacts with the manufacturing departments I decided to go for a blanket procurement linking all sizes to one cost coverage. There was a total of fifty-eight different items (sizes, lengths, etc.) all under the same basic part number. They were all bid as a blanket request for one year with appropriate stock levels to be maintained and delivery on request. I had to furnish the approximate usage of each item per aircraft times the total of aircraft on our contract for a year, adding a small percentage as excess for normal shop loss. I reviewed the average cost over the past year (schedule rate the same) for each item. I took the highest-priced items and the lowest-priced items and got the average price covering the entire lot. This meant that the highest-priced items would be less and the lowest-priced items would be higher. There would be individual purchases placed for each item but the price of all would be the same for each. There was much time spent in developing this information. This research included having our auditor check out the manufacturing cost of the source producing these parts. The supplier and myself could not come to any agreement over the phone so I invited the inside sales manager, the quality control manager, the production manager, and the company comptroller down to negotiate the deal. I found out something that I won't divulge at this time because nothing was dishonest or unethical about it. It is known as CYOA (cover your own ass). This is an acceptable American business practice that is still used. The government and politicians are the granddaddies of this practice. It makes common sense.

Renrut was out of town on a trip. I had the guy (Ross) sitting in for him with me. The gentlemen from the supplier came in at about 10:00 a.m. I guess they were looking for a long negotiation session and so was the fellow sitting in for Renrut. In my opinion most negotiating sessions are like diplomatic meetings—a bunch of beating around the bush trying to reach a conclusion. Go to a negotiation prepared! We went into Renrut's office and sat down. I looked at the inside sales manager and said that we both knew something. He nodded and I asked him for his bid total. He stated over $560,000. I looked everyone in the eye and said I would give $442,000 with no ups or downs to consider. His people looked at him and Renrut's sit-in looked at me. As previously stated, I had had our auditor look over the amount and come to the conclusion that my offer would cover their production plus 15 percent profit. (Any company that could not make a 15 percent profit, in my opinion, shouldn't be in business.) The sales manager asked if he might use my phone. I told him to take all the time he deemed necessary on my nickel. We left them in the office.

After a short while he called us in and simply asked, "Where is the contract?" That contract was signed and the savings to Lockheed was almost $120,000. We went to lunch and they left and were able to check out of their plant by 5:00 p.m. the same day. There was no feeling of having lost anything between the two companies. That company was one of the best suppliers during my time at GELAC and is still one of the biggest producers of aircraft parts (among many other items) in the nation. There was a sense of rapport and support with that company and its people for many years to follow. A very congenial and respectful relationship remained for the balance of my time at GELAC. The savings were based on the difference of what that quantity of parts would have cost if bought on an individual purchase order pricing.

There was another time when I was involved in a negotiation with one of our best suppliers. This concerned a part that was patented; in other words, sole source. Renrut was still with us and I had considered all angles I could think of to get a better price on an item that we could only obtain from one source. This particular part request came from Warner Robins Air Force Base in Georgia. It concerned the modification of the C-141 aircraft. If you have a number of access doors in the wing of an aircraft there is a tendency for cracks to show up in the bolt holes around that area. The stresses may originate out in the skin of the wing or some structure in the area and become cracks at the first edge it encounters, like holes. This was a critical condition and a fix was required immediately. Our source had designed and developed a sleeve (tapered) that was inserted into the hole, creating a tension there that would turn a stress condition back into the stressed area. This had been proven to eliminate the problem of the hole failing (by cracking open). Our internal military group (handling military requirements) had called me and indicated the seriousness of the situation and requested that I procure these new items ASAP. Renrut suggested that we give them all the help that we were able to provide. I called the supplier and requested that because of the urgency of the requirement that they send some of their people down to negotiate the earliest possible delivery and cost.

We went to another part of the plant so as not to be disturbed for we figured this time we were going to have a drawn out negotiation period. The military people had advised that the colonel at Warner Robins had said he was not going to pay over $187,500 for the whole requirement (there were a number of C-141s that had developed this discrepancy). I had my fill of know-it-all superior officers in the navy. They have a tendency to think that their orders are the law outside of military bases also. I always hoped and tried to negotiate for the advantage of Lockheed and our customer (the government) while keeping my suppliers in business. I made a note of the military cost limit and proceeded in my tried and true method.

Renrut, our auditor, and I met with the district sales manager, the plant manager, and the comptroller of the supplier. I had already supplied all info available to our auditor and he was ready. Renrut was there as an observer. Their opening bid was $225,000 for the total. I did not accept so we began to negotiate. I finally got them down to around $200,000. I called the military salespeople and informed them of the offer, but I was told again that the colonel was not going to approve anything more than his original offer and that was final. We negotiated some more, and we got them down to $195,700. The Lockheed group went outside to discuss this last bid. The auditor told me his figures indicated that the supplier was down to about 15 percent profit at the most. The auditor and I accepted this quotation. I checked with Renrut and he said that I was the negotiator and I would be the one to make the decision. (Go Renrut!) I said we buy. We went back in, signed off, and closed the contract.

I told our supplier that we appreciated their effort and we felt we had agreed on a price that was acceptable to both of us. They agreed and left with a firm purchase order to proceed with production and to give us the earliest delivery date. Their commitment was four weeks if no major problems developed. This was their first major order for that part even though it had already proven effective. I never mentioned the colonel's conversation with our military group. I called the military salesperson and told him that we had an order in production for $195,700 with delivery in about four weeks instead of the normal six. He said that he could not tell the colonel that. I told him the order was placed and closed and the colonel could go to hell (in a diplomatic manner). We were his supplier and we meant to see that our product was well supported to fulfill his needs. How we did that was our business as long as it was at the best pricing available. I took for granted that he would be able to do that in his best diplomatic jargon. At least materiel never heard anything further from the colonel (nope, I ain't gonna tell you his name).

Renrut accepted a promotion to fill Dale's position as manager of the Central Procurement Agency at corporate headquarters. I could think of no one who was more qualified, though I sure did hate to see him go.

Chapter 12

This was the year of the great cost reduction effort (1971). I qualified for thirty-five cost reduction certificates. Some of those were Buck Hunter awards (BHAs). This award consisted of a dollar bill in a standard picture frame. One enjoyment I got out of the Buck Hunter awards was that after I had accumulated $14 worth, I bought a case of beer that weekend, cut the grass (front and rear), and washed both cars (the old one and the not so old one) before the beer ran out. Can you imagine how well the grass would have been cut and how clean the cars would have been had I received more BHAs, especially since I had never been able to buy a new car up to this point? I also went back and qualified as a cardiopulmonary resuscitation technique instructor during this year. I taught fellow workers, the ushers at Atlanta-Fulton County baseball stadium, and several other smaller groups. Somewhere down the line I will tell of my own experiences in lifesaving I was able to accomplish.

A group from the NAACP (one of my favorite organizations) came through my area observing how many Negroes were doing this type of work. They were escorted by J. H. "Pat" Patterson (of the community relations department, a part of personnel division). There were only about seven (out of approximately two hundred) other Negroes in the division other than myself. They indicated, according to Pat, that I was too light to be considered Negro and would not be counted. Damn if I didn't think I had left that BS when I stopped riding the public transit system in Atlanta years ago. You know, like, being too light to sit in the back and too olive to sit in the front. I quit when the system switched to buses and I could not sit in the operator's chair in the back of the streetcar. I had developed the attitude that to hell with it (catching hell from both sides) and scraped up my own transportation. The people who knew me accepted me, regardless of race, as just another guy. I acted accordingly, just like any other guy. But I'll be damned if anyone was better than me. Those who had education and achievements and the ones who did not were equally respected by me for what they did know. I gained from all of them. My opinions were developed from people, the ones with a theory and the ones who could not spell "theory" but were able to perform practically any type of job with proper training. Every person in the world can do something in the field of accomplishment. This was my philosophy and therefore I became almost a loner. I developed the two personalities (being Gemini), Hap at work and Dad at home. It was hell at times to keep the two separate but I managed.

The purchasing agent who took Renrut's place was a fellow named Norm Bowker. Norm was one of the guys who had climbed the ladder up the gauntlet of steps and not lost his pleasant personality and ability to work with, while managing, people. Norm, who was also a CPR instructor, and I worked for a long time with the Red Cross in that effort and in recruiting blood donors. (How about over ten years?) We recruited over a thousand donating members for the blood banks, some donating over 15 gallons individually over that time period. I personally donated about 96 pints (over 17 years) to the Red Cross and hospitals for individual friends. As a man, Norm was one of the finest people I have worked for or been associated with. We had a good group and everything operated in a highly professional manner. Norm retired before I did and I know he is enjoying his retirement. He moved North and his one visit confirmed that he is still highly interested in and doing community work.

We had peaked with about 33,000 employees scattered throughout the Southeast in feeder plants and special engineering divisions. In my opinion we wasted a lot of money on engineers but that is the way things are when the DOD says, Go, go! Everybody was busy, working overtime, and some were really screwing up. The Vietnam War and the Cold War were slowing down but management and DOD said we had to be prepared. This I could agree with except that we did not have to plunder the taxpayers to satisfy the whims of some big generals sitting on their fannies in the Pentagon coming up with their own request for changes after the program started. We had enough improvements being made in the systems without their (mostly frivolous) help. I picked up a few more certificates and the best review I have ever received.

The problem with the cracks around the holes in the wing through which the access doors were installed on the C-130 and the C-141 wings at Warner Robins Air Force Base was critical. The colonel needed his repair parts and we all agreed that it was one helluva problem. It must be remembered that the fix required a new steel alloy (bolt to fit the sleeve, mentioned above) but the new design had been completed and approved. This took the coordination of the plant engineering, the vendor's entire crew, and the patience of the colonel. (Colonels don't have patience.) In my opinion he assumed that this should be an item off the shelf in some vendor's plant. He raised pure hell every day and kept his people worrying me and the source constantly. He could not understand why he did not receive his parts. The customer is supposed to get all of their information from the military or commercial sales group and not the company buyers. That is, except for some generals, colonels, and lieutenants who take it on themselves to call the buyer thinking to impress them with their importance. Crap! We buyers catch enough hell from our own management to expedite deliveries. We buyers always fully recognize our need to satisfy our customers more so than sales organizations. Agitation does not improve the problem.

Holy Holy! The great day arrived! It was decided that the time had come for me to travel to the supplier's plant. It was over eleven years that I had been in procurement and now I was finally experienced and qualified to visit the vendor's facility. Do you people who have received graduate degrees remember how you felt after all the years of study? I could now join your ranks for I had finally achieved the same level (you would think). Other than the engineers, no one else at the plant knew more than I did about tapered sleeves and the bolts (including all of the other MSP). The second week in January, one of the assistant directors of materiel came down to my desk and asked the status on one of the items. The bolts had to be of the same alloy as the sleeves. I told him we were looking at four weeks before we could expect delivery. His visit to my desk was one week after the order had been placed. I did not get the impression that he heard me. This was on a Thursday afternoon about 4:00 p.m.

HIM: "Hap, I want you to go to Detroit and pick up those parts and bring them back with you. I am calling RR (his name for the company travel agent) and will tell him to get you on that flight from Atlanta at 6:20 p.m. tonight. He will have a car at the airport waiting for you and you will be in the vendor's plant early Friday morning to get those parts and return on the earliest flight back to Atlanta." (Sounded just like the colonel.)

ME: "Yes sir, I will do my best."

I knew damn well that I would not be able to leave the plant at 5:00 p.m. (the earliest RR could make arrangements and get my tickets and reservations to me), drive home (18 miles), pack some type of bag, and be at the airport (8 miles beyond my home) to catch an airplane at 6:20 p.m. I told RR to make the ticket for the 6:20 p.m. shuttle trip to Detroit and I would come by and pick up the tickets. I arrived in Detroit around 8:30 a.m. Friday morning.

I got a new Ford Torino and the city map and proceeded 35 miles into northeast Detroit. On arriving at the plant I notified the Holiday Inn (further up I-94) that I would not check in until after 5:00 p.m., confirming my reservation. My contact, inside sales manager Joe, picked me up in the lobby and we proceeded to the sales department. There I met my normal contact, Otto. Although I had never met Otto in person, he was everything I expected talking over the phone with him for at least nine years. We were old friends. Joe sat with us and we went over the whole situation with this particular unit. The raw materiel was still in production at the steel plant in Reading, Pennsylvania. Our customer, the air force, could not understand that this was a completely new formula for a special steel requirement.

At noon Joe suggested that we go to lunch. I had been in discussion with engineering, sales, production, and quality control people so I thought that we would go down to the company cafeteria and have lunch. No sir, up shows the plant manager and the others (except Otto, he was an hourly employee) and we proceeded to one fabulous restaurant and had a lunch that must have cost at least $22 (big money in those days) each. Boy, I was eating up on the hog's hipbone. I briefly thought that they might be attempting to influence me, but the thought vanished for I had known them too long. The general sales manager was there also. His name was Lou and we kicked off a relationship that would last for years. After lunch we returned to the plant to follow up on information that had been promised by the steel company in Reading. I was also given a tour of the manufacturing area. I met individual workers plus the union shop stewards. I saw open orders for Lockheed in the process of production. As we walked, they explained the complete types and methods of production on their lines. No one could ask for a better education in the manufacturing process. I decided right then that this would be my standard request—to tour the manufacturing area of each plant that I visited—from now on.

It was about 40 degrees in Atlanta when I left and 14 degrees in Detroit. The wind was not blowing hard and those fellows seemed chilled. They could not understand how I could go about with my collar open, being from the South. I had spent millions of dollars with this company and by their hospitality they showed that it was appreciated. I left and checked into the motel. My room was on the street level. The snow was packed against the wall and it was damp and cold. They claimed that they had no other rooms. I let them know in no uncertain terms that I would not be back on any return visit unless the location of the room was improved. I did not know at the time that I would be back more times than I thought.

I went back to the plant on Saturday morning. We checked with the steel plant in Reading; they were working overtime as promised. Actually, they worked around the clock until that materiel was finished. My supplier was also working overtime on our (and other customers') requirements. I called my big boss and gave him the latest status and told him I would call again on Monday. I then went over to my sister-in-law's house for the weekend.

I returned to the plant on Monday morning and checked on the steel mill. They were holding to their committed schedule with hopes of cutting it down to ship earlier. This was the first week after the original purchase order was placed. The lead time then was four weeks. My reason for being at the vendor's plant was to expedite that delivery as much as possible. I spent the rest of the day checking out the status of my other open orders and a final call was made to Reading. Each step in the manufacturing of this special steel was proceeding on time. The holdup was the time required for each procedure. You cannot rush through a manufacturing process. This was a completely new formula. I returned to the motel and called my boss. I gave him all of the details and asked him why in hell was it necessary for me to remain in Detroit with my desk and work going to pot while it would be at the most three more weeks before we could get a delivery. He told me if I felt that at this time there was nothing further I could do, I should catch the next thing flying. I did, first thing Tuesday morning.

I arrived at Lockheed just after noon. I reported to my supervisor and department manager (the one who had told me to come home). In about an hour I was told to go and report to the third-level manager (assistant director of materiel). His name was Harry also, but he was a heavy-set fellow who wore a size 6½ shoe. I'll call him "Perry." He thought that Georgia Tech was God's gift to the un-anointed engineer. He was not an alumnus of the school but he was their biggest football booster. I sat down and gave him, in detail, every move and reaction I had received in Detroit. This included all the up-to-date information available within the last 14 hours. I told him the best delivery date was still within the next three weeks. His first question was, "Will it ship this week?" After I recovered from being knocked over by that feather I answered, "No sir, but I will be following it every two or three hours to gather the latest status." He said, "Good, stick with it and advise me of any significant changes."

Not only did I have my regular problems going on but the buyer at Warner Robins was calling every two or three hours wanting to know the status on those parts from Detroit. Believe it or not, the value of the open purchase orders on my desk for MSP was $14 million. We are talking about nuts and bolts. On Thursday at about 4:00 p.m., who walked up but Perry wanting to know if Detroit had shipped. I told him no. He said, "Hap, call RR and have him cut the paperwork for you to leave tonight on the 6:20 flight for Detroit so as to get the parts out over the weekend."

If you think that I was going to tell him where to go then you are crazy also. We made the arrangements and I left that Friday morning on the Pan Am shuttle flight from Atlanta to Detroit at 6:20 a.m.

The only difference this time was that snow was as deep as the hipbone of a gravedigger in Detroit. As this big Boeing 747 came in for a landing the wheels were down, the engines were cut, and the glide path was perfect. I was riding in the second seat from the nose, forward under the pilot. All of a sudden something kicked me in the butt, slammed me against the back of the seat, and I spotted the tail of a DC-8 less than 50 feet below us. I had no physical or organic reaction (like crapping all over myself) because it was over before it happened. As we circled around for another landing the pilot announced that we would be slightly delayed because of traffic on the runway. After we were on the ground and deplaning, I stopped at the exit door and looked at the pilot. He looked at me. I said, "I help to build these big sapsuckers and that was some helluva flying." "Did you see that?" he asked. I told him where I was sitting and he said, "Thank you." I replied, "No, we thank you." I hoped I would not have to come to Detroit again soon, especially in the wintertime. Little did I know.

The same routine was repeated at the vendor's plant but this time I went to lunch with Otto. We went to a little restaurant-bar in a Polish American neighborhood. The atmosphere was as if we were in Poland. The tables were covered with red and white checked tablecloths and the waitress was about 180 pounds and wore an apron just like the tablecloths. The menu was mainly soups for lunch. There were all types of old farming equipment and machinery hanging on the walls and from the ceiling. There were several hacksaw type items that had chains of different sizes stretched on them (not blades). Curiosity got the best of me and I asked Otto what were those things. He said, in a matter of fact fashion, that those were "Polack" chain saws. Everyone burst into laughter, including me. Even if I had figured it out, damn if I was going to call them that. The customers were playing checkers and other games. The atmosphere was just like a family gathering. I enjoyed that lunch better than the ones I had with the wheels.

We returned to the plant and Otto got a call from guess who? It was the great colonel from Warner Robins.

Otto: "Good afternoon sir, what can I do for you?"

I could hear some shouting and hoorah over the phone but I could not make it out. Otto turned a little red and began to take short breaths. I wondered why a colonel would be calling the hourly salesperson instead of some manager.

Otto: "Look sir, I don't have to take those insults from you or anybody else. The buyer from Lockheed is sitting at my desk now expediting his orders to fill your requirements." There was a short pause. "Sir, I'm sorry but you don't have any open orders for this materiel received here on file." (Pause.) "Hold on sir! I am not one of your damn airmen and I don't have to listen to this bullshit. I resent you speaking to me in that manner. You get your buyers off of their asses and place some orders for we are going full speed on Lockheed's orders, which we know are for you. If you can't correct your own situation, then call my boss!" With that Otto slammed the phone down on the receiver. It always makes me feel good to see a good man assert himself, especially with some high-ranking dumbass. Otto turned and said that I would probably have a new contact within a few hours for he knew he was going to get fired. I bet him a colonel would not let his (Otto's) manager know that he was as dumb as he presented himself to you. He did not and Otto received no more calls from the colonel.

The balance of my visit went as before. The delivery schedule was still two weeks away, but with hope of improving. Hello, sister-in-law, I'm here again. Hello, boss, can I come home?

My report to my bosses was as expected. Perry came by and asked if they were shipping this coming Friday. Perry just did not seem to understand. I told him that they were making every effort and it might just be possible. That Thursday morning he asked me if they had shipped. I told him no. He blew his stack. "Dammit, you told me they would be here by tomorrow. What in hell are you saying now? Did you lie hoping they would make it?" I apologized (Oh, boy!) to him and told him that I had made a mistake by not giving him the facts in an understandable manner. Perry told me to call RR and get my ticket, etc., etc., and head for "Deetroit." RR asked me if Perry didn't know at least one day ahead when he was sending me to Detroit. I did not answer. Hello, Otto, I'm back again. Hello, sister-in-law, I'm back again. The raw materiel has arrived at the supplier's plant. Otto and all are expediting like hell in production to speed up their process as much as possible. Boss, can I come home?

Meanwhile back at the ranch the buyer from Warner Robins is calling me every hour asking for status. I know from military experience that he can't tell an officer anything when the officer doesn't know from Adam's housecat about what the hell is going on. I knew that that buyer was growing little ulcers on top of his big ulcers. I'd be damned if they were going to give me ulcers again. I told the poor fellow that I would call him every time I had new information, at least three times a day, and if he called me one more time I was going to hang up on him and he could call my bosses from then on. I could feel the hurt in his voice. He did not call me anymore. Hell, I had Perry to deal with.

This is no joke. The following Thursday morning (at least it was not Thursday evening) Perry asked me if the parts had shipped. Since I was talking to Otto two times a day it was a sure thing that the parts would be ready to ship no later than that Monday morning (the fourth week as promised). I told Perry that the parts would ship by air express Monday morning and I would advise him with the air shipment bill number at the same time. Perry said, "Good, now call RR etc., etc., and get there in the morning to guarantee that those parts are shipped." The goddamn parts ain't supposed to ship until Monday morning and he wants me there Friday and the weekend to make sure. Hello, Detroit, hello, Otto, hello, sister-in-law, I'm back but I won't bother you this time. Are they shipping Monday morning, Otto? I believe you. Hello, boss, can I come home? The parts were received Monday evening, went through inspection, were accepted as correct to specs, and were immediately sent to Warner Robins. The colonel was happy, the air force buyer was happy, Lockheed was happy, the vendor was happy, my bosses were happy, Perry was happy, and I was having fits of joy. After all, I had accomplished qualification and experience in four weeks, something I could not do in eleven years. The wheels that be now knew that I was capable of visiting a supplier's plant.

I got a new group supervisor (next up from purchasing agent) and having looked over my past reviews he point blank asked me just what in hell did I do other than buy MSP. From the money value and status of delivery, cost reduction, and comments from other in-plant organizations it was more than just buying MSP. He asked me to write out my job description as I performed it. All the grades were tops in my opinion. If anything was outstanding it would have to be in cost reduction and it wasn't even mentioned. The only reason that in "optional factors" there was no comment is the bald-faced fact that nobody considered me as having any potential for upgrade. This tells me that some bastard somewhere was holding me down. This is one thing for which I will never forgive Lockheed management.

Harry Leo Hudson served in the navy, 1943–46.

The *Atlanta Daily World* carried brief announcements of Harry Hudson's promotion to supervisor.
Photo courtesy of the *Atlanta Daily World*.

Hudson, on the right end, receives a safety award along with members of his integrated crew. On the left end is Lockheed Executive Assistant to the Executive Vice President Charles Wagner (who would become president of Lockheed-California in 1965). Hudson family photograph.

Built during World War II, Air Force Plant No. 9 was among the largest manufacturing facilities in the world. The massive plant formed the setting of Harry Hudson's professional career.
Bell Aircraft Georgia Division Collection, 1942–1945, Kennesaw State University Archives, courtesy of Hugh Neeson.

Hudson on a runway with a C-5 Galaxy, ca. 1969.
Hudson family photograph.

Hudson saved many of his evaluation forms. Shown are forms from June–September 1955, when he supervised a segregated, all-black crew; March 1959–March 1960, when he supervised an integrated crew; February 1962–February 1963, when he served as a buyer; and April 1969–April 1970, when he served as a "semi-senior" buyer. He received consistently high scores on initiative, attitude, and ability to work with others. From papers accompanying Hudson manuscript.

LOCKHEED AIRCRAFT CORPORATION
GEORGIA DIVISION

CERTIFICATE OF TRAINING COMPLETION

THIS IS TO CERTIFY THAT H. L. HUDSON , EMPLOYEE NUMBER 543867 OF DEPARTMENT 21-13 , HAS SUCCESSFULLY COMPLETED COURSE BASIC BLUEPRINT READING (201) CONDUCTED BY O. L. KELLER, SR. FOR A TOTAL OF 20 HOURS ON SEPTEMBER 12, 1952. (GRADE 97)

ATTENTION: DEPARTMENT CLERK

POST THE ABOVE INFORMATION TO THIS EMPLOYEE'S KARDEX SERVICE RECORD SHEET IMMEDIATELY AND INITIAL BELOW. DELIVER WHITE CERTIFICATE TO ABOVE EMPLOYEE AND FILE YELLOW COPY IN HIS PERMANENT PERSONNEL RECORD FOLDER.

TRAINING MANAGER

POSTED BY Sally Jones

Form 4266A-3

Hudson received intensive training as one of what he called Lockheed's first "super Negroes" in 1952. This certificate, for basic blueprint reading, represented forty of more than two hundred hours of training that Hudson and his initial colleagues received in the fall of 1952. Hudson received certification to teach blueprint reading for the Cobb County Public Schools. From papers accompanying Hudson manuscript.

LOCKHEED AIRCRAFT CORPORATION
GEORGIA DIVISION

CERTIFICATE OF TRAINING COMPLETION

THIS IS TO CERTIFY THAT H. L. HUDSON EMPLOYEE NUMBER 543867 OF DEPARTMENT 23-09 HAS SUCCESSFULLY COMPLETED COURSE 127-36 MANAGEMENT DEVELOPMENT TRAINING FOR SUPERVISORS CONDUCTED BY THE TRAINING DEPARTMENT FOR A TOTAL OF 160 HOURS ON DECEMBER 28, 1957. GRADE S

TRAINING MANAGER

Form 4266A-4

Hudson completed 160 hours of "management development training for supervisors" in December 1957. In 1958, Hudson was quietly assigned the first integrated crew at Lockheed-Georgia.
From papers accompanying Hudson manuscript.

LOCKHEED-GEORGIA COMPANY
A DIVISION OF LOCKHEED AIRCRAFT CORPORATION
MARIETTA, GEORGIA

Certificate of Training Completion

EMPLOYEE TIME   Date 03-23-63

This is to certify that H L HUDSON   Employee number 543867   of Department 5314

has successfully completed

VALUE ANALYSIS SEMINAR   Course No. VAS63

Conducted by THE LOCKHEED MANAGEMENT CLUB-GEORGIA   for 6 hours

H L Hudson
TRAINING MANAGER

LOCKHEED-GEORGIA COMPANY
A DIVISION OF LOCKHEED AIRCRAFT CORPORATION
MARIETTA, GEORGIA

Certificate of Training Completion

EMPLOYEE TIME   Date 04-10-63

This is to certify that H L HUDSON   Employee number 543867   of Department 5314

has successfully completed

AMERICAN ECONOMIC SYSTEM   Course No. CD1021

Conducted by THE TRAINING DEPARTMENT   for 24 hours

H L Hudson
TRAINING MANAGER

Hudson continued to pursue training on his own time. Courses varied from value analysis and procurement training to the American economic system and developing our sense of closure. Lockheed maintained one of the most active training departments in American industry. From papers accompanying Hudson manuscript.

CERTIFICATE OF TRAINING - EMPLOYEE'S OWN TIME

THIS IS TO CERTIFY THAT H. L. HUDSON   EMPLOYEE NO. 543867   DEPT. 23-09
HAS SUCCESSFULLY COMPLETED:

DATE	COURSE	HOURS	GRADE
JUNE 14, 1960	DEVELOPING OUR SENSE OF CLOSURE	18	A

CONDUCTED BY:
THE TRAINING DEPARTMENT

R. L. Hudson
TRAINING MANAGER

LOCKHEED AIRCRAFT CORPORATION, GEORGIA DIVISION
FORM GD893-1

LOCKHEED - GEORGIA COMPANY
A DIVISION OF LOCKHEED AIRCRAFT CORPORATION
MARIETTA GEORGIA

Certificate of Training Completion

SHARED TIME   Date 12-18-63

This is to certify that H. L. HUDSON   Employee number 543867   of Department 53-14

has successfully completed

PROCUREMENT TRAINING   Course No. 177

Conducted by THE TRAINING DEPARTMENT   for 18 hours

R. L. Hudson
TRAINING MANAGER

LOCKHEED-GEORGIA COMPANY

Cost Reduction Citation

This citation recognizes your significant contribution to Lockheed's constant effort to reduce costs wherever and whenever possible.

Congratulations and thanks to

H. L. HUDSON

52-24   DEPARTMENT

543 867   EMPLOYEE NUMBER

ORG. CRR. NUMBER: 51-107-24

[X] BUCK HUNTER AWARD
[ ] NOT BUCK HUNTER

SIGNATURE   DATE: JULY 1971

A copy of this citation is in your personnel file.

---

from the desk of **HAP HUDSON**

Cost Savings & Reductions
Approx — Value:
1,223,798.²²
• since 1968
4/76

Hudson received numerous citations for reducing cost in his years as a buyer, including many coveted Buck Hunter awards. Hudson calculated that he had saved Lockheed more than $1.2 million in the years 1968–76 (handwritten note appended to Hudson's cost reduction citations). From papers accompanying Hudson manuscript.

Chapter 13

During this time we lost one of our people. Jack S., our department manager, choked on a chunk of steak while out to dinner and did not survive. From what I came to understand, everything but the Heimlich method was used in an attempt to save him. The restaurant was located across the street and about one block away from one of Atlanta's finest hospital. By the time he arrived at the hospital over fifteen minutes had passed. He was given the best medical attention available. CPR training tells you that after four minutes brain cell deterioration is in process. By seven minutes (if you survive), brain damage is such that you will probably be in a vegetative state. After nine minutes you are dead. Jack S. was put on life support systems for several months but he never regained consciousness. This was a blow to his department because it was accidental. If he had been ill for some length of time it would not have shocked us. As I earlier indicated, Jack S. was a helluva character. A number of people disliked him (including me) but held no hate for him. He would cross our thoughts for some time to come.

Just before we moved to the B-95 building I was walking down the hall in the T-400 building and two people rushed past me going upstairs. I looked up the stairs and someone said something that sounded like "heart attack." I was a CPR instructor at the time so I went up the steps and found several fellows around one of our co-workers on the floor. One man was giving mouth-to-mouth resuscitation and another was doing heart compressions. The fellow giving mouth-to-mouth began to act as if he was going to throw up in the victim's face. When giving mouth-to-mouth resuscitation you have to concentrate on what you are doing and not the fact that the victim is spitting mucus in your face and mouth when the compressed air comes out. Most people are more competent at giving the heart compressions than the mouth-to-mouth breathing because if you pay attention to the mucus hitting you in the face and mouth you are going to throw up. It takes a certain kind of individual to perform that procedure.

I tapped the person giving mouth-to-mouth and told him to go and wash up. I began to give the mouth-to-mouth. Having been a pre-med student (I once ate my lunch sitting next to a partially dissected cat), I had the ability to concentrate on what I was doing rather than the surrounding conditions. After about four minutes we were relieved by another pair. Someone gave me a big wet towel and I then realized how much snot (excuse the expression) I had all over my face. The medics had been called and were on the way. I then had time to examine the victim. Color had partially returned to his lips and his pupils were beginning to contract. I checked his left carotid artery but detected no pulse. I checked his right carotid artery and found a slight pulse. I found a slight pulse in his right arm, nothing in his left arm. Those pulses were coming from the compressions. I thought of an aneurysm, why I am not sure. The medics arrived and immediately put him into the ambulance for transport to the hospital. I noticed that there was only one medic in the back so I went with them to give heart compressions (the equipment they have now had not been invented). Standing up and bending over, I almost developed a hernia in that careening vehicle before we got to the hospital.

I gave compressions right on into the emergency room. The doctor stopped me and said, "What are you doing?" I said, "Hell, I thought I was giving him heart compressions." He said, "What for? Come and look." He pointed out the grayish skin color, the pupils completely dilated to cover the eyes, and the coldness of the body. The doctor said, "Your effort is appreciated but now useless. We thank you for your efforts." He told a nurse to get me some cold towels and stand by. Gentleman Jim, the department manager for that group at the time, came in and sat with me. We talked about the efforts that had been made by all the people with CPR training and the let-down, physically and mentally, that we all felt. The doctor advised us that he would call us as soon as he got the cause of death. We went back to the plant.

The whole department was in a state of shock. The guys who had given CPR were sitting around very depressed. The doctor called and told Gentleman Jim that the victim had died of a massive aneurysm of the aortic arch where the left carotid and other arteries branched off to the left side of the upper thoracic areas. My diagnosis had been correct but that was a guess with no professional background. About three of the clerks and a secretary were sent home. Four of the fellows asked to go home. My desk was in the corner of our office area. I sat with my back to the office looking at the corner walls for about three hours and then felt like driving home and left also. After all of the effort expended we lost our victim. I have never experienced that depth of depression before or since. I promised myself that I would participate in any new situations like that but never ever become emotionally involved to that extent again.

We had air force officers assigned to the materiel group who were monitoring (overseeing) our work (operation). If they noted in our procurement methods that they did not understand, one would have to go to their office and fully explain. We had a captain who had an emblem depicting a parachute hanging over a set of wings over his left pocket. I asked him what type of pilot that emblem signified. He said that he was not a pilot but had jumped from an airplane. After that experience they must have decided to send him into a defense plant to monitor the manufacture of aircraft. He impressed me as one who would prefer to parachute into a lake instead of a plowed up field. Explaining a procurement function to him was like explaining to a 6-month-old baby why it was not such a good thing to soil his diaper. He was not going to sign anything that he could not understand. He reminded me of Mr. Hal. After a few visits with him I told my department manager that I could not have another argument with this gentleman anymore and asked if we could get another person to check my work. We went to the assistant director and he reviewed my workmanship, overrode the captain's objections, and approved the job.

With the thousands of units of MSP items we were procuring, it is understandable that at the end of each shift there would be quite a bit all mixed together. In the course of a year we would accumulate barrels of the stuff. It was too costly for us to separate them and return them to stores. We would sell it as salvage on the open market at five cents a pound. Someone thought of a small organization for the blind in a small city south of us that indicated that they had the capability of separating these items and returning them to us in a like new condition. I think that they rigged a magnet to separate the aluminum from the steel alloys. Then strictly by feel or touch they separated by length, diameter, thread size, head types, and logo identification into trays and returned them with about 98 percent accuracy. We were glad to pay the relatively small charge as compared to what we originally paid and the extremely low salvage price we had been getting. Whenever we had a critical shortage for a particular part you can bet they had some of those parts on hand or in process and could send us enough to get out of trouble immediately. We were really proud of that connection. Instead of our helping them they were actually doing more for us and saving cost at the same time.

I mentioned the above because in this year I was offered a job with one of our largest suppliers. This vendor was a worldwide organization. I made no firm reply until the opportunity came for me to visit this source on company business. The international sales manager was a fellow I had dealt with when he was national sales manager. He was the one who offered me the job. I was given a tour of the plant and the surrounding community (management and employee residences). I was introduced to the company CEO and most of management down the line. The increase in salary would have been about

$5,000 the first year with all relevant benefits, moving expenses, and no obligation for rent or ownership until my house was sold. The house they showed me was equivalent to mine but $15,000 more in cost. My lot was much larger. The job (with my manufacturing experience and a period of training) was a mid-level management position in the high-speed transmission division. I told them I would give the offer top consideration.

That company was one helluva organization (otherwise they could not have been worldwide with the diversity they maintained). They had one area that was the most impressive I have ever seen. There was a handicapped section that had people with serious disabilities—sight, hearing, mobility, etc. The supervisor over that group could communicate using hand signals and touch when necessary. He was somebody in his own right (incidentally, he was a black guy). Those people produced more standard work hours per person than any other group in the whole plant. Their mistakes and errors were almost none. They were not distracted by noise or lighting effects and other things that could interfere with their attention to their work. By testing how far they would actually go in realization they reached an output of 250 percent of the average non-disabled worker and never complained. The problem was slowing them down to 150 percent without making them feel that they were not doing an up to par job. After considering the move to a colder climate, the transfer of the kids to another school, and the adjustments required in the cost of living, I decided I would rather build airplanes at the good old Lockheed-Georgia plant. I am not quite sure I didn't make a mistake. That company was Standard Pressed Steel.

Chapter 14

The 1970s were rolling in and a lot of things were happening. The government was fighting the Cold War at its worst. We were letting the CIA and some in the State Department do a lot of our diplomatic work. We were letting political markers pay for our diplomatic corps. We were training diplomatic representatives but most of the ambassadors were appointed as a result of their contributions during political campaigns and not on their ability. The CIA was making crappy deals all over the world without civilian knowledge (like the president, etc., in my opinion). Kickbacks were the order of the day. Reciprocal propositions came into being, that is, "scratch my back and I will return the favor." If you deal with a foreign country they may buy something if you kick back enough to pay all the boys and still show a profit for the country. I remember we sold about $57 million worth of C-130s to a well-known so-called ally with the promise we would purchase over $20 million in reciprocal (not equivalent) products. We could not always use the crud. I guess the government ate it as they usually do.[1]

My interpretation of ethics and integrity went out the window during these years. Companies had levels of ethics and integrity that they most times maintained. Governments (including our own) included some of the biggest crooks that ever existed. Everyone was guilty of being greedy and going for that which was most to the advantage of the chosen few. The heads of certain governments (regardless of philosophy) were out for the most profit to their personal bank accounts. It seems that everything was a deal regardless of whether it was a government or civilian operation. If you wonder why I should be concerned with a situation like this, well mainly because nobody seemed to give a damn about conditions like this and I was tired about all the propaganda of how great and ethical the world's governments were. In my opinion, ethics and integrity were at their lowest levels during the 1972–77 years. After the Richard Nixon fiasco I blame Jimmy Carter; he should have been a crook like 80 percent of the rest of politicians. Since he seemed to be honest many politicians did not work with him.

Lockheed was caught up in some deal about paying a gratuity to a big Japanese politician for procurement of some L-1011 aircraft for their commercial airlines. At the time Lockheed was doing about 75–80 percent military aircraft and defense work for the United States. Naturally, we had nothing to do with State Department deals with other governments for their military needs, which the State Department handled and we fulfilled. All kinds of cruddy deals were being pulled by the government authorities to fulfill these requirements. When politicians cannot get certain contracts for their states they have the right to investigate the contracts that other states get for their areas. They forget that there is a big difference in dealing within the United States and overseas. There are different laws and ethics. The ethics of the country you deal with rule the negotiations. Even though we think that democracy is a good form of government, other people around the world sometimes do not see it the same way (maybe it's the way we practice it: "them that's got, gets," and "do as I say, not as I do").

I was taking advantage of all training classes available and my old buddy from the manufacturing days as in-plant transportation manager was now the director of materiel. Here I was at two levels below supervisor and salaried and he was now upper branch level reporting to the vice president and I was reporting indirectly to him through five levels of management. Twelve years had passed. One thing I can say for him is he never forgot that relationship of teamwork and his door was always open without the necessity of getting approval to go in as you will see throughout the rest of this narrative. His name was Wally F. Kalmbach. Wally's brother, Herbert, was one of Nixon's lawyers and got caught up in the Watergate scandal. Wally was a guy who wanted to know your opinion of what was happening and he would take the time to let you tell him. He might come in with something that had happened in his experience that was similar to some experience of yours and you could really get down to specifics on the problem.

You could always follow a decision of Wally's because you knew it was based on something other than the spur of the moment. He was the guy looking important while walking down the hall and an hourly person would pass by and he would stop them and say, "Aren't you so and so? Yeah, I thought I remembered you. You did such and such last Friday and that enabled us to move a shortage down the production line. I'm glad I ran into you and I can tell you that we appreciate your help, keep it up, that was a good job, thanks." Did you ever think about how much a worker appreciates a big boss recognizing him and saying, "thank you," especially if there are other workers around? The big boss's stock rises about 20 points.

Over the past few years I had been asked to go to engineering for different reasons concerning fasteners and their usage in certain areas. This was not because of any exceptional knowledge of engineering but because of my overall knowledge of fasteners and their availability. One of our major competitors had a contract to manufacture the B-1 Bomber. This baby was so complicated that it was necessary that the DOD requested that certain elements of the design (and some aspects of production) be accomplished by several other major aircraft manufacturers. This would eventually become a normal practice as technology advanced. Our advanced engineering group requested my presence among their elite group in the design and production of the B-1 wing slat configuration. The prints were supposed to be complete and all we had to do was integrate the components into the overall wing structure. I went over and the program director, W. A. "Andy" Pitman (I'm in tall grass again, working with the director), gave me all of the prints containing the configuration and different types of fasteners (that included sizes and lengths, etc.). I never saw such a screwed-up bunch of crap in all of my years in the aircraft industry. No joke! The grip lengths were too long as called out, the diameters in certain areas did not meet the callouts, and the whole layout was the sorriest piece of work that I had ever seen. I told Andy that I had never seen such shoddy work and I would have to do a major critique on the whole operation with all the associated blueprints required. Andy seemed quite perturbed until I showed him the complete setup. Engineers do not like to see where members of their profession have made a real screw-up. He asked me if I could straighten it out and I responded in the positive as the dimensions were all given as to the thickness of materiel and the degree of thickness as we got to the trailing edge of the slat. If I had not been able to correct the errors, then Andy would have had to assign another engineer to the job. A professional is required in any endeavor where a problem exists outside of the normal range of the general expert (is there such a person?). I spent three weeks going over prints, MSP callouts, and requirements. Finally, I came up with all the glue necessary to hold together all the components of the slat program.

I had the pleasure of getting a pat on the back for my work on the B-1 slat a little later in the year. I was told one day that I had to report to the B-2 building. The B-2 building is Mahogany Row. Top executives from the president on down inhabit the B-2 building. It seemed that the DOD, the air force, the Handbook Five Committee, and all the other big wheels that be were meeting for a conference on the progress of the B-1 Bomber. The other aircraft manufacturers concerned had representatives there as well. What in heaven did they want with me?

I went over to the B-2 building and the number of big shots was very impressive, including a few generals. I did not know anyone but our own people. We buyers always wore suits and ties so I stood around trying to look as if I was someone important also. I was offered a martini. After all, I was in tall grass, so therefore I could imbibe. (It was before lunch.) I walked around listening to all the wheels expressing their knowledge of nothing that I could understand until one big fellow walked up to me and said, "Are you Hap Hudson?" I replied that I was, and said, "My name is Bill Carey and I am the director of materiel of North American Rockwell." Rockwell was the prime contractor of the B-1 Bomber. I may be wrong on the spelling of the last name but the first name is right.

ME: "It's my pleasure to meet you, Mr. Carey." (He looked like old Harry Carey, the movie cowboy, but much younger.)

CAREY: "Andy tells me that you are the fastener expert (WHAT?!) who found all the errors on our initial prints for the B-1 slats. When I came over I told him that I wanted to meet personally the man who found those errors. I just want to shake your hand and express our appreciation for your expertise and the thousands of dollars saved by your ability to detect the original errors in the design prints."

ME: "Thank you, Mr. Carey, I did what I thought was best for the quality of the aircraft." (There were a number of people [Lockheed folks] listening to our conversation and wondering what this big wheel was discussing with me. Thanks, Lockheed, for not issuing a commendation, for I guess Mr. Carey said it all.)

One day I was going from the B-27 building toward the B-2 building (the administration offices and the main entrance to the plant). I noticed this group of very important-looking people coming out of the B-2 building with a tall four-star general with them. This general happened to be a Negro so I took another look and recognized him as an old buddy of mine from previous years. I first met him when he was a lieutenant colonel. We were not what you would call close friends but more of the casual acquaintance type. On a number of occasions we had met at a certain watering hole and spent several hours going over experiences common to the both of us, though I had not seen him in a number of years. He also knew many people who were acquaintances of mine.

Since there were several people I moved over to the next walkway to pass. We caught each other's eye at about the same time. I nodded and he said, "Hey, Harry, what the hell you mean by walking past me and not saying hello?" I was taken aback a little because I didn't think I was supposed to say anything with so many wheels in the group. I was so surprised to see him that I can't tell you today who else was in the group. I returned his greeting in the proper manner and moved on.

The general's name was Daniel "Chappie" James. He was the commanding general of the North American Aerospace Defense Command (NORAD) system. I understood that after the president, the commanding general of NORAD, not the head of the Joint Chiefs of Staff, was second in line of command in a Red Button situation. Chappie had been a civilian instructor at Tuskegee when the original members of the 99th Pursuit Squadron—the famed Tuskegee Airmen, the first group of Negro fighter pilots—had gone through training. He was in the second group. He continued to train pilots for the remainder of World War II. He flew over one hundred combat missions in the Korean War and seventy-eight missions in Vietnam. He held a number of high command positions, including a deputy assistant secretary of defense and then command of NORAD. Hell, 99 percent of the American people did not know that! Little media or governmental coverage was given to the ability of Negroes during those wars mainly because of prejudice. Very few knew or gave a damn what Negroes were doing other than being good grunts. He was standing first in line when that beautiful C-141 landed with the first Vietnam prisoners of war returned. A lot of viewers wondered who the hell that black general was. In later replays he was cut out of several versions that I saw. As time rolled on he had to be recognized for who he was and he received much recognition after that.

General James made many trips to manufacturing plants in line with his command responsibilities and was at Lockheed at the time the C-5A was in full swing. His recognition of me probably raised my stock with some levels of management about 3 points up from "horseshit." At least they seemed impressed that I would know someone at such a high level in the organization of our prime customer. Chappie was one of the most "I don't give a damn, full speed ahead" pilots I have ever known. He once told me that his philosophy was do your best at all times, don't ever worry about what danger you may face in performing your job, and when your number is up there is nothing you can do to avoid that date. General James suffered a heart attack in his middle fifties. He probably realized that his date was approaching and he retired. About three months or so later he died of another heart attack. He told me that of all the hot planes that he had flown the one he liked best was the F-94 Starfire, one of the first U.S. Air Force jet-powered fighters in the late 1940s. Guess who built that plane?

Chapter 15

In 1977, the biggest screw-up of all of my time with GELAC came to pass. This is the year of the longest strike ever experienced by the division. The following is strictly my recollection of my experiences and opinions of that time. Our production had slowed down and we were awaiting follow-on contracts and bidding on a number of products. The current agreement between the company and the union expired. Instead of going into negotiations for a new contract before the current one expired, (in my opinion) the "Willies" that be (both union and company) waited until the last minute to begin their talks. The union stated that "we want this and the other." The company answered, "We ain't got no money to do anything." The contract expired in August and by the first week of October no agreement had been reached, so a strike was called.[1] One would think that the strike of 1958 had taught all of us a lesson. Everyone had been fairly prosperous during the eighteen years we had worked with good labor and management relations. The last quarter of 1977 indicated that if we did not get new contracts ASAP, it would be necessary to have a layoff. The normal routine in the aircraft industry was one of ups and downs. There was one helluva lot of hourly and salaried employees who had used the prosperous period to buy new homes and automobiles, and who had accumulated high levels of indebtedness. Without thought for the future, they all reacted like the "Chess Cat" as he sat his dumbass on the hot griddle for the second time.

GELAC was on schedule and had a few "Hanger Queens" sitting on the line unsold. A strike would not hurt the company. If the strike lasted over thirty days all employee benefits would automatically cancel. Those salaried employees who wanted to cross the picket line would be welcome to work in any capacity. Some hourly employees would also cross the line (known as scabs). The financial situation of some employees forced them to come to work, returning threat for threat. A few even said that they would kill if necessary to maintain their right to work (Georgia had a right to work law at the time). This turned out to be a very nasty strike that would last over seventy days. Things that I will relate here deal strictly with my own personal experiences.

The first few days of the strike were rather hectic as the strikers blocked the plant entrances and verbally raised hell. The names that the salaried people were called by their co-workers and friends were insulting and derogatory. If you saw these people later on they would explain that that was the way the strike organizers had told them to react. I had to go down and tell one of my neighbors that the next time he called me a scabbing SOB on that line he and I would settle it when we got home. He said that he had to show unity with the strikers. I told him he could show all the unity he wanted but if he looked me in the eyes and called me names like that again he had better bring some of his fellow strikers home with him. Those of us going to work had to wait as the strikers marched across the access streets to the plant. Some of them would just drag along to agitate you. We were told to be cool and exhibit restraint, don't talk back at all, regardless. After the first week things became routine as far as the inconvenience on entering and leaving the plant. The local city and county police were doing their job as required. The state patrol was maintaining order on the incoming streets and expressways, unlike during the 1958 strike.

After the first week the plant had to function simply to receive materiel supporting our spares program. A minimum amount of manufacturing work had to be accomplished. All salaried employees with any experience in the other processes were sent to work in those areas. Three of the big manufacturing wheels requested my presence in their areas. (Ha!) This included old BG himself. I hurriedly called my friend, manager of the receiving inspection/quality control department, and told him to tell everyone that might call that I had volunteered to work for him during the period of the strike. He told me to hurry on over. No amount of persuasion could change my mind. After all, those were the same guys who had railroaded my backside out of manufacturing to make room for someone else to be upgraded. After a day or so familiarizing myself and getting updated on the new quality control equipment, I hit the incoming line.

The first day I received and accepted thirty-four different items after thorough inspection. Those items that needed more technological examination by electronic methods were covered by the supervisors and managers in the QC division. After the first week I was averaging about thirty items a day. The average for the hourly workers prior to the strike had been about seventeen a day. The other guys like me were doing about the same as my average and the department manager asked his supervisors what the hell their people were doing before the strike. There was one thing for sure and that was we had to do the work of all the strikers or be backed up to the flight line with uninspected materiel. We did what was necessary and the line continued to move.

The strike created some catastrophic individual situations. One of the guys in the product control section, an hourly employee, had suffered for some months with a back problem that was very painful. Naturally, he was in no financial condition to have to go out on a prolonged strike. I might mention that, to the best of my knowledge, he was a charter union member. After the third week as far as I know the union had no strike fund and nobody was getting any funds except possibly the union officials. This fellow called in and asked his supervisor if he could ride in with him in the trunk of his car if necessary. Naturally, this was a no-no. He was told that this would be against all agreements between labor and management during a strike and so no one could help him. His supervisor told me later that this employee cried and told him that his insurance was expiring in a week and he would not be able to get medical treatment and he could not stand the pain much longer. There was nothing his management could do for him under the circumstances. The thirty-day grace period expired and all the hourly people covered by the contract lost their life insurance and medical coverage (think about that for a while). The following week this fellow was waiting for his wife to take him to the doctor or hospital and he went into another room of his house. She heard a loud pop and rushed into the room and found he had shot himself in the temple with a .22 caliber pistol. Thus ended the life of a valuable Lockheed employee. Fortunately, the company reached into its own funds and gave his wife the total of his expired insurance. (This was commendable, but which do you think she would have preferred?) There was a rumor that there was another suicide but I can't confirm it. Everybody was shocked and upset, especially those people who knew him well. The strike continued on.

The materiel group got their offices remodeled. That is, all the men (those who could only buy) cleaned the walls and woodwork and painted the whole area. You wouldn't think that we had so many professional painters among those buyers. The place certainly looked good. Those of us in receiving inspection rolled on and really picked up experience in the quality control field. The good people in manufacturing again requested my participation, but the QC manager explained that I was needed more in the quality control area. Some trucks had trouble crossing the picket lines to make deliveries, but for those critical items that had to come through, the DOD took care of those deliveries. (Showing such a delicate intent that the impression was given that one did not screw with those anointed deliveries.) Those military planes had to be maintained because of hot spots throughout the world at the time. We fulfilled all of those requirements and made on time deliveries on most of our commitments to our customers. The strike continued and the financial plight of the strikers went to hell. I felt real bad for some of my friends who got caught up in that stupidity. No negotiations were in process and the strike just lingered and lingered.

We continued to come through the picket lines every day. We were harassed daily and insulted but we became used to that. It was hell to look at our co-workers on the line, recognizing the financial situation they were getting into, and not being able to speak or give some form of encouragement. If we even looked at some too long while waiting to pass through the line they were ostracized by their fellow workers as wanting to be scabs. Management had instructed us not to speak under any circumstances to the strikers on the line. It was necessary to show our badges on request to the leaders (normally business agents for the union) when coming to work. They even wanted to search our vehicles for scabs. Damn if that was going to be. We could get fired by the company for slipping any hourly workers into the plant. One morning one of the business agents stopped me (we both knew each other). I had two salaried people riding with me (they were afraid to drive in themselves because some damage was being done to the automobiles by scratching with nails and slashing tires) and this guy requested that we show him our badges. The two people with me exhibited theirs and this is exactly what I told the agent. I called him by name and said, "You know damn well who I am." He requested again and I flashed my badge real quick. I leaned out the window of my pickup and asked him to step closer. I said, "You know I have the right to enter this plant. This crap about identifying myself every morning is a bunch of shit. If my pickup is ever scratched, my tires slashed, or my windows cracked, your natural ass belongs to me if it takes six months. I hope you fully understand what I am saying." I was looking him straight in the eye with no smile and I meant every word of it. Later when I thought about it, that was maybe stupid but my promise I would have kept. He looked a little stunned and backed away and I drove through. Whenever he was on the line after that I had no problems. My two riders got real upset but I told them they could drive themselves after that day because I had my gut filled with that stupidity long enough. It may have taken a year but I meant every word that I said. They continued to ride with me for I had no more trouble coming into the plant.

One advantage I had was that I knew one helluva lot of hourly people after working in the manufacturing division for those nine years. I had been a charter member of the union and most of them knew that. It is not an easy thing to go through a situation like that of being on opposite sides of the fence and having to accept the hardships you knew your friends were going through. I can't begin to go through the problems these people were experiencing because their elected officials (both union and company) did not have the ability to solve the problems without the method of striking. I would bet half of them didn't even know what a strike entailed when they voted for it.

In all of my experience I have never known any side to win a strike up to that time. It takes about three years to regain what is lost by the average worker following a strike. What the hell, it takes an intelligent cat to realize you don't sit on the same hot stove the second time around. Put your negotiators in a room and lock them up for a few days (or weeks) without pay and the whole lot of problems could be solved in a short period of time.

After three months no progress had been made on a settlement. I began to smell a rat. To this day I will not identify that rat except to say I felt that there was some sort of conspiracy in the works. My respect for certain business ethics (labor and management) went to hell. The grunts always lost. There were no Christmas parties for the kids, no checks for the families, and nothing but hardship all around. The two parties of negotiators were drawing their paychecks and so were we management people. One can come up with all the reasons why such conditions are allowed to occur and don't give a damn for one reason—going home and attempting to explain to the kids why Santa Claus ain't coming this year.

Right at Christmas it was announced that some progress had been made and there was the possibility that the strike could be settled by the first of the year. An agreement was reached and all employees were notified to return to work January 2, 1978. Glory be to miracles! With very few improvements made, everybody returned to work and did not gain a goddamn thing of significance. Most of the workers were in debt up to their nostrils. It took almost four years to get over the setbacks accumulated during the seventy-seven days of the strike. The animosities that had developed took much longer to be resolved. The trust of the people (both hourly and salaried) was the hardest thing to regain. Since in my opinion the only people hurt by the strike are the workers, strikes ain't worth a damn. In all my years in aircraft there has never been a problem that could not be eventually solved, that is, except negotiations between management and labor.

We all reported to work January 2, 1978, and after giving each other leery looks, we proceeded to work together again. It took a long time before the spirit of teamwork was fully back into place. All the propaganda spread during those seventy-seven days took a long time to dissipate. Trying to solve the conflict between my hardnosed character at GELAC and my friendly and congenial self at home—my Gemini nature—I came to the conclusion that honesty, principles, and integrity had gone to hell. Life stops for no individual. We continued to work and after some years the past passed and the future began to take over. The family of Lockheed workers bypassed the problems of dissentions and continued to produce the quality aircraft that they were famous for over the years.

Chapter 16

After the strike things came back gradually to normal. We began to implement the Zero Defects (ZD) program. This was a system to practice in eliminating errors and screw-ups in all phases of workmanship. It was initiated to cover all improvement possible from the government through the smallest manufacturer. All workers (from grounds maintenance to top management) were instructed to check methods to improve quality, delivery, and cost. The findings (ideas and suggestions) were to be passed up in writing to your immediate supervisor and on up to the Zero Defects committee for consideration and implementation. There were some initial hold-ups because previously one might have been told that it would not work or some supervisors had taken the idea for their own and passed it up, thus the hourly or first line supervisor did not get credit for many of their suggestions. The earlier attitude had been "to hell with it."

As confidence developed that their ideas and suggestions were getting attention, however, the volume of Zero Defects suggestions took off. The best place to find out if improvements can be made is from the worker on the job. More than likely they have found ways to cut time, improve quality, and save cost in their particular operation. Now they would be given Buck Hunter awards and cost reduction certificates. The Zero Defects program was proving to be a very good cost-effective operation. In the materiel division it was the responsibility of the buyers to see that their suppliers got the necessary literature, as they were required to participate in the program. I thought that the sooner that Lockheed could award a ZD certificate to a business (especially a small business), the better for the program and the morale of suppliers.

Some years back I had been helpful in increasing involvement by a small company in supplying small quantities when shortages existed and the prime suppliers could not deliver. As time moved on I found that this source could find practically any part I needed immediately, including the traceability and certification of those items back to the manufacturer, batch numbers, and production dates. The owner had established a network throughout the United States to similar small shops having the same capabilities as he possessed. They all specialized in aircraft fasteners and other small items used commercially and by the military. They were all able to supply records on these items that were traceable to the manufacturer, thus meeting the specific standards as required.

I went down to visit this source, located a little south of the plant in the Atlanta area. If I had not gotten the surprise of my life to find the most perfect small business then this source would be mentioned as another well-operated small business. The company was located in a relatively small business complex. On entering you went into a small reception area. The office was behind plate glass dividers. Although there was up-to-date communications equipment available, they were in the process of installing and programming a completely new computer system. All of this was the latest state-of-the-art (it took four weeks to complete the installation and programming). The owner showed me his library. He had the original volumes and the latest editions of leather-bound encyclopedias on all the aircraft, automotive, and whatever fasteners ever used in the United States and other countries covering the period from the Wright Brothers up to 1975. He had a total of about thirty-five volumes (not books). I had never seen such a collection on this subject nor have I seen anything like it since. This was one expensive set of books. I asked him why he would need such a volume of information. He informed me that he received requests for materiel from all over for different types of aircraft fasteners. He did not stock this materiel, but he knew where to find it if it was still in existence. Thus he established his wide network of sources. For easy access, this information was going into his new computer system, which would be constantly updated.

We went into his receiving, stocking, and shipping section. Everything was as clean as a whistle. No dust, no wrapping refuse, no parts on the floor, and no misidentified materiel anywhere. There were certification papers with each unit holding parts with a received and quantity shipped record with each storage container. There was no rust, grease, or contaminated parts to be found. I could see thousands of fasteners of all sizes. According to size and usage, he had from fifty to maybe one thousand units in each container. He had proven to me that he could furnish practically any critical shortage requirement we might need in a very short time, immediately if in stock and (believe it or not) on the average of twenty-four hours if not in stock. He introduced me to his crew, which consisted of himself, about three members of his family, and six others. I have never seen another team as tightly organized. His inspection was equipped with the latest instruments and he had sources to send out to for the types of inspection that he did not have the capability of performing. That was a happy place.

I went back to the plant and concentrated on their record over the past several years. I could not recall one time having to return anything because of discrepancies. I thought of all the times I had been helped out of tight spots by this small company. I made the decision that this would be the first company that I would recommend for a Zero Defects recognition certificate. I processed the request up through the channels and got approval that this was surely the type of source we would want to receive such an award. Thus Mr. Henry Price, owner, president, and CEO of Dutch Valley Supply, became the first outside source to be awarded a Zero Defects certificate by the Georgia division of the Lockheed Aircraft Corporation. Mr. Price appreciated that as much as I did. There is one more interesting incident that occurred that I will write about a little later involving Dutch Valley. By the way, that award boosted the morale of all of his employees and they continued to try and outdo themselves in rendering a valuable service to Lockheed. There were other awards given, but the above seems to me to have been especially remembered because it was the first.

To show that progress was being made by some Negroes within the company I must mention that my old buddy (shop steward-supervisor grievance writing partner) J. B. Mabry was promoted to manager of the C-130 production assembly and paint quality control department in 1978. He had gone into quality control not too long after I went to procurement. There were quite a few Negroes in first-line supervisory levels of management in a number of divisions such as production, inspection, parts control, and several other areas. There were no black purchasing agents in materiel nor would there be one for many years. There had been one fellow hired in materiel and upgraded to purchasing agent before I knew that he was with us. He could only make as much as his most senior buyer ($120 a week) and he needed so much more training to become qualified (the primary reason for existing) he began to look around. It seems he was promoted to show the DOD that all effort was being made to show that Negroes were moving up in the company. This fellow had the education and the experience to out-rate his management so he took it as long as he could (several months) and quit. A few years later he was director of materiel for one of the major manufacturers in the country. His name was Ronald Paine, if anyone is interested in checking. Meanwhile "Old Hap" was still trucking along.

Chapter 17

Work picked up in 1979. We had started a hot modification program for the C-141 with a very tight delivery schedule. Fasteners were the highest-volume parts to be required. As noted in the last chapter, quite a number of those items were already in the procurement cycle. We needed oversize pins and other types of fasteners that were not commonly used or stocked. We intended to hit a delivery of one ship per day after we got through the initial startup. The first delivery was for around June 1, 1979.

I asked all of my major suppliers to send their salespeople in with quotations and information on their best delivery schedules. We had been involved in helping the patent holders develop licensees and those sources were now producing. I was surprised to find that practically all of the major aircraft manufacturers were backlogged with new aircraft orders, especially those in the commercial field. I had not noticed this in reading the industrial magazines, where I kept up with the raw materiel backlogs and pricing changes. I guess I was pretty busy myself. All of the big boys (I don't have to name them) had orders on the most popular fasteners and were backed up at that time for at least two years. I had heard rumbles of an intensified buildup but we were holding stock levels and ordering parts under the impression that the lead times were solid for some time to come. We got caught sitting not on it but in it. All the other divisions could now use materiel as the scapegoat that was causing the behind-schedule conditions. Damn the fact that we knew that the C-141 deal was in the works and regardless, GELAC was the only source capable of modifying that particular plane (lots of original tooling still available). At the time I don't think that GELAC recognized the speedup in the whole industry and the effect this would have on our suppliers (including me).

I got the estimated usage for all the parts required for the program and requested a stock level check. We would have to change our philosophy of on-hand levels (kept low because of inventory taxes) and get parts orders in to the production lines of the suppliers. I decided that I would increase quantities on purchase orders to the next quantity price break where it seemed cost effective and place orders for the earliest delivery without going into overtime. I utilized every method I could without having to get prior approvals. We had corporate purchasing agreement (CPA) contracts on a number of the items so I re-negotiated volumes on those contracts (naturally with Renrut's CPA bunch) to get lower prices since we were exceeding the original usage figures. This was the only time I felt that more documentation was required on each PO and made it a habit to keep individual records in my file for later reference when required. Sometimes I stayed over until six and eight o'clock at night (no overtime, stupid) as this exhibited my enthusiasm to do my part in keeping shortages at a minimum. Some days I was away from home for fourteen to fifteen hours at a time. I don't think my family missed me as much as they did because I did not make any overtime pay.

With all this hustle and production, I went to my department manager and told him that the time was past due for a promotion and a raise. I reminded him that the young buyer that I had helped and trained on the extrusion desk a few years ago was now a senior buyer and still purchasing extrusions. The department manager was up to date on my performance and many other critical situations. I told him that I was going to take two weeks of my backed-up vacation time and when I returned I expected to be a senior buyer. If not then my plans were made to do something else. I don't think that any member of management had ever suggested that I deserved a promotion. I wonder if these characters thought that I was blindly happy to trudge along without a decent raise or promotion for the past eighteen years. If you can't get the gist of what was going on damn if I'm going to enlighten anyone at all.

I returned and walked into the department manager's office. Eighteen years after leaving manufacturing as a manager and coming into materiel as a buyer, then making semi-senior buyer in seven years, here is my department manager giving me a promotion to senior buyer with a half-assed decent raise (bless his heart). Upgrades are based on merit (what's merit?). I was so overjoyed that I think I shed a tear or two (actually, I felt like kicking somebody's butt). Although it was late as hell I felt good that I had finally gotten an upgrade. The only supervisory classification below purchasing agent was subcontract administrator. I would never make it. I continued to my own satisfaction of helping and training the younger buyers as they came into the department. I don't think that some members of management appreciated the effort because I taught them to have confidence, be hardnosed, and perform the job to their highest standards. I told them not to consider anything as right or complete until they were satisfied and the result would be above average each time.

I made a statement earlier that I had no desire of going to California any time soon. The reason I felt that way was because one morning early in January 1971, I heard that California had suffered one terrible earthquake. It was 7:00 a.m. in California when I learned this so I called one of my contacts who lived and worked in the city (Los Angeles) to find out what the damage may have been. Believe it or not but he was at work. Less than thirty minutes later all contact with L.A. was lost. He told me that he was shaving at about 5:30 a.m. and a low rumble started and he felt his house shaking. He rushed out of the bathroom and told his wife to get to a doorframe and spread-eagle to brace herself. His 6-foot refrigerator came out of the kitchen through the den, through his plate glass sliding doors, onto the patio. He made a quick check of the house and surroundings and made sure that his wife was getting settled down, for the quake seemed to be over. Fortunately, neither he nor his family was hurt but their loss in material things was great after all the aftershocks. That fellow was Frank Alfultis, one of my best contacts.

I made it my business to find out all I could about that San Andreas Fault. At the time no one could have sent me to California. I knew, though, that eventually I would have to go. Up until this time (1979) I had nightmares of coming in for a landing and just as we set down a crack about 25 feet wide opened on the runway and in we went. Imagine that happening and you are on a big L-1011. No sirree, I had no intentions of going to California. We had a woman in the group and she was a whiz. They sent her on the first trip to go and expedite our requirements. She got back safely (and that's about all) so I knew I had to take the next trip. This I would do in a few more weeks.

Our special little baby was the Jetstar, known in the military as the C-140. This aircraft was designed, manufactured, and accepted by the military (and later the commercial) customers a little more than nine months after the concept was requested. The greatest aeronautical engineer at the time was responsible for the whole development. His name was Clarence "Kelly" Johnson. He was instrumental in the concept and design of about 90 percent of all aircraft developed by Lockheed Aircraft during his forty-five plus years with the company. On retirement he remained as a consultant until his health restricted him. The manufacture of this little bird was delegated to the GELAC division.

Kelly and his crew were right up there with the so-called experts when it came to developing and building advanced aircraft systems. With the time to design, build, and fly the Jetstar naturally there would be a lot of modification to prints and other specifications to be completed before scheduled production could be started. Our engineers fell in and corrected the rivet patterns and other minor problems that could have grown into major problems during production. Finally, we met the requirements set down by Kelly and his people and we produced a top-quality aircraft. The C-140 came on line before the C-141. We had developed much experience with the B-47 (Boeing design) and the C-130 (which Kelly and his crew also designed).

During the end of the production of the Jetstar, it was necessary to keep the cost of production to a minimum. We were on a firm fixed contract for the changes required for the constant updating of developing technology. There were always improvements made in the performance of certain components used in aircraft. Production ship number ten would be advanced above number one. This was to be expected as the advancing technology in safety and reliability became available. Every conscientious worker was always looking for ways to reduce cost and making suggestions to improve realization (efficiency in production) and reliability. A good team consists of people who respect the expertise of the others and work together to accomplish a high-quality result in their endeavors. In my opinion, a young engineer who comes in realizing that he mastered the theory (by graduating from an engineering school) and is now ready to gain the experience and who keeps his mouth shut and his ears open until he finds out what is going on, is going to be successful. Some of the just out of school guys think (they have finished certain schools) they are the greatest and have all the knowledge (after all, they finished BS Tech) so therefore they can come up with the most brilliant ideas. Their best orientation would be to go to the floor and stay with several hourly workers for a week. This would give them a firm base to start their careers. Some of those guys had the idea that "I am the engineer, therefore you will do as I say." They usually found out in a short while from the more senior engineers that that was not so. A good team never let one monkey stop the show.

I had one of my few encounters with such a young fellow near the end of the Jetstar program. He sent forth a requirement that we buy a new fastener that cost twice what we were paying for the present one. He emphasized the stress, shear, and yield characteristics of the new part. On researching the requirements and what we had on hand I called him and told him that we could cover the higher requirement with what we already had in stock. He impolitely told me that he was the "goddamn" (he said it) engineer and what he had requested would be procured. Poor fellow, he had never dealt with me as a buyer. I won't say that I smelled hanky-panky but one damn thing was for certain, I did not intend to spend any unnecessary funds just to satisfy a young engineer. I promptly sat down and wrote a memo to his division manager stating his request and the fact that I had no intention of spending excessive funds to satisfy anyone increasing the cost of the Jetstar program this late in the contract. I need not say how the memo was worded. After my boss (I requested his approval) had reduced my memo to a more diplomatic message to the upper management, the division manager called and agreed.

Later, the young engineer called me and said that he had misunderstood me and my substitute was completely acceptable.

The time came when it was necessary to go to California. It was not reasonable to send anyone out there who was not completely knowledgeable of our critical fastener problems on all of our programs, especially the C-141 modification. I had gone to California in 1974 on vacation to visit two of my brothers and never felt a tremor so I figured that things would remain calm. Actually, there was no fear on my part regardless of the earlier impression given.

One of the guys I had helped to train years ago was now an assistant manager in the requirements department. After my urging, my management personnel finally convinced that group that we had to change our method of procurement because of the glut of our competitors' orders placed with our suppliers was creating long lead times for our urgently needed requirements. Preston Upshaw and I joined together and had an inventory run on our full stock. We checked engineering requirements for oversize and other not normally stocked items. This included checking most of the modification blueprints (my expertise). We went through scheduling plans for eventually we would be committed to deliver one a day of the C-141 modified aircraft. We worked from 8:00 a.m. until sometimes 11:00 p.m. for a week compiling this information (I didn't get any overtime, him I don't know, probably not). I called all of my sources in California and informed them that I would be in their plants beginning the following Monday. I gave them a synopsis of what our problems were in much detail over the phone and let them know the scope of my visit. I made firm appointments to be in their plants on certain days. I carried piles of data sheets three inches thick and hoped we had covered everything. I was going out there with fifteen years of markers. Our long and fruitful business relationships, in my opinion, were coming down to the test.

At this time we did not have millions of dollars in open orders, we only had hundreds of thousands. After making sure that the plane I would take was an L-1011, I boarded that big baby at 11:00, Sunday, October 21, 1979. As we set down in L.A. there was no big crack in the runway.

The five days that I was there I practically toured Southern California without seeing anything except freeways and the backs of automobiles and trucks. The times I was not at a vendor's plant, I was stuck in traffic. It sure did seem strange that traffic had not been better with all of those freeways. The quake damage was mostly repaired, so I didn't see any results of the quake. I felt no tremors, or so I thought. One evening while writing up my daily report in my hotel-motel bottom floor room, I was using the table lamp.

I kept hearing a squeaking noise. I could feel nothing or any sensation of movement. Finally, I looked up and the ceiling light held by a chain was doing a perfect circle over my head. I looked out the window and everything seemed normal, people were going in and out of the parking lot showing no indication of anything being wrong. I did not sense anything to become alarmed about but I thought about those seven stories over my head. I went to the lobby and all of the hanging lights were doing a little dance. I asked the man on duty what the hell was going on. He looked around and said, "Oh, that's just a small tremor, we get two or three hundred a year." He had responded in such a matter-of-fact manner that I decided I would go outside. Everybody was going about their business in a normal way. I began to wonder about that old description of "Nuts, Fruits, and Flakes." Anyway, since it all seemed normal I ignored the tremors also. I wanted to appear as normal as the rest of the people.

There is one more incident that happened in late 1978 that covers one of the greatest tragedies that occurred to our C-130 aircraft. I will go to another chapter for that story.

Chapter 18

The incident mentioned in the last chapter occurred in December 1979, but we were aware of the problem long before. There had been indications that a problem was developing with the flight controls that could result in major difficulties controlling the aircraft. We had a Negro who was a retired lieutenant colonel from the air force in our military sales department. I have mentioned Don Thompson in an earlier chapter. When Don came to Lockheed he worked in the personnel division. After a few months he transferred to the military sales department. Don was a qualified pilot of a number of military aircraft, including the C-130. Incoming reports had indicated that one of the control cables was showing a problem in correcting from a right turn. Among others, Don was assigned to investigate the problem and come up with a suggestion hopefully leading to a solution. It was determined that one and maybe more of the control cables would have to be replaced with a corrected and improved design. Meanwhile, Don was sent out with a few of our other pilots to all the Air National Guard bases to instruct the pilots on the corrective action to take if they experienced this problem in flight. Guess who bought control cables—ME!

Don was highly qualified in flying jet fighters and twin- and four-engine transports. He had served over twenty-five years on active duty and served in World War II, Korea, and Vietnam. He had rows of ribbons and decorations to prove it. I got to know Don pretty well because of my acquaintance with other air force pilots and the Tuskegee group; plus, his daughter worked for Lockheed in our group and I helped to train her. Don was teaching the Air National Guard pilots how to use the engines to correct the right wing drop when this discrepancy occurred; otherwise you had no control on pulling that plane out of a spinning dive. If you did not have decent altitude you had no chance anyway. He took the pilots up and simulated the condition and supposedly taught them the method of making the adjustments to correct and survive. Would you believe it—he told me this himself—that some of those units indicated that they didn't need no nigger to teach them how to fly. Just about all of the pilots in the Air National Guard were white. A unit in Kentucky was among those indicating that attitude. Guess who in hell went into the ground killing the whole crew plus a number of civilians in a café—that Kentucky group. All of a sudden the groups began to pay attention to Don.

That crash grounded every C-130 flying. I mean all over the world. At the time I think we had about forty countries flying our plane, military and otherwise. If you think all hell didn't break loose, consider every customer wanting their replacement cables at the same time, which was immediately. I felt like the little rabbit dying from road kill looking at fourteen buzzards wondering which would take the first bite. I had everybody from staff sergeants to second lieutenants calling for replacement parts, bypassing all channels. Some of them gave the impression that they were colonels. They didn't know me (I ain't askeered of no colonel). It was two weeks before Christmas and we only had two sources for those cables.

The Shah of Iran had thirty C-130s in his fleet and he wanted his cables now. One officer called from Fort Lewis and told me if I could not furnish his requirement right away he knew where he could buy them. He mentioned some source that I recognized as a scrap yard and told me he could get them for $110 each. I told him to help himself for he would never install that junk on a military aircraft. I only paid $5.95 each plus expediting, but no cables of the improved design were in stock. They had to be assembled. Meanwhile, I told him to go through channels and not to waste my time again. The Shah said that he wanted his parts and would buy the manufacturer if necessary to guarantee delivery. I was told he put up the money and bought the plant, which would have been closed for the holidays. The manufacturer actually only charged for the overhead and overtime required for the employees volunteering to work over the holidays. We were able to get many parts, with the first thirty going to the Shah. If you think that some member of upper management was doing all those negotiations, think again. Those cats went on holiday leave. Ole senior buyer Hap was motivating. "Good job, good job." Thank you. It took about a month but eventually all C-130s were back in flight.

After the cable fiasco was settled, things remained in their rush-rush situation. That is the race to secure enough parts for the C-141 modification program to stay on schedule. I had supplied our sources with all the necessary information and requirements to fill our needs for this critical program. After trying to get all of the standard parts available from all the qualified sources, I remembered an engineer (ole Floyd Poss) whom I had known for some time. He was now working for Boeing Aircraft. The markings on Boeing MSP and probably some other small parts carry the identification logo BAC. I called my acquaintance at Boeing, knowing that Boeing was the main culprit in tying up all the parts manufacturers' production schedules. I requested that he check their MSP stock and find out if they could sell us some of their high-stock quantities on hand. If they would, then I could get our engineering to approve BAC parts usage to fill our shortage needs. Air force approval would be required also. Once he told me that they would agree to sell us the quantities of our immediate needs I expedited the necessary approvals and we purchased the Boeing parts. They were identical except for the head markings. This kind of cooperation from competitive aircraft companies under certain conditions is beneficial to all concerned. It works both ways. Thus utilizing all methods and sources we were beginning to catch up and meet our delivery schedules. We called back all layoffs and then had to go to new hires to fill our worker openings. Things were on the upswing again.

Unfortunately for him, the Shah was kicked out of his country (Iran) and fled to Egypt. For political reasons among others the new regime did not care for the United States. We didn't care for them either. This happened in February 1979. To emphasize their point, the new Iranian government retained about fifty-two of our embassy people and other Americans that they could grab. As long as they retained our hostages they held the hole card. There was nothing diplomacy or negotiation could accomplish to get those people released. A few weeks after this incident I was told that certain parts had to be procured to facilitate modification of a C-130 and would be needed within ten days. I was firmly instructed that this program was restricted and highly confidential. In other words, don't discuss with anyone under any circumstances unless authorized to do so.

I was given the specifications for four big bolts. They would need to be about 30 inches long and 3 inches in diameter, and yield, stress, and shear requirements were out of range of anything that I had ever purchased before. To find bolts of those specifications I looked everywhere except the west side of hell. I called every source I thought even had a possibility of producing such. No help, except with long lead times like six to eight weeks to produce. I finally called a small business just on a hunch to see if they had anything near those requirements. (Even Dutch Valley could not find anything.) I hit lucky. A small business had five bolts of the required specs but they were 5 feet long. They had done a special job for a customer two or three years previously and had these left in stock. They could rework them and ship in three weeks. Raw parts, yes; finished parts delivered, no. I called Dutch Valley and asked if they knew anyone who could rework those bolts and get them to us in a few days. Mr. Price said yes but he would have to handle it. I got in touch with engineers (with approval) and asked if I could get the prints right away for the bolts. I told them the whole story about what I had found. I was asked if I thought that Dutch Valley could do the work. Most of the fastener engineers knew Dutch Valley and their reputation for quality. They did not believe that the job could be accomplished in that short period of time. I told them that if they would give approval, I would worry about delivery. They sent me the prints immediately and I called Mr. Price and told him to get ready. The West Coast source was instructed to take the parts to the airport in a cab and ship Jetair directly to me for ASA delivery.

All of this action had come to a close at about 2:00 p.m. on a Thursday. I got the bolts for a good price for I reminded my supplier, Mr. Paul Briles of PB Fasteners, that my taking them from his stock would save him paying inventory tax for another three years. I never did tell Paul what the requirement was for but he would have given them to me at a good price anyway. Hell, actually I didn't know exactly what they were for myself. The urgency of my request was good enough for him. Friday morning the parts arrived and the Dutch Valley representative was standing at the front gate. I gave him the parts and the engineering paper and told him to motor. I needed those parts finished and delivered by Monday. I called Mr. Price and he informed me that the parts were at his source and they were going to work around the clock to guarantee that delivery date.

Those bolts had to be annealed (heat treated to make the metal workable), cut to length, re-threaded, re-plated, and baked. It was hard to believe that it could be done in the time required. I was a little uneasy over the weekend. I never called for a progress report. When I arrived at work Monday, Dutch Valley's man was waiting at the gate with the finished parts. Away they went to engineering for one of the most intense inspections I had ever seen given to an item. By noon, those parts passed all inspection. I never asked Mr. Price his source and he never divulged it to me or anyone else to my knowledge. Naturally, I did not tell him what the parts would be used for as at that time I did not know. The word was that we would be ready to deliver the finished production schedule or else (what I did not know). Anyway, we paid a pretty penny for the bolts and it was worth it. It never occurred to me what type nuts were used. Those big bolts were probably screwed right into a heavy metal backup plate.

Later I found out the purpose of the effort. Quite some years ago I had seen a C-130, loaded with about a 1-hour fuel supply, turn on full power (not jet-assisted take off [JATO] bottles) with the brakes locked. I knew that they were testing for quick takeoff capability. With the release of the brakes that big baby jumped 2 feet into the air, bounced, and cleared the ground in exactly 408 feet from a standstill. Since I witnessed it, it was not hard for me to believe. Because the Iranians were holding our people hostage and were not contemplating letting them go until they were ready, the powers that be deemed it necessary that we go in and get them. The problem was how, when, and with what. The C-130 had presented to the world its capability of performing seemingly unnatural functions for an aircraft. I guess that is why the C-130 was selected to be the "with what" as far as method was concerned. Much more power was needed to perform this mission. The plane had 8 JATO bottles (4 at each parachute jump door with a thrust of 14,000 pounds each for 30 seconds), so they decided to add 2 rocket engines to the fuselage over the wheel covers to give more power. That was what the big bolts were for—to attach them. From what I heard the hostages were still at the American Embassy on the main drag in Tehran. This was a pretty wide street. This would be the rescue location.

This special C-130 would take off from a friendly base and pass over Iraq, dropping to 200 feet in altitude as it came into Iranian radar space. They would be escorted to this point by jet fighters, which would lay back at the Iranian border until the C-130 had taken off on its return. The C-130 carried three 6 by 6 trucks and I think four jeeps (possible with a tight squeeze). The jeeps carried troops with 50 caliber machineguns. The plane would fly in under the radar scopes, land on the street, and stop within a quarter mile of the Embassy. This would occur at 2:00 a.m. The vehicles would rush to the Embassy, rescue the hostages, and load them into the trucks and the jeeps would lead back to the plane firing like hell into the buildings to create panic. The time limit was very short. On arriving at the plane the hostages would be loaded, the vehicles would be left on the ground, and the juice shot to the motors and rockets. At this moment the jet fighters would be alerted and come in to protect the return of the C-130 with no regard for the fact that this would be considered an invasion. Sound feasible? It was possible with the element of surprise. Could it have been accomplished? Yes. What happened? Some (deleted) character warned the Iranians and they moved the hostages the day before the raid. (Years later I would come to a conclusion about who that bastard was, right or wrong.) If you can't believe or don't want to believe, that is what happened, I know that it did. This was the result of President Carter's first attempt to get the hostages out of Iran. The media didn't know about the attempt beforehand (that's why it was not published), so why tell about it after it was never used? The second was more of a disaster because of military stupidity since the services do retain a high number of such people.

The hanky-panky started long before the election was over. This action would cost us dearly in years to come. (Watergate who? What about Iran-Contragate?) Well, that's politics and the only reason it is mentioned here is because of the loss of some fine aircraft and military personnel because of the stupidity of a few. The above happenings did not interfere with our operations so we kept going at a fast pace. That C-141 modification was rolling along.

Chapter 19

I thought that I would never say anything about what happened during this time. Now that the period that was considered strictly confidential is over, I feel that this is a significant part of this story.

In 1980, there was a lot of secrecy going on about an area being established for special emphasis similar to the Skunk Works in CALAC. We were advised not to discuss it under any circumstances. There were certain people leaving our area that we did not discuss. Sometime in May I got a call from one of my former upper managers to meet him on the shipping dock. He told me just to get up there and be there, not to discuss it with anyone. We met and he drove me around the base and into the city and about.

He requested my complete silence on what he had to say and that it should not be repeated. It is a rough type of thing to promise this silence but it is also surprising to know how well you can adjust to zipping your mouth when it is considered necessary. I was told that because of my expertise in fasteners and the past record of doing a respectable job, he was requesting that I join his crew. Coming from him, this was quite a compliment. I did not know that seventeen weeks of FBI and other types of investigation were in store. I accepted with glee, anything to finally get into something new.

Top management in my division was notified that on clearance I should be released without comment. Although my current work assignment continued, I started the long process of getting an AO1 security clearance. They accepted the fact that I did not know the exact date that both of my grandparents had their first sex experience but considered that they were married when my parents were born. No problems were incurred to indicate that my parents were not married when I was born. After being under the Social Security system since 1937, I was considered a good boy who had never been arrested as a child, served in the navy during World War II with an honorable discharge, completed college with a BS (that is, bachelor of science degree, thank you), worked for Lockheed-Georgia company for twenty-eight years, never pissed into the wind or farted against a breeze, other items in my ancestry, and that I had probably paid more taxes than was due (which was of no interest to them). All of this was taken into consideration with the information available from the thirteen digital numbers that I am known under and believe it or not but I was then considered a good American with doubtful ancestry. I got the AO1 security clearance. As the newborn baby said, "I didn't do nothing."

It was now September and I went down to the area of the new job. I parked as instructed to have my entrance interview. Before I could complete the interview I had an in-plant ticket for parking in a restricted area. You don't know what a relief it is to toss a ticket to your boss (or local police chief) and say, "Take care of this." I was told to report to the area the following Monday morning with the proper identification. I walked into the arena of the covert and secret world on that day.

Unless you have worked under these conditions you would not know the requirements and I will only give you a hint. You learn to button your lip. It becomes a habit and there is no stress. You don't even dream of your job after you have left for the day. You become two characters, one for work and the other for home life. As far as my neighbors were concerned I worked for Lockheed. As far as Lockheed was concerned, I had quit to become an independent aircraft fastener consultant. I had two badges. My business mail did not come to the plant. I had a post office box. My phone number could never be traced to Lockheed. My office phone could be divulged to my family with the order never to give it out. My phone number at home was changed to private (no phonebook listing). It would be stupid and unnecessary for me to divulge any part of the work location. You were accepted by management for your ability and knowledge and because the investigation had proven you capable of performing the job required.

It is a helluva thing to have to deal with prejudice everywhere one goes but the thing to remember is that the average white person (that is, 80 percent of them) believe that they are the chosen few with all the intelligence of the world inherited. Usually, a person with a good knowledge of history will be one of the most rational people. It's hell to be stupid and not realize it. History should give a great knowledge of the accomplishments of all the people of the world. We know it does not factually present that information. I found a small degree of prejudice exhibited in some of the groups I had to work with and this was normal.

I think I have explained that the most irrational people that I have worked with are engineers, especially the young inexperienced ones and the old know-it-alls. These comprise about 15 percent of the total. The balance are those engineers who would rather be developing, researching, and designing than being managers. I found exceptional people in engineering management positions but they were not in the majority. I think I had better leave the engineers alone or it will seem that I don't like or respect them, and nothing could be further from the truth. The one good thing I will never forget is that the majority respected me and my efforts to cut cost, consistently improve quality, and deliver our product on schedule.

The value and cost of this type program was usually high. One reason was that the top management of all the suppliers and their designated people had to have the same level of security clearance. These were the only people we could contact at the supplier's facility. All of them had set aside areas for this type of work. The suppliers were well versed and experienced in this type of work over many years. We had the same expert category in our R&D departments.

We really hustled at our jobs and the program was making schedule and quality but cost was something no one seemed to emphasize too much. I have two more incidents to relate dealing with certain engineers that I have described (indicated, in my opinion, as the stupid ones). The first was a young fellow who was "gung-ho" in his efforts. His attitude was snotty and one of the buyers had already cussed him out. He brought me a piece of paper with a rectangle drawn in the center of it. He dropped it on the desk, said buy 200 each right away, and he wanted a ³⁄₁₆ hole drilled in the center. He walked back to his area. There were no dimensions as to length or thickness, the location of the hole, and no alloy specified. I looked at it and wondered 200 each of what? I went to his desk in engineering and requested more information, including the anticipated use of the item. He said he knew what he wanted and he was the "goddamn engineer" (heard that one before, too) but if I was too stupid to purchase it then he would do my job and (with a big laugh to impress his buddies) I could do his. I told him that if I did not know my job any better than he indicated that he knew his, I'd be damned if I wanted his job. I did not bother to consult him on any more engineering requirements. I wonder if he ever got his rectangles.

The other was with a high-level character who was the top boss in his division of engineering. I knew his background but I don't feel that it is necessary to mention. He was highly thought of by his flunkies. The other people just did their jobs. He had the habit of intimidating and insulting his subordinates and others on many occasions due to his position. I inherited the opportunity of going to a top-level shortage and schedule meeting with my boss where this character was officiating. He always looked with contempt on anyone other than engineers. He made the statement that "if the sorry procurement department got off their asses and got deliveries in on time we would not have the behind schedules that we face." My boss turned red in the face and did not say anything. Then all of a sudden that voice that I usually recognize as my own after the fact burst forth, "If you goddamn engineers would let us know what you want yesterday we probably could have it on dock today!" The silence that followed would have allowed one to hear a rat pee on wet cotton. I was never invited to another top-level shortage meeting (what a relief). But I would miss increasing my glossary of excuses.

I received a bunch of drawings detailing the plumbing (I bought that equipment also) required on our bird. Enthused that I knew the exact source that could supply same (with all clearances), I eagerly jumped forward to make contact. After sending the prints and specifications and requesting earliest delivery the contract was placed. The first error I made was not checking the prints myself. Remember that I had taught blueprint reading at Lockheed years ago and also worked with R&D engineers on the B-1 Bomber wing slats and other engineering areas. It should be, but seldom was, utilized for every person working on the aircraft to check the quality of all the work done previous to commencing their own job portion. I had made a habit of doing this most of the time. The source broke a few production records and sent the beautiful top-quality parts to us. The parts were highly acceptable for they were made perfect to the prints we had sent them. They would have made good plumbing installations in the governor's mansion or the Taj Mahal but were not worth a damn for our requirement. The parts were twice the size needed. We paid for the engineering error and the supplier's production.

A lot of thinking and vapors were evident but they came from hell-raising. The prints were given a complete going over and the new prints were ready in a few days. I rushed those out to the supplier and they cut loose again, expedited production, and delivered the parts in a little over a week. This was the result of around-the-clock effort. The parts received were suitable for the city hall but not for our bird. We again paid for the engineering effort plus that of the source. I went to another high-level management meeting. My second boss was fed up so he made a clear-cut request. He looked at me and said, "Hap, what will it take for us to get the right parts in here immediately?" Damn if everybody didn't look at me. I told him that I needed engineering to correct the prints and they should immediately give them to me with a design engineer (I requested one by name) and we would take them to the supplier. This was on a Friday and we intended to leave on Sunday as to get an early start first thing Monday morning. This they committed to and we went to transportation for tickets, etc. Engineering made the flight request for their man and my department did likewise for me. They arranged for their man to leave Sunday morning at 11:00 a.m. at $808 for the round trip. Since materiel has always been cost conscious my reservation was to leave on the redeye special Sunday night for $404 round trip. What was he supposed to do?

Wait for me in the airport. He admitted that he had never been to California before. Hell naw! We would fly together so both of us went on the 11:00 a.m. flight, naturally an L-1011. It is embarrassing to go to the engineering of a supplier and admit that your own engineering department is knee deep in it. The engineer who went with me changed any impressions that they may have formed. By the way, there was no crack in the runway on our arrival. Fortunately, the supplier recognized our dilemma and put all effort in giving us what we needed. We were able to bring the parts back with us and through a lot of effort we regained schedule.

I had another of my wild experiences on this job. I was sitting in my chair at my desk and all of a sudden the whole room started to spin. I had experienced this sensation a couple of times previously but not to this extent. I clamped my eyes tightly shut and held on to the chair. I felt nauseated but not too sick. I told the guy next to me to call medics. This he did and told them that I was having a heart attack. It's funny how a lot of people think of a heart attack first. Since I had, at one time, bought most of the medical supplies for that unit they immediately recognized my name and made a real rush to get to me. No doctor was with the ambulance but a nurse and one of the top paramedics were in that vehicle. I knew both of them well. Normal security was reduced and they took me and the chair to the ambulance. On reaching the medical department one of the doctors I also knew was ready and waiting. My eyes were clamped shut and I was still spinning. He recognized vertigo, often caused by an inner ear infection. He gave me a mild sedative and told me to try and sleep. He came back in thirty minutes and asked me how I felt. I felt real good and normal. I remained there for about two hours. He gave me some antibiotics and told me to go home if I wanted to do so. I went back to work. This was, in my opinion, the first indication of the trouble I would experience caused by the loss of hearing I was having in my left ear.

I made several trips with my supervisor to the West Coast. We never sat in adjoining seats nor did we offer any recognition of each other. I remember the time we went to L.A. together and on deplaning, one of those skin-headed disciples of something stepped in his face and shouted, "Do you believe in war?" He ignored him and kept on walking. The fellow stepped in front of me and shouted the same thing in my face. For some stupid reason, may have been his bad breath, I shouted, "Hell yes!" right into his face and almost bumped him. Since it seemed that I was the only one who had answered him it drew attention. The little incident was over in a matter of seconds but later my boss asked me why I did that. I did not have a good reason for my action. If I had been by myself I probably would have knocked hell out of him. I don't think anyone would expect a 007 to do that so I never forgot my role after that.

A lot of interesting things happened, like the time I had to have my nose opened up as I was having difficulty breathing. The nose had been broken back in 1951 (an automobile wreck) and I had straightened it myself with a right hook. The septum had been a little out of place for a long time. During the operation there was a "secret service" man observing to make sure while under the anesthetic I did not give away any classified secrets. The only thing I noticed was that I lost a lot of blood and used a heap of oxygen. One Saturday I had all of my teeth pulled and replaced with plates during the same operation and was back to work the following Monday. Since I would be asleep and the dental surgeon would have my mouth full of hands it was not necessary to make sure I might divulge any secrets.

We were told not to walk fast between our buildings as this would draw attention. Who? They said that the Russians had a satellite directly over our location and were monitoring each and every move. That was a little hard to take. I had seen some odd-looking stuff going on in California opposite the Skunk Works at a so-called camera shop across the street. They had a video type lens sticking from between the blinds on the second floor and taking pictures of the whole location, who went in and out. Our attitude seemed to be to ignore them by being careful going in and out and maybe they would think we did not know that they were there. It had to be true about the satellite for we heard one morning that the night before there was a distress signal that a plane was down in the vicinity of the plant. It seems no one, the CAP or military had picked up that distress signal. A call came in to the local authorities from Washington, D.C., alerting them to the fact that a plane was down near the Bear Creek area (not too far from the plant). The government had received a call from the Russian Embassy indicating that they had evidence to believe that an aircraft was down in that vicinity. Investigation discovered a small aircraft at a small landing area near Bear Creek with an electrical short or something causing the mayday signal to go off. Since our alert systems had indicated nothing, how did the Russians know? The satellite, boss, the satellite!

After three years it was required to move this program back to the West Coast. A few of the people, including the director, went to the West Coast. Those remaining were absorbed back into the regular workforce. We were debriefed (which means that you were told to forget everything that you knew and never mention where or what you did, or somebody would beat hell out of you) and sent back, mostly, into our old work areas. Fortunately, by performing a decent job at the above duties my salary increase over the two and one half years totaled $102 per week. At the rate I was going in the old workplace, it would have taken almost five years to attain that size increase.

Chapter 20

With some regret I went back to my old group. The aircraft industry is one where you maintain your employment as a salaried person by your performance. You have no seniority, unless you came up through the hourly ranks. From my attitude of doing the best job that you can I have been able over the years to remain employed. A lot of people hold their jobs by their ability to become the best yes-man, better known without hesitation as brown-nosers. An employer appreciates the person that will take a management decision and act on it even after stating to management (face to face) that in his opinion it may not work. Never fear to make that opinion known to your boss. A real manager knows that he does not know all the minute details of an operation and the ones who realize this will appreciate knowledgeable employees saying so. Then there are some people so ignorant or impressed with their position that they may not appreciate this approach so just let them know that you are doing what you have been told. They will blame you anyway if it's wrong.

This was a time that I consider the most stressful of the many I experienced in my career at GELAC. It was downright stupid. The volume on the desk was gradually increased and became almost impossible to maintain. I got an appointment with the president of the division for an interview and we talked about some of my problems and the fact that I had been overlooked many times for advancement. The main issue discussed was the possibility of an advancement or promotion based on my seniority and record. I now had thirty-one years with the Lockheed-Georgia division company. No one between me and the president (called "proper channels") to my knowledge had ever placed my name before the management selection committee (except in 1953) for promotion. If it ever was, then, as I later found out, a high percentage of my records were missing in the package presented to the committee. I suspected two characters who were capable of doing such and I would almost swear that they did. Not a goddamned thing was heard from the interview with the president, not even an answer or acknowledgment that it ever took place. 'Nuff said.

I negotiated a large requirement of electrical wiring that we had been purchasing by lots to be manufactured and held by the source until needed and then shipped. This gave us the advantage of paying the volume price and only paying (the volume price) for the quantity shipped at intervals. It saved the supplier production time and unnecessary paperwork to the both of us. The nitpicker tried to take it apart and I went to the department manager and got it approved. My cost reduction report was never filed. The savings totaled over $25,000.

Earlier I had gone to the assistant director of materiel and asked him to pull my folder so we could review it with the intent of finding information that reflected that what I had in my records was comparable. We found that there was a sheet supposedly indicating that it contained copies of my training records. It stated that I had three training courses (this was 1983) during my time at GELAC. One of the courses it listed stated was, "How to build an aeroplane." Even an uninformed fool would know we were not talking about model aircraft. The other two were seemingly just as simple. This was the sheet that had been sent to the Management Selection Committee (MSC), not the whole folder. The big boss agreed that that was what happened with the information he had at hand. I had a good friend who built model aeroplanes for GELAC. It took him nine months of training and they used his models in the wind tunnels. (Hello, O. P. Burns.)

Strangely, all of the certificates I had earned were in my folder, including many cost reduction awards. The procedure of sending a record to the MSC was to get a computer printout of one's record so that all pertinent information would be easily available to the reviewer. What some exceptional bastard had done was sent the printout as outlined in the previous paragraph. The most insulting part was that I had a certificate from Cobb County Vocational School indicating that I had completed sixty hours of instruction in reading blueprints dated 4–30–56. The only training I had in blueprints is the interpretation of blueprints, not just to read them. This certificate was signed by the head of the GELAC training department. His last name is the same as mine. (Hopefully no kin.) At the time I was supposed to be taking this training course at CCV I was actually teaching blueprints (primary through advanced design) in the training department at GELAC with a Cobb County Vocational Teacher's permit effective for one year dated 7–1–55 and expiring 7–1–56 (temporary certification, time limited). I taught for almost a year and have retained a copy of those two items. I made a copy of my original permit and gave it to the boss and watched him insert it into my folder. The assistant director wanted to know what the hell was going on. I told him that I was finding out a lot of crap that I had no idea was being carried out. There had been a ceiling put on my progress within the company for many years. There was nothing the boss could do or attempt to do. I had been standing behind the fan for many years and never realized it. I decided that the wheel still rolled and from time to time all I had to do was wait and watch a whole bunch of characters get their turn to be smashed in one form or the other. At least that is better than shooting up a bunch of characters as I felt like doing. I have lived long enough to see most of them take their turn under that wheel. As silly as it may sound, I went back and retrieved my hip pocket salt that I had left when I was working under tight security and placed it back in its position.

I had a conference with the fellow sitting in for the assistant director (who was on vacation) and we discussed the issue man-to-man (lay it on the line, no holds barred) concerning the situation with my "Whiz-bang" supervisor. I was told to go and take two weeks of vacation and when I returned to take my desk, lock, stock, and barrel, to another buying group and report to the purchasing agent there. The new purchasing agent was a guy named Joe. Joe was a supervisor I had worked for some time previously and we had turned out the group raising hell with each other and I was moved from his group. Over the years since we had gotten to know each other well and learned to respect each other and it was no problem to work for Joe (we understood each other). We got along well for the months I worked for him. Joe called together his group and introduced me, giving my background and suggesting that if they ran into problems to consult me as I had experience in practically all procurement methods and materials. (After thirty-two years somebody was expressing that I probably had experience and was now qualified.) He asked me when time was available to take some of the younger buyers over and walk them through the manufacturing plant to familiarize them with the areas in which their procurement items were being used, including the more complete aircraft so they could see their parts on the actual aircraft. I developed confidence in Joe and worked my usual hard hours and did a good job. I liked for Joe to get a raise for then I would get one also.

During this time Joe moved laterally to another position and my new boss (department manager) was a young fellow about fifteen years my junior. I had known him for some years but he had never done anything overly impressive to my knowledge. But here he was. He did impress me with his first department meeting in which he said that he expected each member to do his or her job, to come to him with problems, to do the things we were experienced in, and to get the job done. This indicated to me that he was letting everyone know that he did not know everything about all the operations. If you ever get a new boss who gives the impression that he knows it all, beware! I later learned of some of his prejudices and his lack of rational thinking that I could not accept according to his level of intelligence. Everyone has a problem with the atmosphere that they grew up under. I think over the years he grew with the experiences he was having and would have. He did express an appreciation for my ability to do a good job and my overall knowledge and this was appreciated.

My next supervisor (purchasing agent) was a young fellow about 27 years old who was the biggest bullshitter I had ever run across. He had a big mouth (bigger than mine), twice the size of his brain. This guy could open his mouth at the most inopportune times recorded. Ninety percent of the time he didn't know what the hell he was talking about. In other words, he was of that class of ignoramuses who knew everything while espousing nothing. I won't even guess how he got the position. His type has been described in earlier chapters. He agitated everyone with his fountain of knowledge and manner in which things were to be done. Those of us not completely bulldozed just kept quiet. I knew damn well that I would not be able to have some dumbass telling me how to run my job so that made me the exception as usual. This boils down to the fact that we just did not get along with each other. He was the boss but it was hell trying to carry out his decisions. Actually, he gave the younger people hell but seemed to hold off on me so the explosion would come later.

My new office mate was a woman of the Jewish faith who was right out of school (college) and on her first job. Being a little shy, she was making every effort to prove capable of doing the job. You have to appreciate the joy of having a new employee to train, knowing nothing of the procedures and methods required to be a good buyer. You can start from scratch with the basics of character, principles, honesty, and integrity that are the priorities of a good buyer. You can teach the basics of quality, reliability, delivery, and cost. A person like this has not had the chance of having an attitude spoiled by association with the slicks of the profession (it is a profession). I had her listen to me when I would be discussing delivery or quality with a supplier who was behind schedule. I taught her the proper aircraft language when it was necessary to emphasize a condition. I taught her how to distinguish between truth and bullshit from a supplier representative when discussing problems. I taught her everything I knew about the product she was purchasing. (I don't have to brag and say there was very little that I did not know about just about everything materiel bought.) I took her into the shop and showed her the items she purchased and their location on the aircraft and the importance of her job to the overall product.

I told her that she was somebody and not to fear anyone once she learned her job requirements. I told her that I would rather hear her use profanity (the aircraft type) than ever to see her cry after a tough phone conversation. I advised her on when to cancel a purchase order for failure to deliver when committed, and how to place with the next highest bidder who had stock and document same. She became a very efficient buyer and had confidence in herself. There were other young women brought into the larger department who did not have this type of training. I tried to help all of the young buyers coming into the department as there were certain basics that one needed that just weren't laying around. They all did well but not in the time that our little lady (Fay) did.

I went into the office one day and she was crying. I jumped her and was giving her hell about what I had said about crying. She told me that this stupid supervisor of ours had been riding her lately and had made some remarks that became known as sexual harassment later on. I asked her what she intended to do about it. She said that she did not want to cause any trouble. I told her to tell me if any other incidents occurred and to tell me everything that was said. I went into my supervisor's office and made this short statement: "I want you to lay off of my office mate. I'm not going to say a goddamn thing more. You understand exactly what I'm talking about so it stops right now, understood?" He looked at me sort of stunned and I walked out before he could answer. No more crap was given to my partner after that. I told her what I had done and if it ever occurred again I wanted to be the first to know. Things rolled along a little smoother. After all, I was about 59 and she was about 23 and I had never had a daughter.

Review time rolled around and this super-duper supervisor gave everyone their performance reviews except me. He told me he wanted to see me at the end of the shift. I went into his office after everyone had left and he handed me my review. It was the lowest graded review that I had received in over twenty years. Everything reflecting on my ability was marked "usually meets requirements." I looked at that bunch of bullshit indicating that I needed further training, more experience, and a change of attitude for my grades to be higher. This was from a character that had never read my folder and knew nothing of my history with Lockheed and was giving me grades according to his stupid interpretation of where I belonged. He had the audacity to try and give me reasons for his grading. What he was trying to say was that I did not brown-nose (kiss ass) to his satisfaction. Well, this was no lady supervisor and I had said that any man that showed this level of ignorance I would probably kick his ass until his nose bled. I took the review, balled it up, threw it on his desk, and told him to ram it up his ass. I had worked at Lockheed-Georgia years before he was born and this snot-nose was telling me how I was rated and I'm supposed to say "yassir" and believe that crap. I told him I would see him on Monday morning in the manager's office.

I went to the manager's office with about ½ inch of resume type information. The manager had known me for some time but not too well. I told him that if I had to take that type of BS after all of these years then I would just check back out to manufacturing. He knew that was a lie for I would have thrown more crap into the fan than it had ever experienced. Within five minutes after he heard my complaint and read the information I had furnished him I had a new supervisor. I noted the discrepancies between the original review ratings and the comments on the copy of a new review. The super supervisor was around a few more months but finally rammed his foot so deep in his own mouth that he got the opportunity to resign rather than be fired. No one missed him.

My new supervisor was a young kid, born about four years after I started working for Lockheed. I now had seniority of over thirty-three years. I don't know where he came from for I can't remember seeing him around the division. I don't bite my tongue when I say that he was someone's prodigy (I knew later) and was able to move on up the ladder. I have no objection to a person who has that opportunity when they are capable and have ambition with common sense. Very few who get this opportunity have the other qualifications. This fellow seemed to possess those characteristics. He came into my office and stated that he had little knowledge of his responsibilities or the product lines and asked my help in familiarizing him with the problems. What the hell do you tell a person who admits his shortcomings? At least he admitted his capabilities and asked for help. I recognized him as being smart as hell or completely honest. He proved to be honest and I eventually recognized him as being smart as hell also (I never recognized the brown-nosing syndrome) and he got my wholehearted support. My days of working with and for him were very pleasant. He always had my support.

Chapter 21

The department manager and my new supervisor came to my office and informed me that I would take the desk responsible for managing the support of our Air National Guard, military (navy and coast guard mainly) requirements, and all foreign customers as to their warranties, maintenance, and repair needs. This did not seem too great until I realized that the Air National Guard was from the East Coast to the Mississippi River, the U.S. military was everywhere in the world, and about fifty-four foreign countries were utilizing our aircraft. The aircraft were the C-130 and the C-140 including the Jetstar. This support included everything that was on these airplanes—maintenance kits, repair kits, items like brakes, tires, small assembly spares, generators, cables, electrical harnesses and light bulbs, all flight instruments, assemblies pertaining to troop seats, requirements for cargo handling, glass, control cables, pilot compartment accessories, toilet seats (yeah!), tool kits, life rafts, survival kits, sanitation kits, life jackets, and every damn thing else including the most important, the engines.

There had been about three buyers doing this job in a rather unreliable manner so here I was again, because of previous experience, being given the opportunity to take on this load.

How many times would I get such marvelous opportunities? This seemed to be getting close to number ten. Take advantage of all opportunities and you will get ahead. As Paul would so eloquently have said, "Horse feathers!" (By the way, Paul is now a purchasing agent after many years and he earned his long ago also.) Actually, I am a glutton for punishment and I get a kick (self-satisfaction) out of knocking out challenges.

After almost thirty-three years of ulcers, hemorrhoids, high blood pressure, stress problems, a blocked artery in the heart, four or five operations, and two bouts with cancer (fortunately both benign), having been bar-b-cued plus a set of new teeth, here I am with the opportunity to prove my ability. It is to my own advantage that I have ignored all of these ailments with proper medical treatment. I give the credit to my belief that the mind is the open door to God. Therefore, mind over matter is my most religious belief. Put physical problems out of your mind, let the body take care of itself, and believe in God. He will take care of all of your problems. Try it. The scars left in certain places always seem to amaze doctors. Doctors don't seem to realize that most of the medicines they prescribe have been here all the time. The best medicine is to go to the Source. Then you go to the doctor with the ability to describe your ailment.

Have you ever seen a C-130 engine flown into a Middle Eastern sandstorm? Have you ever known of a Jetstar flown beyond the time specified on the forward energizers (or whatever)? What about all of the other flight safety items past their maintenance or replacement time? Have you realized that the customer requires immediate replacement? Oh, it's all right that they failed to monitor the maintenance schedules. They need the damn part now to sustain flight operations. They are losing money and it's the manufacturer's fault. Remember the guarantee? What the hell, the damn tires wore out regardless of the cargo weights carried and the braking required to stop. The altimeter indicates that I am flying 10 feet under water and I damn well know by eyesight that I'm at 10,000 feet. Boy, howdy! We were flying at 22,000 feet and lightning struck the left outboard engine and the only thing left is the engine support. When are you going to replace the engine? (That actually happened.) We haul a lot of cattle in our aircraft and the urine has corroded the floorboards. When can we expect replacements? Some of the oil equipment broke loose and damaged the side panels on our C-130. When can your field representative repair same? Sounds crazy? Remove what humor may have been inserted but leave the emphasis and those above give you some indication of the complaints we receive.

Now consider the fact that this desk is also responsible for ground handling equipment. These include the work stands, the gurneys, the tugs, and all of their maintenance, the tug engines, and everything else required for aircraft maintenance on the ground. Think of anything that is necessary to maintain the ground handling equipment in top shape (including new units when required) and you are running one helluva garage and stock shop. Every requirement for this equipment came across this desk. Someone was trying to kill me and I was falling for it or there was one helluva lot of confidence placed in me and I was trying to confirm it. If there was a reward for this volume of work being accomplished by one person, damn if I ever realized what it was.

The purpose of this desk (and it should have been at least two buyers) was to support all of the requisitions and keep those planes in operation for our customers. With the support of our repair sources and the original suppliers we were able to satisfy most of the needs on an expedited basis. Without the help of our different support organizations and the knowledgeable people involved none of this would have been possible. It is a great relief to talk to support people with experience who know what can be done in a given time limit. You won't find a bunch of idiots in these organizations telling bosses what they would like to hear. The bosses get the facts from their field people. The character that threatens and intimidates thinking that a miracle will occur is a fool. Communication is the greatest tool available and as long as communication is in effect customers recognize the effort being made to solve their problems. We had so many fine repair shops developed to handle our requirements that I won't attempt to name them. Any aircraft and repair company person reading this, and remembering me, I say your efforts and help will never be forgotten.

Although I had dealt with many fine companies over the years who had exhibited those qualities of principles, honesty, and integrity that I looked for in my sources, there was one that simply amazed me. The C-130s (all models) were powered by the T56 turbo prop engine manufactured by the Allison division of General Motors Corporation, Detroit, Michigan. In comparison with the big radial engines of the pre-jet types this was a very streamlined smaller type of the transition period (propeller turbo jet). Our goal and theirs was to produce an engine that developed 1 horsepower to 1 pound of weight. If I remember correctly the weight of the original engine was 1,750 pounds. The horsepower was a little less. Quite a few years ago the weight of the engine was 1,833 pounds and the horsepower (1,983) was 4,050. On all the aircraft we produce and sell, the customers have their own maintenance crews, trained by Lockheed and the manufacturers. The major overhauls are done by Lockheed or the unit manufacturer.

Allison had all the capability to overhaul and maintain their engines. When an engine shows up with a certain type of damage they request that it be sent back to the main plant for diagnosis and disposition. They have samples of soil from all parts of the world and classified as to damage that can be done by the different types of soil. They have accumulated evidence and information to almost tell where the aircraft has flown in the world without reaching a state of teardown and analysis of the complete engine and its components. They have sales engineers (so has Lockheed) around the world servicing the aircraft that use their engines. They once sent me a list of soil from around the world with the physical and chemical characteristics of each sample and the location from which it was obtained. When an engine was returned for analysis and repair I was sent pictures of the component parts and the damage done to each, indicating what had caused the breakdown. The physical damage caused by foreign objects (especially soil) was the same as fingerprints. During this time a new engine cost about $800,000. If the repair cost were beyond $375,000, usually the damaged engine would be replaced with a new engine. Normally, the repair was much less than this amount but any components found worn to a certain degree and still under warranty were replaced with new parts. Once the customer's engine went for repair he always got back a practically new engine with full warranty on all parts. Engines were damaged by other things than soil and sand. FOG (foreign objects on the ground) was a big problem also.

Remember when I noted that I had bought nuts of all sizes, pea and gravel rock, ducks, chickens, geese, turkeys, and several items indicating practically any type of object that would hit the windshield and other parts of the aircraft. These were used also to test damage done to turbo and jet engines when ingested in flight or on the ground. (Don't stand behind the fan-jet that is.) You could get splattered with all of that crud. A firm cost could not be estimated until an engine had gone through all of the inspection procedures. As stated above, I would receive a brochure of pictures of the damaged parts showing extent of damage to each part to be replaced, parts being replaced under warranty, and a cost breakdown for the complete repair of components replaced. You talk about documentation, I had it.

There were a number of small business shops who kept our customers supplied with reworked and reparable components. Their workers consisted of veterans with experience from the military who maintained, in the field, the operation of aircraft under the most severe conditions. A very high percentage of these aircraft were always ready for battle or the performance of their missions. These men and women knew the value of reliability. We were fortunate to develop these sources for the services we needed. I am happy to say that none ever let us down. It is surprising to talk to the workers in these small facilities and experience the level of knowledge and the attitude that just passing is not good enough. The other part is that most of managers of these sources were younger than the workers. Some shops have the father (usually the founder) as the general manager, taking care of the full operation of the workforce and quality/reliability, and the sons and daughters handling sales, bookkeeping, and customer relations. The workforces consisted of people averaging about twenty years or better of experience each. No major decisions seem to be made concerning operations without the input of the workers. Even when there were only ten people involved, the unit functioned as a team. You did not receive poor quality from such companies. They had the same problems of getting components as everyone else, but usually were able to meet their commitments. When necessary, some of these little repair shops had their salesmen bring parts to the plant to make their schedules. This helped to guarantee that we made our schedules. A good buyer never forgets such service.

Other than the small businesses in the local area I never got the chance to visit many of the small businesses that supported us unless they were in the area of the larger suppliers whom I did visit when I had problems. One of my best was in Oldsmar, Florida, and specialized in repair and maintenance of small aircraft components. Brian was the president and CEO and Jeff was the marketing director. Small companies could have big shots just like the larger ones. You could always identify the top management in a small shop—they were the ones who worked the hardest. Most small shops were family-operated concerns. Brian's wife took care of all the paperwork and business and was as knowledgeable of the aircraft parts as the others. You could bet on the fact that you would find a quality operation when dealing with the usual tight team performing in an operation of this sort. I will mention a number of small businesses that I have dealt with because they were above average in their workmanship and delivery. The only influence that they attempted was the quality of their work and developing the customer's confidence in the level of their integrity. Jeff had been a young buyer at GELAC before going with this small company, Gulf Aerospace, Inc. He understood my problems and reacted accordingly when they were awarded orders after competitive bidding. I had excellent competition for this type rework with a number of small companies.

One of my other good small shops was on the east coast of Florida in Titusville. Both the top salespeople at Gulf and this shop, Air Marine Sales, Inc., were good friends and competitors on a number of items but differed on most of them. One would loan the other component parts to fulfill a commitment and be paid back later. This often worked to GELAC's benefit. Robert was the production manager and he did as much selling as he did production. Air Marine was founded by Robert's father. Robert and Jeff were in their twenties and real go-getters. They were a little over 150 miles apart but they sometimes planned their field trips together and if you saw one the other would be there also. It was like dealing with two hotshot brothers. They would razz each other on who had the best reputation for quality, delivery, and lead time (turn-around time for rework). I saw one of the two of them about every four or five weeks. Communication was good and the rapport was great.

One of my most memorable moments was experienced while talking about deliveries with Robert one morning. We knew that the *Challenger* was flying that day and I had told him earlier that I would call about that time for information pertaining to rework problems. I knew that he could see the cape from his backdoor for he had told me of watching earlier shots. We were talking and he told me it was time for the shot. He went to his backdoor with the phone on an extension line and described the takeoff. I could hear that initial blastoff real good. He said it was beautiful and he wished I could see it. Perfect takeoff, trailing that big plume of white smoke. All of a sudden he gasped and said, "What the!!!!!" and then he hollered into the phone, "It exploded! It exploded!" He sounded as if someone had shot at him and missed. He was really excited and started describing the scene to me. "It is breaking into two—no! three pieces and exploding and falling. Hap, the *Challenger* is gone, just blown apart. I can't see how there could be any survivors. I got to go, I can't talk, will call you later."

I told my nearest co-workers what had happened. Within five minutes everyone in the building knew about it. Lockheed had a lot of components on that bird. It was a very sad moment for us because of the lost crew. Later it was on all the news with pictures of the catastrophe on television. This was a great blow to all of us in the aerospace industry. That incident rammed home to all of us the importance of quality and reliability. Just about every aircrafter is interested in the causes of such disasters and since it happened we subconsciously hoped that it was human error and not product failure. It really raises the efforts for quality workmanship. The cause was determined to be a bad O-ring in the big takeoff tanks.

Chapter 22

By this time the whole company was becoming computerized. I did not like computers until it dawned on me that this was the way things were going regardless of my likes or dislikes. They put computers and printers in each cubbyhole (these little offices were divided by removable panels) for the two buyers to utilize in all phases of their work. A programmer was sent down to schedule our units into the main system or bank.

We had a young fellow (below 30 years old) who had finished a course in computer technology and he was my office partner at the time. The bosses assigned him to teach the rest of us the basics of computerization. He did a good job, but I still did not seem to feel that what he was teaching would be of any value to me in my oddball responsibilities and the variety of problems that I encountered. I learned to put in my orders and follow through on updating the delivery status. This was mainly what the bosses wanted. I wanted more. I had some definite ideas about how my program should be set up and be beneficial to me and the reports that were required. My partner's name was Mike and he was a young gung-ho buyer. Sharing an office, we had a lot of opportunities to discuss the possibilities of the computer being a great help in what I wanted it to do for me.

Mike did not have the experience to program the computer like I wanted it. I went over to the main bank and requested that a programmer be sent to give me some help. Kevin came over and we talked for a long time as I told him what I wanted available in my computer. Mike was in on the conversations and Kevin determined that Mike could put in the exact program I wanted after he had made the initial programming required. After Kevin finished and Mike took over, I told him what I wanted and how I wanted it. Kevin had set up my own bank and gave me the key punches to gain access to it. No one could get into my bank except Mike, as he was the only one other than me who knew the correct entrance keys. Mike programmed the things that I wanted and the results would be what I needed. I would have to go to the department computer to complete my program initiated on our little office computer.

I had Mike set me up about thirty-five components to follow initially. I had the manufacturer, part number, ship-to date (sent for repair on purchase orders), the return date committed, item on schedule, item behind schedule, the original cost value, the repair cost, the percentage or repair cost against the original cost, and the actual delivery date received. I had spaces provided for fifteen items of each part number and could always tell the average cost of repair against the original cost. I updated this record weekly. At any time I could pull up-to-date information for the boss on demand. At the bottom of the page there was the quantity of the particular part out for repair, average repair time, average original cost, average repair cost against average original cost, average turn-around time, percentage on or behind schedule, and the total value of the units out for repair. Imagine the amount of information in that system when all orders were entered. I would sit at that computer and make it smoke. Everyone thought that I was a computer whiz. I still put up-to-date information available to anyone in the little computer in our office but nothing to compare to the (gem of) information in the department bank. Finally Mike fixed it so I could pull down charts (in color) indicating status. I did not know a damn thing about the computer but I sure could work my system. I posted my weekly computerized chart status on the wall next to the entrance to the boss's office. He got a big kick out of it as the wheels-that-be could always see it when they came to his office.

I had finally reached the stage where I appreciated the computer. The two main items to be considered as I moved along at GELAC had always been organization and communication. I had reached a point where it really paid off. The job of handling and monitoring the thousands of rework, repair, and maintenance requirements of our customers, overseas and otherwise, came down to a well-organized and accountable system. The job developed a level of routine. The volume of work did not decrease, it just became more manageable. More foreign countries were buying our C-130 because it was a workhorse. Before I retired I think the number of foreign customers had increased to over sixty utilizing our "Fat Albert."

Of course, with all these aircraft being sold to the U.S. Air Force and foreign countries, Lockheed did much of its business with governments. President Eisenhower warned the American public to beware of the military-industrial complex. What he should have said was beware the military-industrial-political complex. I cannot think of any other person more qualified to make such a statement. Since I was a cog (unknowingly) and not a wheel in the process, I won't attempt to make any further statements about this so-called complex. I will say that a whole lot of wheels from the military and political theaters got some helluva high-level jobs within the industrial system of defense contractors after their retirement. If you guessed that that was your tax money, you are right.

My performance reviews in this period indicated the inconsistencies of grading and comments. It seems the grader did not know what he was talking about because he had never read my history. Same old crap.

Chapter 23   I have now worked for Lockheed-Georgia for thirty-four years. I am one of the first ten Negroes who actually bought a permanent ticket into the field of skilled labor in the aircraft industry (the opinion of the wheels-who-be at GELAC). We have proved that anyone given the opportunity of training and the possibility of advancement can build aircraft to meet the tough competition of the industry. The obstacles put in one's way by idiots can be overcome. Given the chance, one can exceed in all levels of the manufacturing field. By the pursuit of training opportunities I have proven to others and myself that even though you may not get the authority, you are capable of assuming the responsibilities of any position. I have seen Negroes (now known as blacks) reach the positions of department managers, division managers, and other positions of upper management. I have seen one old production friend of mine go all the way to acting (for a limited time) as labor relations manager (branch level). These positions were reached through study, hard work, and ability. A black always had to be twice as good as the next to attain these positions. I think that I have attempted to get away from the use of aircraft language but I must say that that is the goddamn truth. Since I knew most of these people I know that their success came about from enthusiasm, training, and dedication to the success of Lockheed. I can say that I know of no one who practiced brown-nosing (ass-kissing) to any great extent. There were rumors but I don't have firm proof of such. There were some who followed my path of learning as much as possible by the training offered by Lockheed. Others had returned to college on a part-time basis and completed their degrees. One of the fellows who worked with me in the nose section in manufacturing went back and became a doctor (schooled in Pennsylvania, not Georgia). With my knowledge and personality I became the devil's advocate in many instances. A lot of people never forgot that and my lack of advancement is probably the result. One thing is known and that is my loyalty to Lockheed was never in question. I think one of my biggest faults was that I loved the damn place and the aircraft industry.

Time was rolling around and I began to think, what am I doing? My responsibilities are in order and I don't have any major problems. One thing is for sure and that is I ain't gonna get no promotion. I had seen too many younger people come in and get promotions and move on up the ladder. The experience they had attained, in my opinion, didn't amount to a drop in the bucket. Those who have learned to respect the people under them as the only tools that they have and treated them accordingly are the most successful. The ones that think they know it all don't make such good impressions. Usually, they don't last too long. Too much political maneuvering seemed to be the order of the times. I don't know if it was age or seniority working, but I felt that the time was getting close to make another major decision in my life.

I had a comprehensive physical examination in 1987. The doctors found lumps in my prostate gland. Since I had been smoking since I was 14, my lungs were 2 years older than my body. I started with beer and had been drinking on occasion since I was about 18. (Ulcers did not come from drinking.) I drank when I pleased (or was able with money) and never had an alcoholic problem in my working years (ever heard of relaxation time?). I would have gone to a urologist immediately but my brother-in-law died the next morning. This was June 27, 1987, a Friday. After helping my wife make the funeral arrangements until about 2:00 p.m. on that date, I returned home and got a call from my eldest brother in California that I should try and get there right away as my younger brother was dying. Through connections with the airline in Atlanta, I left at 5:30 p.m. that night and arrived in L.A. at 11:00 p.m. the same night, after a Chicago delay. My younger brother died at 8:00 a.m. that Saturday morning June 28, 1987, twenty-four hours and thirty minutes after my brother-in-law. I went to my brother's funeral the following Monday and returned on Wednesday to attend my brother-in-law's funeral on Thursday. A helluva week.

I went to the urologist that Monday and he asked me when I wanted to have the operation. I told him yesterday. He said, "Good, how about tomorrow?" I said fine. He told me that under the circumstances it would be what in layman terms is called a roto-rooter job. I would take a spinal (injection) anesthetic. The anesthesiologist missed my spinal cord four different times and after almost electrocuting me (that's what it felt like), another was brought in and made a good injection. Although groggy, I was awake during the complete operation. Instead of spending three days in the hospital I stayed for twelve days. If I had known at the time the trouble I would have in later years I would have sued the whole bunch (back and sciatic nerve problems). I was out from work for ten weeks. The fellow who took my desk on my retirement had been watching over it while I was out.

The desk was in good shape when I returned in October 1987. It occurred to me that I had now worked for Lockheed for over thirty-five years. I'll be damned if I intended to stay until I dropped dead. "Fool, there is no future at

Lockheed anymore," I told myself. Like the Gross brothers, Dan Haughton, Clarence "Kelly" Johnson (everyone at Lockheed was a link in the chain), and on down the line, the time has come to quit! You may feel that Lockheed owes you something, but you don't owe Lockheed a damn thing more. I went into the office and told the boss that effective December 14, 1987, I was going to take six of the seven weeks of vacation I had coming and return on January 31, 1988, for full retirement. He expressed surprise and stated that I had a lot of nerve to take retirement at 62 years of age. What he did not know was that I was in the gray financially and that seemed about as close as I would get to the black. The average length of life after retirement in 1987 for Lockheed retirees was eighteen months. Hell, I intended to live much longer because I had planned to retire at 55 but couldn't financially. I decided to wait no longer. I had many good working buddies who retired and got one to twelve retirement checks before croaking. I think this was mainly the shock of realizing that their working life was over and they had made no plans for their retirement. If you have not made plans for retirement it can be quite a shock. The sudden realization that you have reached the peak, you either fall off the mountaintop or leisurely slide to the level plane of life. I hoped that I would be ready to take the slow slide. After almost twelve years I am hobbling along with my half deaf self and screwed up back, including the sciatic nerves down both legs, under the impression that if I pay the pain no attention I will not feel it. For quite a while I took about two or three nonprescription pain pills a day and ignored the pain. After two major back operations four years ago and two years of constant back and leg pain, I finally stopped having the constant pain and now just suffer from getting old with the normal aches and pains. I still believe that my open door to God (the mind) and my belief in mind over matter has worked and is still working.

    I started to put all effort into closing the problems on the desk and getting everything in order for the person who would take over my responsibilities. I hoped I was giving him the knowledge to operate as I had and to utilize the system that I had set up in the computer. I called my local sources and informed them of my plans. They all congratulated me and expressed their pleasure at working with me over the years and wished me a happy retirement. I received many cards and quite a few personal phone calls. From the large companies and corporations I received cards and calls from the presidents on down to my daily contacts.

Chapter 24

It seems it will only take twenty-four chapters to cover almost thirty-six years of working with Lockheed Aircraft. With all of the memories and backup data I have it would probably cover over eight hundred pages. The basic experiences have been given and about one-half of the backup data used. I have worked with thousands of people—for, over, with, against, agreed, disagreed, been cussed out, and cussed back but the thing I appreciate most was there was no physical contact in anger or otherwise. I have never been disciplined for insubordination or disrespect. By being honest and straightforward, I always had a good understanding with my managers. Quite a number of managers did not like the way I would discuss things, but there was never an indication that their decisions would not be followed.

Racism was prevalent (color, creed, ethnic or national origin, gender, and anti-Semitism) right up to the end. The condition improved slowly with only those changes necessary to meet the government's defense contract demands. Individuals of all groups were able to make improvements in their status because of their enthusiasm, training, ability, and efforts. The hiring practices changed for the better for individuals having these capabilities. A company demands a worker be able to perform at a level of earning his own pay and making a profit for the company. Ability and capability came to the forefront and race gradually slid out of consideration. The problem, in my opinion, is the manager without the qualifications to be able to determine the qualifications of the person attempting to qualify (complicated but true). Some of us may live long enough to recognize the fact that today, there are no races in America, just a melting pot of people (multiracial) making up that group of humans known as Americans. I recognized that long ago and have acted accordingly. One probably won't make many friends or influence too many people with that attitude. You will find that you have good individual friends but not a large diversified group of friends. The only people who can be considered better than one's self are the ones with a better knowledge in a specific field, an overall general knowledge, ability, or natural perspicacity for leadership. Over the years and across the country I made many good acquaintances (and some real friends) through my straightforward and honest interactions and business dealings. They respected my position and I did the same toward them. This resulted in satisfactory and profitable relationships for all of our companies.

By the fourteenth of December 1987, I had cleaned house or put everything in order for the next buyer. I was glad to be informed that Lindsey McDaniel would take over my desk. He was well qualified (I was qualified and had assisted in the training of Lindsey quite a few years back and knew that he was qualified). All the ladies in the materiel division (it seemed) and some of the gents cooked and made salads, cold cut spreads, ham, all types of bread, finger sandwiches, soft drinks, and really made up a table of food as if the CEO was coming or leaving. My wife and oldest son and his wife were there, many cameras were flicking, and messages of good will and best wishes were being expressed all over the main conference room. The group gave me a fine fishing rod and reel outfit, including a tackle box which was well stuffed with all the ingredients required for many fishing trips. All of top people in management in the division were present. Each had very complimentary remarks to say to me. (They meant it.) People from several other divisions were there that I had not seen in years. The suppliers' representatives were there, including the manufacturing air force inspector (whom I mentioned earlier having retired), some of the union representatives (mainly JC from the good old days), engineering, manufacturing groups, quality control groups, the medical section, and many others. There was enough food for everyone.

As mentioned earlier, sometimes you have to blow your own horn. I had spent many years working with community groups, civic organizations, charitable groups, and politicians (even was a scout master once). I informed some of my political friends of my retirement intentions and the date. On that date the Honorable State Senator Horace Tate, from my district, presented me with a Declaration from the Governor of the Great State of Georgia, His Excellency Joe Frank Harris, making me a lieutenant colonel, aide de camp, governor's staff, formed for the defense of the state. It went on to outline what a great citizen I had been and all the rights and responsibilities of the position. It stated that through the years my activities and efforts had helped to make our state a great place to live and this was recognition for that reputation. I had also paid my state taxes on time (that's a joke). I really appreciated that award. The governor, the senator, and myself are now retired and on inactive duty (subject to recall).

My co-worker and longtime friend, Jim Maddox (still city councilman), took care of the other two awards. The Honorable Andrew Young, Mayor of the Great City of Atlanta, Georgia, issued a proclamation indicating that the tenth day of December 1987 would be known as H. L. Hudson Day in the city. His comments also stressed appreciation for my many citizenship achievements. (I paid my city taxes on time also.) That plaque is on my wall and proudly exhibited. The Atlanta City Council gave me a plaque recognizing the efforts I had put forth to make the city a better place to live (for I did). That is on my wall also. Jim Maddox is now retired from Lockheed but still a member of the city council. Andrew Young has accomplished many distinguished achievements. I appreciate what both did by their good deeds.

The only one of the original ten present at my retirement was Ike Jones. He was also a buyer. Ike died one week after my retirement and was buried on December 23, 1987. I gave thanks to everyone who participated in my retirement party. But I especially thank Fern Hoinowski, for she took many pictures, put them into a brochure, and gave them to me later. (Fern, you did not get one of yourself.) I wish it were possible to put everyone's name in this narrative but I won't try as I may miss too many. Anyway, we made a damn good team, didn't we, y'all? The party was over and my wife and family went home. I shook a lot of hands and kissed a bunch of gals (all ladies).

I slowly strolled through the department, caught the elevator, and went down and looked into the bank. I walked out to my van and slowly got in, and drove around the parking lot for the last time as an employee. I went up to the main parking lot and parked by the Glerc building. I got out and stood looking at that big plant for about ten minutes. All of the almost thirty-six years rolled through my mind. The good and the bad. The good overruled the bad. I had first seen that place when I was 27 years old. Now I was 62 years old and looking at it in the sense of I no longer worked at the Bomber Plant. It sure didn't seem that it had been that long. The sun seemed to shine brighter and I realized that the days of getting up early, meeting schedules, writing documentation, negotiating, trying to be diplomatic, being congenial yet hardnosed when necessary, the personal responsibility I always felt when trying to satisfy our customers, getting along with all of those other grunts, and the stress of keeping up with changing technology—it was over! Gone! Not required anymore!

A feeling of peace came over me. It was wonderful. I got back into the van and pulled out of the lot onto the road in front of the plant. I took one last look and wheeled on home. To this day I have never looked back with regret (except one mentioned in the next paragraph) nor missed being at dear old Lockheed (the Bomber Plant). All in all I guess it was a wonderful time.

I went back on January 31, 1988, and got my checks and signed all the papers required. The regret that I had was why in hell didn't I get the promotions that I had earned. I try not to feel that it was other than out and out pure rotten prejudice. I couldn't get that thought out of my mind. If I was too independent, then I'm satisfied that I am still independent. My father told me that whatever I did or accomplished, I was still myself, so be true to yourself. I can just about name every bastard who held me back, I supported them all. I feel no sorrow in stating that most of them are gone (period). Today I hold no animosity toward anyone. The retirement benefits I have received are considered good (could be a helluva lot better). The amount of money I saved Lockheed was over $3 million. I believe that that amount has paid my salary, retirement, and benefits. That's history and I'm retired.

Epilogue When I retired from Lockheed and pulled away from the plant, I did as I had all of my life. I closed the last page on that time in my life. When I finished college and could not get into medical school, I closed that page. When I could not expand the service station business I was in, I closed that page. When I realized that there was nothing else for me at Lockheed, I closed that page. I developed the ability to recognize and have a sense of closure when a goal had been accomplished or I had gone as far as I could toward attaining that goal. Sometimes goals were set too high. If you did not make it, then accept the fact that you attempted and did the best that you could for it was never a failure. You just did not move as fast as you thought. The same thing happened when I was sued for divorce after forty-six years. What the hell, close the page.

I would like to say that I got in a lot of fishing but that would not be true. That boat rides rougher than a sleigh on a rock pile. The one thing I really enjoyed was getting this book together. If you think that was easy, try it. I know many stories concerning my boys and their friends who went to the Vietnam War that I will more than likely write of their experiences in a fictional way based on facts. There are fishing and hunting stories full of interesting episodes. There are unlimited stories to be written about politics and local governments to keep one busy for months to come. There are numerous benefits and charities to participate in now that it is known that you are retired with time on your hands. There are hundreds of subscriptions to take out on magazines you don't need, many senior citizens requesting your participation in their activities. (I ain't that old yet.) Once you have retired you have unlimited cash reserves to donate to everything. Major credit card manufacturers, big banks, and home improvement associations all give you preapproved credit up to the thousands of dollars. Now you can increase your insurance even to perpetual maintenance of your gravesite. Refuse courteously and go on with your retirement life.

You never get an increase in your retirement benefits. Your Social Security benefits average about a two percent increase per year. Your Medicare goes up about four dollars or so every year. If you don't have a supplemental type insurance already you can't afford it now. Learn to cut your lifestyle to fit your income. Do not get into debt if you can possibly keep from doing so. DON'T GET SICK!!! (Nor your wife.) The best thing is that you are retired. How long do you think you are going to live anyway? The nicest thing is you don't have to live by a tight schedule. Go when you please and come when you please (unless your wife has other ideas). I am enjoying my association with other retirees and the time I have, unlimited to the best of my knowledge. I can accept any pains that go with being a senior citizen and enjoy what I have. May everybody attain the same status one day. With the way things are going these days that last sentence might be a joke!

Notes

Chapter 2

1. Lockheed's production workers were represented by the International Association of Machinists, a union with a notorious history of racial exclusion. Although the IAM had abolished its racially exclusive initiation policies, the union remained one of the least progressive on racial issues in the 1950s. The aircraft industry faced intensive organizing efforts by trade unions in the late 1930s, the heyday of the modern labor movement. Lockheed's Robert Gross was opposed to any form of union organization among his employees, but faced with a strong labor movement backed by (in Gross's view) pro-labor federal government, he chose what he considered the lesser of two evils. Rather than risk losing a representation election to the United Automobile Workers, a member union of the more progressive (radical, in Gross's view) Congress of Industrial Organizations, Gross negotiated an agreement with the more conservative American Federation of Labor–affiliated IAM. Gross described his decision to negotiate with IAM explicitly as a move to "combat this infectious spread of radicalism which is sweeping the country." See Hartung, *Prophets of War*, 41. Lockheed recognized the International Association of Machinists as the bargaining agent for Lockheed production workers in 1952 without the necessity of an election. While IAM had improved its racial policies somewhat (the union initiation ceremony no longer barred blacks), the organization clearly was less progressive on race than most CIO member unions. Lockheed company officials insisted that the firm offered "no contest" recognition to IAM to preserve labor peace and avoid antagonizing the union's locals in California. But in a sense, whether intentionally or not, IAM representation would in some ways delegate the race problem to the union. Dobbin, *Inventing Equal Opportunity*, 53. Hudson mentioned a union election at Lockheed in 1952, and there was an election. The CIO-affiliated International Brotherhood of Electrical Workers challenged the existing IAM for leadership of Lockheed-Georgia's skilled workers. IAM won the election, and the merger of the two federations in 1955 ended such internecine warfare. *Atlanta Daily World*, September 24, 1952, 1.

2. Hudson appeared convinced that top management at Lockheed, at least within

the Marietta plant, opposed racial discrimination or wanted to avoid difficulties with the Department of Defense (DOD) over the issue, or both. Hudson, perhaps like many locals, placed too much emphasis on James Carmichael, whose chief function, according to some company officials, "was to introduce [Dan] Haughton to the community." Of the numerous men who managed the Georgia facility or led the Lockheed company during his career, Hudson singled out Dan Haughton for the highest praise. In this, Hudson echoed the common sentiment of Lockheed workers from those early days. Uncle Dan, as Hudson and virtually everyone else called him, was, like Carmichael, a native southerner and graduate of a major southern state university (the University of Alabama). Unlike Carmichael, Haughton had entered the aircraft industry in the 1930s, eventually ending up at Lockheed. Haughton absorbed everything he could and made himself indispensable. Haughton served as assistant general manager of Lockheed-Georgia during Carmichael's introductory year, and assumed the position himself in 1952. Scott, *Cobb County*, 216–17, 220–26.

Chapter 4

1. Alfred "Tup" Holmes was a member of a prominent African American family in Atlanta and, for a brief time, a union shop steward at Lockheed. Holmes's nephew, Hamilton, would become one of two African American students (along with Charlayne Hunter) to integrate the University of Georgia in 1961. Tup Holmes also played a role in the civil rights movement. In 1951, Holmes and three others filed a lawsuit challenging segregation on public golf courses in the city of Atlanta. After delays and appeals, the suit finally reached the Supreme Court in November 1955. The Court ordered Atlanta to desegregate its golf courses. Over the protests of arch-segregationist Governor Marvin Griffin, Atlanta's boosters, led by Mayor William Hartsfield, elected to comply with the Court's order and desegregate public courses. Yet Hudson never mentioned Holmes's successful fight to desegregate Atlanta's golf courses or his relationship to Hamilton Holmes. The way Hudson deals with the Tup Holmes story is indicative of his style. On Holmes, see David Andrew Harmon, *Beneath the Image of Civil Rights and Race Relations: Atlanta, Georgia, 1946–1981* (New York: Routledge, 1996), 68–69.

Chapter 14

1. Lockheed officials consistently blamed unrealistic contract requirements imposed by a new system adopted in the mid-1960s, total package procurement, which required bidders for defense contracts to submit bids that would cover design, research, development, and production in a single cost estimate. Senator William Proxmire, perhaps the most famous budget hawk in congressional history, argued that Lockheed's management and the Defense Department had developed such a close relationship that they had become nearly indistinguishable. Lockheed was ostensibly a private firm that relied more and more on a single buyer for its products. The sheer size and complexity of Lockheed's operations is hinted at in Hudson's narrative, with hundreds of buyers purchasing parts and supplies of all kinds. Proxmire and his allies believed that the Lockheed organization had grown overly dependent on large, guaranteed government

contracts, exemplifying exactly the danger Eisenhower had identified. Indeed, many believed that the Pentagon had awarded the C-5A contract to Lockheed rather than Boeing mainly to keep Lockheed afloat as a contractor, to maintain that manufacturing capacity in case it was truly needed in a crisis. Hudson echoed the company's management in arguing that the country owed Lockheed a debt of gratitude for its service to national security. On the C-5A controversy, see Hartung, *Prophets of War*, 69–94. On the bribery scandal, see a profile of Karl Kotchian, the Lockheed president who was caught up in the scandal, *The New York Times*, July 3, 1977, 73.

Chapter 15

1. The strike grew out of Lockheed's massive financial difficulties in the 1970s. Lockheed management negotiated what it considered overly generous seniority provisions in the late 1960s to avert potentially disastrous strikes. Lockheed faced a crisis in its relationship with its prime customer, the federal government, related to cost overruns on the C-5A Galaxy super transport plane. After giving away the store to buy labor peace and keep assembly lines moving, from the company's perspective, Lockheed tried to pull back some of the generous seniority provisions in an effort to reduce costs. Lockheed had agreed to an elaborate "bumping" system that necessitated extensive retraining to shift more senior workers from "surplus" jobs to assembly lines that remained active. The struggle over seniority reflected the serious conflicts between skilled workers who demanded a measure of job security in a notoriously "boom and bust" industry and a company struggling to survive in an uncertain environment. In the end, Lockheed agreed to maintain the seniority benefits for existing workers but to eliminate them for workers hired in the future. The strike and the settlement are summarized in *The New York Times*, January 4, 1978, A14.

Index

African American employment:
aircraft industry, 5–6; Atlanta area
progress by late 1960s, 23; impact
of segregated labor market and,
2–3; at Lockheed-California, 6; at
Lockheed-Georgia, 19
Air Force inspectors, 67
American Red Cross blood program,
68–69, 146
Atlanta Daily World, 1, 10, 11, 16, 20
Atlanta Urban League (AUL), 7, 12–13

B-1 bomber, 159
B-29, 7
B-47, 12–13; Hudson begins work on,
45; problems in production of, 52–55;
strike impact on production, 96
Bell Aircraft, 6–7, 34
Boeing, 177
boosters, 6–7, 14–15
Briles Manufacturing, 138–39
Brown decision, 19–20, 63

C-5A, 129, 131, 138, 141, 161
C-130, 74, 82–83, 106, 108, 126, 131,
146, 157, 175, 193–94; 1979 crash,
176–79
C-141, 100, 106, 108–9, 111, 131, 143,
146, 161, 170, 177, 193

cardiopulmonary resuscitation (CPR),
146, 153–54
Carmichael, James V., 6–7, 10–11,
12–13, 14, 17, 24, 34, 50, 79
Carter, Jimmy, 157, 179, 180
Challenger space shuttle disaster, 197–98
Committee on Government Contracts,
Truman administration, 10
Congress of Industrial Organizations
(CIO), 21
Cooper, Shan, 28
cost reduction awards, 145

Delta Airlines, 110, 111
Delton, Jennifer, 7–8, 26
disabled workers, 156
Dobbin, Frank, 22
Dutch Valley Supply Co., 168–69

Eskew, Glenn, 26
executive orders and equal employment
opportunity, 4, 10, 22

F-94 (Starfire), 161
Fair Employment Practices Committee
(FEPC), 4, 5, 7, 8, 10
federal government and equal
employment regulations, 34
Ferguson, Charles, 23–24

G.I. Bill of Rights, limited impact for African Americans, 9, 35
Gordon, Hugh L., 16, 23, 24
Grady Hospital, 136
Gross, Robert, 5
gubernatorial election of 1946, Georgia, 14, 34
Gulf Aerospace, 197

Hamilton, Grace Towns, 12
Hartung, William, 5
Haughton, Dan, 19, 50–51, 95, 102
Hill, Herbert, 18
Holmes, Alfred "Tup," 81–82
Hudson, Edith, 17–18, 28
Hudson, Harry L.: B-1 project, 159–60; becomes buyer, 102–3; classified work, 181–86; corruption scandals of the 1970s, 157–58; cost reduction awards, 145; CPR to co-worker, 153–54; fasteners, expertise in, 132; female buyer, mentoring, 190–91; illness, 61–62; injury in boating accident, 134–37; job offer from Standard Pressed Steel, 156; military-industrial complex, 200–201; minority suppliers, 118–23; presidential committee and, 114–15; promotions, 57–58, 140, 171; recruitment by Lockheed, 34–36; Red Cross blood program, 68–69, 146; religious experience, 136–37; retirement, 204–8; supervises an integrated crew, 84–87

industrial accidents, 76–78
International Association of Machinists, and the race issue, 20–21
Iranian hostage rescue attempt, 178–80

James, General Daniel "Chappie," 160–61

jet assist take-off (JATO), 88
Jetstar, 106, 108, 131, 172, 174
Johnson, Clarence "Kelly," 172

Kalmbach, Herbert, 158
Kalmbach, Wally, 158
Kennon, Robert, 13
Korean War, impact on defense industries, 9–10

L-1011 aircraft, 100, 158
labor market segregation, 2–4, 5–7
Lockheed Aircraft Corporation, California division (CALAC), 37, 64–65, 94–95, 129
Lockheed Aircraft Corporation, Georgia division (GELAC), 37, 96; feeder plants established, 100
Lockheed National Management Association Club, 101–2, 132–34
Lockheed Vega, 5
longerons, 45–47
Loughead, Allan and Malcolm, 4–5
Lydon, James P., Lockheed director of industrial relations, 12–13, 17, 19–20

Mabry, J.B., 104,
Marable, Manning, 26
Marietta, Georgia, 6, 10
Merit Employment Association, 23
minority suppliers, 118–24
moon photographs, purchasing, 118

National Association for the Advancement of Colored People (NAACP), 1, 8, 11–12, 14, 17, 18, 21, 24, 25, 145
National Urban League (NUL), 8, 15–16, 19, 22
Nixon, Richard M., 157, 158
North American Aerospace Defense Command (NORAD), 161

organized labor, 20–21, 45, 81–82, 93–99, 162–66

PB Fasteners, 139–40, 179
Pet Milk, advertisement featuring Harry Hudson, 17–18
Plans for Progress, 22–23, 24
plant security (plant protection), 52, 57, 63, 69–70; female employees visiting "Negro" clubs and, 71–73
President's Committee on Equal Employment Opportunity, visit to Lockheed, 24, 114–15
Price, Henry, 168–69

racial attitudes, white workers and managers, 34–40, 42–44, 84–85, 90, 101, 112
racial integration: difficulties of, 202, 205; mobile food carts as alternative, 86; plant facilities and activities, 93; single drinking fountain, 49–50
Reece, Amos, controversial court case, 20
Rhyant, Lee, 28
Robeson, Paul, quoted, 12
Russell, Senator Richard B., 8–9

Shah of Iran, 177–78
Shultz Steel Co., 109–10

skin color, impact within the African American community, 25–26, 145
Skunk Works, Lockheed experimental shop, 48, 100
Standard Pressed Steel, 156
strikes, 21, 93–99, 162–66
"super Negroes," 35–36, 42, 44

Talmadge, Eugene, 6, 13, 14
Talmadge, Herman, 13, 14
Taper-Lok pin, 138–39
Temco, 47, 51–52, 54
Truman, Harry S., 1

U.S. Postal Service, as source of African-American social mobility, 3–4

Warner Robins Air Force Base, 143, 146
Weaver, Robert C., 5–6, 19
white primary, 13–14
Wright, Gavin, 8, 14, 27

Young, Andrew, 206
Young, Whitney, quoted, 202

Zero Defects program, 167–69

CPSIA information can be obtained
at www.ICGtesting.com
Printed in the USA
LVHW042146270919
632507LV00002B/222